Mastering matplotlib

A practical guide that takes you beyond the basics of matplotlib and gives solutions to plot complex data

Duncan M. McGreggor

BIRMINGHAM - MUMBAI

Mastering matplotlib

First published: June 2015

Production reference: 1250615

Published by Packt Publishing Ltd.
Livery Place
35 Livery Street
Birmingham B3 2PB, UK.

ISBN 978-1-78398-754-2

www.packtpub.com

Credits

Author
Duncan M. McGreggor

Reviewers
Francesco Benincasa
Wen-Wei Liao
Nicolas P. Rougier
Dr. Allen Chi-Shing Yu

Acquisition Editor
Meeta Rajani

Content Development Editor
Sumeet Sawant

Technical Editor
Gaurav Suri

Copy Editors
Ulka Manjrekar
Vedangi Narvekar

Project Coordinator
Shweta H. Birwatkar

Proofreader
Safis Editing

Indexer
Hemangini Bari

Graphics
Sheetal Aute

Production Coordinator
Komal Ramchandani

Cover Work
Komal Ramchandani

About the Author

Duncan M. McGreggor, having programmed with GOTOs in the 1980s, has made up for that through community service by making open source contributions for more than 20 years. He has spent a major part of the past 10 years dealing with distributed and scientific computing (in languages ranging from Python, Common Lisp, and Julia to Clojure and Lisp Flavored Erlang). In the 1990s, after serving as a linguist in the US Army, he spent considerable time working on projects related to MATLAB and Mathematica, which was a part of his physics and maths studies at the university. Since the mid 2000s, matplotlib and NumPy have figured prominently in many of the interesting problems that he has solved for his customers. With the most recent addition of the IPython Notebook, matplotlib and the suite of the Python scientific computing libraries remain some of his most important professional tools.

About the Reviewers

Francesco Benincasa, master of science in software engineering, is a software designer and developer. He is a GNU/Linux and Python expert and has vast experience in many other languages and applications. He has been using Python as the primary language for more than 10 years, together with JavaScript and frameworks such as Plone, Django, and JQuery.

He is interested in advanced web and network developing as well as scientific data manipulation, analysis, and visualization. Over the last few years, he has been using graphical Python libraries such as matplotlib/Basemap, scientific libraries such as NumPy/SciPy, Pandas, and PyTables, and scientific applications such as GrADS, NCO, and CDO.

He is currently working at the Earth Sciences Department of the Barcelona Supercomputing Center (www.bsc.es) as a research support engineer. He is involved in projects such as the World Meteorological Organization Sand and Dust Storms Warning Advisory and Assessment System (http://sds-was.aemet.es/) and the Barcelona Dust Forecast Center (http://dust.aemet.es/).

He has already worked for Packt Publishing in the past as a reviewer for *matplotlib Plotting Cookbook*.

I would like to thank my wonderful future wife, Francesca, for her constant support and love.

Wen-Wei Liao received his MSc in systems neuroscience from National Tsing Hua University, Taiwan. He is interested in the development of computational strategies to interpret the genomic and epigenomic data that is produced from high-throughput sequencing. He works as a computational science developer at the Cold Spring Harbor Laboratory. More information regarding him can be found at http://wwliao.name/.

Nicolas P. Rougier is a researcher at INRIA (France), which is the French national institute for research in computer science and control. His research lies at the frontier between integrative and computational neuroscience, where he tries to understand higher brain functions using computational models. He also has experience in scientific visualization and has produced several tutorials (matplotlib tutorials, NumPy tutorials, and 100 NumPy exercices) as well as the popular *Ten Simple Rules for Better Figures* article.

Dr. Allen Chi-Shing Yu is a postdoctoral fellow who is currently working in the field of cancer genetics. He obtained his BSc degree in molecular biotechnology at the Chinese University of Hong Kong (CUHK) in 2009 and a PhD degree in biochemistry at the same university in 2013. In 2010, Allen led the first team in CUHK to join MIT's prestigious International Genetically Engineered Machine (iGEM) competition. His team, a 2010 iGEM gold medalist, worked on using bacteria as an obfuscated massive data storage device. The project was widely covered by the media, including AFP, Engadget, PopSci, and Time, to name a few.

His thesis research primarily involves the characterization of novel bacterial strains that can use toxic fluoro-tryptophans, but not the canonical tryptophan, for propagation. The findings demonstrated that the genetic code is not an immutable construct despite billions of years of invariance. Soon after these microbial studies, he identified and characterized a novel marker that causes Spinocerebellar Ataxia (SCA), which is a group of diverse neurodegenerative disorders. This research about the novel SCA marker was recently published in the Journal of Medical Genetics. Recently, through the development of a tool that was used to detect viral integration events in human cancer samples (ViralFusionSeq), he entered the field of cancer genetics. As a postdoctoral fellow in Professor Nathalie Wong's lab, he is now taking part in the analysis of hepatocellular carcinoma using the data from the high-throughput sequencing of genomes and transcriptomes.

Special thanks to Dorothy for her love and support!

---

www.PacktPub.com

Support files, eBooks, discount offers, and more

For support files and downloads related to your book, please visit www.PacktPub.com.

Did you know that Packt offers eBook versions of every book published, with PDF and ePub files available? You can upgrade to the eBook version at www.PacktPub.com and as a print book customer, you are entitled to a discount on the eBook copy. Get in touch with us at service@packtpub.com for more details.

At www.PacktPub.com, you can also read a collection of free technical articles, sign up for a range of free newsletters and receive exclusive discounts and offers on Packt books and eBooks.

https://www2.packtpub.com/books/subscription/packtlib

Do you need instant solutions to your IT questions? PacktLib is Packt's online digital book library. Here, you can search, access, and read Packt's entire library of books.

Why subscribe?

- Fully searchable across every book published by Packt
- Copy and paste, print, and bookmark content
- On demand and accessible via a web browser

Free access for Packt account holders

If you have an account with Packt at www.PacktPub.com, you can use this to access PacktLib today and view 9 entirely free books. Simply use your login credentials for immediate access.

Table of Contents

Preface

In just over a decade, matplotlib has grown to offer the Python scientific computing community a world-class plotting and visualization library. When combined with related projects, such as Jupyter, NumPy, SciPy, and SymPy, matplotlib competes head-to-head with commercial software, which is far more established in the industry. Furthermore, the growth experienced by this open source software project is reflected again and again by individuals around the world, who make their way through the thorny wilds that face the newcomer and who develop into strong intermediate users with the potential to be very productive.

In essence, *Mastering matplotlib* is a very practical book. Yet every chapter was written considering this learning process, as well as a larger view of the same. It is not just the raw knowledge that defines how far developers progress in their goal. It is also the ability of motivated individuals to apply meta-levels of analysis to the problem and the obstacles that must be surmounted. Implicit in the examples that are provided in each chapter are multiple levels of analysis, which are integral to the mastery of the subject matter. These levels of analysis involve the processes of defining the problem, anticipating potential solutions, evaluating approaches without losing focus, and enriching your experience with a wider range of useful projects.

Finding resources that facilitate developers in their journey towards advanced knowledge and beyond can be difficult. This is not due to the lack of materials. Rather, it is because of the complex interaction of learning styles, continually improving codebases with strong legacies, and the very flexible nature of the Python programming language itself. The matplotlib developers who aspire to attain an advanced level, must tackle all of this and more. This book aims to be a guide for those in search of such mastery.

What this book covers

Chapter 1, Getting Up to Speed, covers some history and background of matplotlib, goes over some of the latest features of the library, provides a refresher on Python 3 and IPython Notebooks, and whets the reader's appetite with some advanced plotting examples.

Chapter 2, The matplotlib Architecture, reviews the original design goals of matplotlib and then proceeds to discuss its current architecture in detail, providing visualizations of the conceptual structure and relationships between the Python modules.

Chapter 3, matplotlib APIs and Integrations, walks the reader through the matplotlib APIs, adapting a single example accordingly, examines how third-party libraries are integrated with matplotlib, and gives migration advice to the advanced users of the deprecated pylab API.

Chapter 4, Event Handling and Interactive Plots, provides a review of the event-based systems, covers event loops in matplotlib and IPython, goes over a selection of matplotlib events, and shows how to take advantage of these to create interactive plots.

Chapter 5, High-level Plotting and Data Analysis, combines the interrelated topics, providing a historical background of plotting, a discussion on the grammar of graphics, and an overview of high-level plotting libraries. This is then put to use in a detailed analysis of weather-related data that spans 120 years.

Chapter 6, Customization and Configuration, covers the custom styles in matplotlib and the use of grid specs to create a dashboard effect with the combined plots. The lesser-known configuration options are also discussed with an eye to optimization.

Chapter 7, Deploying matplotlib in Cloud Environments, explores a use case for matplotlib in a remote deployment, which is followed by a detailed programmatic batch-job example using Docker and Amazon AWS.

Chapter 8, matplotlib and Big Data, provides detailed examples of working with large local data sets, as well as distributed ones, covering options such as numpy.memmap, HDF5, and Hadoop. Plots with millions of points will also be demonstrated.

Chapter 9, Clustering for matplotlib, introduces parallel programming and clusters that are designed for use with matplotlib, demonstrating how to distribute the parts of a problem and then assemble the results for analysis in matplotlib.

What you need for this book

For this book, you will need Python 3.4.2 or a later version of this as is available with Ubuntu 15.04 and Mac OS X 10.10. This book was written using Python 3.4.2 on Mac OS X.

You will also need graphviz, HDF5, and their respective development libraries installed. Obtaining the code for each chapter depends upon the Git binary being present on your system. The other software packages that are used in this book will be automatically downloaded and installed for you in a virtual environment when you clone and set up the code for each chapter. Some of the chapters explore the use of matplotlib in Cloud environments. This is demonstrated by using Amazon AWS. As such, an AWS account will be needed for the users who wish to go through all the steps for these chapters.

If you are new to Python 3, the first chapter provides a brief overview of the same. It will provide you with the level of comfort that is needed when dealing with the examples in the book.

Who this book is for

If you are a scientist, programmer, software engineer, or a student who has working knowledge of matplotlib and now want to extend your usage of matplotlib to plot complex graphs and charts and handle large datasets, then this book is for you.

Conventions

In this book, you will find a number of text styles that distinguish between different kinds of information. Here are some examples of these styles and an explanation of their meaning.

Code words in text, database table names, folder names, filenames, file extensions, pathnames, dummy URLs, user input, and Twitter handles are shown as follows: "The axes and projections directories form a crucial part of the artist layer."

A block of code is set as follows:

```
#! /usr/bin/env python3.4
import matplotlib.pyplot as plt

def main () -> None:
  plt.plot([1,2,3,4])
  plt.ylabel('some numbers')
```

```
    plt.savefig('simple-line.png')

  if __name__ == '__main__':
    main()
```

Any command-line input or output is written as follows:

```
$ git clone https://github.com/masteringmatplotlib/architecture.git
$ cd architecture
$ make
```

New terms and **important words** are shown in bold. Words that you see on the screen, for example, in menus or dialog boxes, appear in the text like this: " For instance, when the **Zoom-to-Rectangle** button is clicked, the mode will be set to zoom rect "

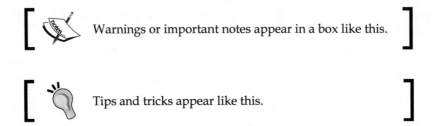

Warnings or important notes appear in a box like this.

Tips and tricks appear like this.

Reader feedback

Feedback from our readers is always welcome. Let us know what you think about this book—what you liked or disliked. Reader feedback is important for us as it helps us develop titles that you will really get the most out of.

To send us general feedback, simply e-mail `feedback@packtpub.com`, and mention the book's title in the subject of your message.

If there is a topic that you have expertise in and you are interested in either writing or contributing to a book, see our author guide at `www.packtpub.com/authors`.

Customer support

Now that you are the proud owner of a Packt book, we have a number of things to help you to get the most from your purchase.

Downloading the example code

Each chapter in *Mastering matplotlib* provides instructions on obtaining the example code and notebook from Github. A master list has been provided at `https://github.com/masteringmatplotlib/notebooks`. You can download the example code files from your account at `http://www.packtpub.com` for all the Packt Publishing books you have purchased. If you purchased this book elsewhere, you can visit `http://www.packtpub.com/support` and register to have the files e-mailed directly to you.

Downloading the color images of this book

We also provide you with a PDF file that has color images of the screenshots/diagrams used in this book. The color images will help you better understand the changes in the output. You can download this file from `https://www.packtpub.com/sites/default/files/downloads/7542OS_ColoredImages.pdf`.

Errata

Although we have taken every care to ensure the accuracy of our content, mistakes do happen. If you find a mistake in one of our books—maybe a mistake in the text or the code—we would be grateful if you could report this to us. By doing so, you can save other readers from frustration and help us improve subsequent versions of this book. If you find any errata, please report them by visiting `http://www.packtpub.com/submit-errata`, selecting your book, clicking on the **Errata Submission Form** link, and entering the details of your errata. Once your errata are verified, your submission will be accepted and the errata will be uploaded to our website or added to any list of existing errata under the Errata section of that title.

To view the previously submitted errata, go to `https://www.packtpub.com/books/content/support` and enter the name of the book in the search field. The required information will appear under the **Errata** section.

Piracy

Piracy of copyrighted material on the Internet is an ongoing problem across all media. At Packt, we take the protection of our copyright and licenses very seriously. If you come across any illegal copies of our works in any form on the Internet, please provide us with the location address or website name immediately so that we can pursue a remedy.

Please contact us at copyright@packtpub.com with a link to the suspected pirated material.

We appreciate your help in protecting our authors and our ability to bring you valuable content.

Questions

If you have a problem with any aspect of this book, you can contact us at questions@packtpub.com, and we will do our best to address the problem.

1
Getting Up to Speed

Over the past 12 years of its existence, **matplotlib** has made its way into the classrooms, labs, and hearts of the scientific computing world. With Python's rise in popularity for serious professional and academic work, matplotlib has taken a respected seat beside long-standing giants such as Mathematica by Wolfram Research and MathWorks' MATLAB products. As such, we feel that the time is ripe for an advanced text on matplotlib that guides its more sophisticated users into new territory by not only allowing them to become experts in their own right, but also providing a clear path that will help them apply their new knowledge in a number of environments.

As a part of a master class series by Packt Publishing, this book focuses almost entirely on a select few of the most requested advanced topics in the world of matplotlib, which includes everything from matplotlib internals to high-performance computing environments. In order to best support this, we want to make sure that our readers have a chance to prepare for the material of this book, so we will start off gently.

The topics covered in this chapter include the following:

- A brief historical overview of matplotlib
- What's new in matplotlib
- Who is an advanced, beginner, or an intermediate matplotlib user
- The software dependencies for many of the book's examples
- An overview of Python 3
- An overview of the coding style used in this book
- References for installation-related instructions
- A refresher on IPython Notebooks
- A teaser of a complicated plot in matplotlib
- Additional resources to obtain advanced beginner and intermediate matplotlib knowledge

A brief historical overview of matplotlib

The open source project that we now know as matplotlib had its inception at the beginning of the millennium when John Hunter and his colleagues were conducting epilepsy research using proprietary data analysis software. They migrated to MATLAB as it was more flexible and less expensive. However, it was not designed to handle the data formats and diverse data sources that they had to contend with on a daily basis.

It was with this realization that John Hunter created the first version of matplotlib—a **GTK+** visualization tool for *electroencephalography* and *electrocorticography* analysis. Having been built in Python, adding support for new features as the team needed them was a straightforward task. Before long, this led to the idea of providing a similar interactive command mode to generate plots on the fly, as MATLAB does.

One of the oldest sources available for matplotlib code online is the GitHub repository. The first commit in this repository was with regard to migration from Subversion to Git, though the original repository was CVS. This commit was authored in May 2003, though this repository records a CHANGELOG file whose first entry was made in December 2002. By the time this book goes into publication, matplotlib will have celebrated its 13th birthday.

What's new in matplotlib 1.4

In the past 12 years, a great deal has happened in the matplotlib codebase. Of particular interest are the new features that have been added to the most recent release at the time of writing this book—version 1.4.3. Here are some of its highlights:

- A new IPython Notebook backend for interactive matplotlib plot support
- A new style package that allows for greater control over the visual presentation of plots
- The new **Qt5** backend
- Google App Engine integration
- New plotting features
- New configuration options

The intermediate matplotlib user

If you've read the preface, then you know who this book is for—developers with intermediate or advanced knowledge of matplotlib as well as the motivated beginners. But who are they exactly? What do such users know?

Answers to such questions are fairly open-ended. We have the following guidelines. The intermediate matplotlib user should have some limited knowledge to passing experience with the following:

- Installation of matplotlib in multiple environments
- Creation of basic to moderately complicated matplotlib plots
- Basic matplotlib APIs, styling, backends, and customizations
- Using matplotlib objects, subplots, and overlays
- Advanced third-party tools such as **Seaborn**, **Pandas**, **ggplot**, distributed **IPython**, and **StarCluster**
- Completed reading most or all of the following books, *Matplotlib for Python Developers, Sandro Tosi, Packt Publishing*, and *matplotlib Plotting Cookbook, Alexandre Devert, Packt Publishing*

Prerequisites for this book

This book assumes that you have previous experience with matplotlib and that it has been installed on your preferred development platform. If you need a refresher on the steps to accomplish that, the first chapter of Sandro Tosi's excellent book, *Matplotlib for Python Developers*, provides instructions to install matplotlib and its dependencies.

In addition to matplotlib, you will need a recent installation of IPython to run many of the examples and exercises provided. For help in getting started with IPython, there many great resources available on the project's site. Cyrille Rossant has authored *Learning IPython for Interactive Computing and Data Visualization, Packt Publishing*, which is a great resource as well.

In the course of this book, we will install, configure, and use additional open source libraries and frameworks. We will cover the setup of these as we get to them, but all the programs in this book will require you to have the following installed on your machine:

- **Git**
- **GNU make**
- **GNU Compiler Collection** (gcc)

Your operating system's package manager should have a package that installs common developer tools—these tools should be installed as well, and may provide most of the tools automatically.

All the examples in this book will be implemented using a recent release of Python, version 3.4.2. Many of the examples will not work with the older versions of Python, so please note this carefully. In particular, the setup of virtual environments uses a feature that is new in Python 3.4.2, and some examples use the new type annotations. At the time of writing this book, the latest version of Ubuntu ships with Python 3.4.2.

Though matplotlib, NumPy, IPython, and the other libraries will be installed for you by set scripts provided in the code repositories for each chapter. For the sake of clarity, we will mention the versions used for some of these here:

- matplotlib 1.4.3
- NumPy 1.9.2
- SciPy 0.15.1
- IPython 3.1.0 (also known as *Jupyter*)

Python 3

On this note, it's probably good to discuss Python 3 briefly as there has been continued debate on the choice between the two most recent versions of the programming language (the other being the 2.7.x series). Python 3 represents a massive community-wide effort to adopt better coding practices as well as improvements in the maintenance of long-lived libraries, frameworks, and applications. The primary impetus and on-going strength of this effort, though, is a general overhaul of the mechanisms underlying Python itself. This will ultimately allow the Python programming language greater maintainability and longevity in the coming years, not to mention better support for the ongoing performance enhancements.

In case you are new to Python 3, the following table, which compares some of the major syntactical differences between Python 2 and Python 3, has been provided:

Syntactical Differences	Python 2	Python 3
Division with floats	`x = 15 / 3.0`	`x = 15 / 3`
Division with truncation	`x = 15 / 4`	`x = 15 // 4`
Longs	`y = long(x * 10)`	`y = int(x * 10)`
Not equal	`x <> y`	`x != y`
The unicode function	`u = unicode(s)`	`u = str(s)`
Raw unicode	`u = ur"\t\s"`	`u = r"\t\s"`

Syntactical Differences	Python 2	Python 3
Printing	`print x, y, z`	`print(x, y, z)`
Raw user input	`y = raw_input(x)`	`y = input(x)`
User input	`y = input(x)`	`y = eval(input(x))`
Formatting	`"%d %s" % (n, s)`	`"{} {}".format(n,s)`
Representation	`'x'`	`repr(x)`
Function application	`apply(fn, args)`	`fn(*args)`
Filter	`itertools.ifilter`	`filter`
Map	`itertools.imap`	`map`
Zip	`itertools.izip`	`zip`
Range	`xrange`	`range`
Reduce	`reduce`	`functools.reduce`
Iteration	`iterator.next()`	`next(iterator)`
The execute code	`exec code`	`exec(code)`
The execute file	`execfile(file)`	`exec(fh.read())`

Exceptions	`try:`
	
	`...`
	
	`except val, err:`
	
	`...`
		`try:`
		
		`...`
		
		`except val as err:`
		
		`...`

Coding style

The coding style used throughout this book and in the example code conforms to the standards laid out in **PEP 8**, with one exception. When entering code into an IPython Notebook or providing modules that will be displayed in the notebook, we will not use two lines to separate what would be module-level blocks of code. We will just use one line. This is done to save screen space.

Something that might strike you as different in our code is the use of an extraordinary feature of Python 3—*function annotations*. The work for this was done in **PEP 3107** and was added in the first release of Python 3. The use of types and static analysis in programming, though new to Python, is a boon to the world of software. It saves time in development of a program by catching bugs before they even arise as well as streamlining unit tests. The benefit of this in our particular case, with regard to the examples in this book, is quick, intuitive code clarification. When you look at the functions, you will instantly know what is being passed and returned.

Finally, there is one best practice that we adhere to that is not widely adopted in the Python programming community—functions and methods are kept small in all of our code. If more than one logical thing is happening in a function, we break it into multiple functions and compose as needed. This keeps the code clean and clear, making examples much easier to read. It also makes it much easier to write unit tests without some of the excessive parameterization or awkward, large functions and methods that are often required in unit tests. We hope that this leaves a positive, long-lasting impression on you so that this practice receives wider adoption.

Installing matplotlib

Given that this is a book on an advanced topic and the target audience will have installed matplotlib and the related dependencies more than once (most likely many times), detailed instructions will not be provided here. Two excellent books on matplotlib that cover this topic in their respective first chapters are *Matplotlib for Python Developers* and *matplotlib Plotting Cookbook*.

That being said, each chapter will have its own Git repository with scripts to install dependencies and set up Python's virtual environments. These scripts are a great resource, and reading them should provide additional details to those who seek to know more about installing matplotlib and the related libraries in Python virtual environments.

Using IPython Notebooks with matplotlib

Python virtual environments are the recommended way of working with Python projects. They keep your system, Python, and default libraries safe from disruption. We will continue this tradition in this book, but you are welcome to transcend tradition and utilize the matplotlib library and the provided code in whatever way you see fit.

Using the native `venv` Python environment management package, each project may define its own versions of dependent libraries, including those of matplotlib and IPython. The sample code for this book does just that—listing the dependencies in one or more `requirements.txt` files.

With the addition of the `nbagg` IPython Notebook backend to matplotlib in version 1.4, users can now work with plots in a browser very much like they've been able to do in the GTK and Qt apps on the desktop. We will take full advantage of this new feature.

In the IPython examples of this book, most of the notebooks will start off with the following:

```
In [1]: import matplotlib
        matplotlib.use('nbagg')
In [2]: %matplotlib inline
In [3]: import matplotlib.pyplot as plt
```

Downloading the example code

Each chapter in *Mastering matplotlib* provides instructions on obtaining the example code and notebook from Github. A master list has been provided at https://github.com/ masteringmatplotlib/notebooks. You can download the example code files from your account at http://www.packtpub. com for all the Packt Publishing books you have purchased. If you purchased this book elsewhere, you can visit http:// www.packtpub.com/support and register to have the files e-mailed directly to you." This configures our notebooks to use matplotlib in the way that we need. The example in the following section starts off with just those commands.

A final note about IPython—the project has recently changed its name to Jupyter in an effort to embrace the language-agnostic growth the project and community has experienced as well as the architectural changes that will make the adding of new language backends much easier. The user experience will not change (except for the better), but you will notice a different name and logo when you open the chapter notebooks for this book.

Advanced plots – a preview

To give a taste of what's to come, let's start up a matplotlib IPython Notebook and look at an example. You will need to download the example from a GitHub repository first:

```
$ git clone https://github.com/masteringmatplotlib/preview.git
$ cd preview
```

You only need to do the following in order to bootstrap an environment with all the notebook dependencies and start up the notebook server:

```
$ make
```

This will do several things for you automatically, some of which are as follows:

- Clone a support repository holding various `include` files
- Create a Python virtual environment
- Install matplotlib and other scientific computing Python modules into this virtual environment
- Start an IPython Notebook server that runs on local host
- Open a browser window and load the `preview` notebook in it

In this browser window, you can run the code yourself by selecting each code section and hitting the *Shift* and *Enter* keys to execute it. Let's go through an example.

Setting up the interactive backend

As mentioned above, our notebooks will all start with the following, as does this preview notebook:

```
In [1]: import matplotlib
        matplotlib.use('nbagg')
        %matplotlib inline
In [2]: import matplotlib.pyplot as plt
        import seaborn as sns
        import numpy as np
        from scipy import stats
        import pandas as pd
```

These commands do the following:

- Set up the interactive backend for plotting
- Allow us to evaluate images in-line, as opposed doing the same in a pop-up window
- Provide the standard alias to the `matplotlib.pyplot` sub package and import other packages that we will need

Joint plots with Seaborn

Our first preview example will take a look at the Seaborn package, an open source third-party library for data visualization and attractive statistical graphs. Seaborn depends upon not only matplotlib, but also NumPy and SciPy (among others). These were already installed for you when you ran `make` (pulled from the `requirements.txt` file).

We'll cover Seaborn palettes in more detail later in the book, so the following command is just a sample. Let's use a predefined palette with a moderate color saturation level:

```
In [3]: sns.set_palette("BuPu_d", desat=0.6)
        sns.set_context("notebook", font_scale=2.0)
```

Next, we'll generate two sets of random data (with a random seed of our choosing), one for the *x* axis and the other for the *y* axis. We're then going to plot the overlap of these distributions in a hex plot. Here are the commands for the same:

```
In [4]: np.random.seed(42424242)
In [5]: x = stats.gamma(5).rvs(420)
        y = stats.gamma(13).rvs(420)
In [6]: with sns.axes_style("white"):
            sns.jointplot(x, y, kind="hex", size=16);
```

The generated graph is as follows:

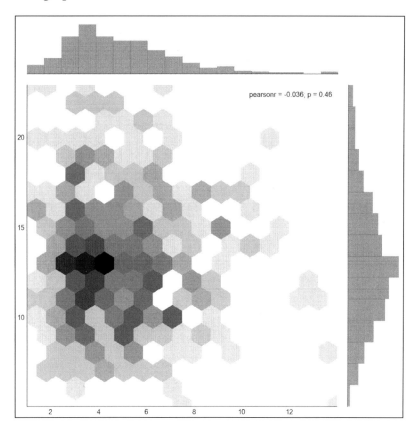

Scatter plot matrix graphs with Pandas

In the second preview, we will use Pandas to graph a matrix of scatter plots whose diagonal will be the statistical graphs representing the kernel density estimation. We're going to go easy on the details for now; this is just to whet your appetite for more!

Pandas is a statistical data analysis library for Python that provides high-performance data structures, allowing one to carry out an entire scientific computing workflow in Python (as opposed to having to switch to something like R or Fortran for parts of it).

Let's take the seven columns (inclusive) from the `baseball.csv` data file between *Runs* (r) and *Stolen Bases* (sb) for players between the years of 1871 and 2007 and look at them at the same time in one graph:

```
In [7]: baseball = pd.read_csv("../data/baseball.csv")

In [8]: plt.style.use('../styles/custom.mplstyle')

        data = pd.scatter_matrix(
            baseball.loc[:,'r':'sb'],
            figsize=(16,10))
```

The generated graph is as follows:

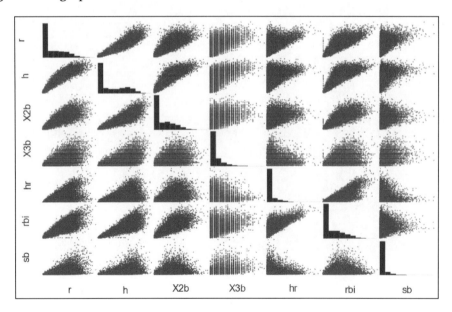

Command 8 will take a few seconds longer than our previous plot since it's crunching a lot of data.

For now, the plot may look like something only a sabermetrician could read, but by the end of this book, complex graph matrices will be only one of many advanced topics in matplotlib that will have you reaching for new heights.

One last teaser before we close out the chapter — you may have noticed that the plots for the baseball data took a while to generate. Imagine doing 1,000 of these. Or 1,000,000. Traditionally, that's a showstopper for matplotlib projects, but in the latter half of this book, we will cover material that will not only show you how to overcome that limit, but also offer you several options to make it happen.

It's going to be a wild ride.

Summary

In this chapter, you got to learn a little more about matplotlib's origins and the latest features that were released at the time of writing this book. You've seen the software that we're going to use, including the version of the Python programming language that we've chosen. Furthermore, we've given you a peek into the future of this book (and matplotlib) with a custom IPython Notebook, which highlights the Seaborn and Pandas projects.

In the next couple of chapters, we're going to focus on matplotlib's internals. In particular, *Chapter 2*, *The matplotlib Architecture* will cover the architecture of the project, giving you an insight into how it all works together.

2
The matplotlib Architecture

As software systems age, they tend to undergo a natural evolution through processes such as feature addition and debugging. The resultant codebase embodies the familiar tension between maintaining the old code and at the same time offering the end users an improved product. Architectures for long-term projects are not something that were originally carved in stone and adhered to monomaniacally ever since. Rather, they are living, adaptive concepts that guide the plans and activities of a project's contributors.

The matplotlib module arose out of such an environment, and it has continuous goals of refining and improving its architecture and updating its older bits to follow the best practices of and the latest advances in not only the project itself, but also the wider Python community over the years since its inception.

In this chapter, we will perform the following tasks:

- Review the original design goals of matplotlib and explore its evolution
- Examine the current architecture at a high level using the metaphors put forth by the core developers of matplotlib
- Dive into the details of the three major layers of the matplotlib architecture
- Explore the matplotlib namespace in relation to the architectural layers
- Create a dependency graph for a standard matplotlib script to gain additional insight on a project's structure in relation to the user scripts
- Take a look at the additional packages that were not a part of the matplotlib release and identify their connection with the overall architecture

The original design goals

As mentioned in *Chapter 1, Getting Up to Speed*, the creators of matplotlib were originally focused on building a GTK+ application for researchers and providing a command interface for the interactive plotting of data, not unlike that provided by MATLAB.

Both of these aims helped drive the development of improved abstractions for matplotlib. It was in this dual crucible that the top-level object of the rendered plots in matplotlib gained its rightful prominence — the **Figure**. These ideas led to various foundational objects in matplotlib, and the relationships between them ultimately provided the basis for the architecture of this library.

The current matplotlib architecture

The current matplotlib architecture revolves around the operations that are necessary for the users to create, render, and update the Figure objects. Figures can be displayed and interacted with via common user interface events such as the keyboard and mouse inputs. This layer of interaction with common user interface is called the **backend layer**. A Figure needs to be composed of multiple objects that should be individually modifiable, but it should be implemented in such a way that it has a positive and predictable impact on the other aspects of the Figure. This logical layer is responsible for the abstraction of each visual component that one sees in a Figure. Due to its highly visual nature, this layer was identified as the more general concept of *creating visual art* and is thus referred to as the **artist layer**. Lastly, the Figure needs to support programmatic interaction and provide the users with the ability to manipulate Figures with a syntax that is as clean and intuitive as possible. This is called the **scripting layer**.

The following figure shows the relation between the three layers of matplotlib architecture (backend, artist, and scripting):

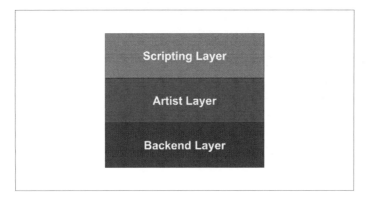

The backend layer rests at the bottom of the matplotlib architecture and it only knows about its own interfaces. The subsequent layers at the top of the stack know only about themselves and the layers below. Thus, complexities are properly isolated to the higher levels. In describing this, we are taking some liberties with the simplification that we've generated, which is a small sacrifice that was made to help clarify the roles of the layers. We will cover each layer of this stack in detail in the following sections. We will provide examples, references to code, and diagrams. Part of this will include revealing the complexity behind the initial sketch that you just saw.

As we explore the depths of matplotlib in the following sections, it might be helpful to keep a mental placeholder for the layers as they relate to data and the Figure object for a given plot in the following way:

- The user creates either the data that he/she wants to plot or the functions that generate this data
- This data is either created or loaded in the scripting layer
- The data is transformed into various objects in the artist layer; it is adjusted as scripted
- These objects are then rendered by the backend, which ultimately provides the configured toolkit with the raw data necessary to place an image on the toolkit's canvas

Let's explore this in more detail now, starting from the bottom — the backend layer.

The backend layer

Seasoned computer scientists, engineers, and software developers all know that one of the subtler and trickier problems that arise in our industry is *naming*. It sounds a bit silly and it is repeatedly the subject of jokes, but the difficulty remains—how do you speak or write explicitly on a subject whose very nature requires exquisite precision and yet has great ambiguity that arises in different contexts?

We have the same problem with the term *backend*. Here, as in so many other instances, the context is everything. Our context is matplotlib, a set of tools, and a framework where everything is done in support of the visualizing of data and their relationships. The term *backend* has to be viewed from this perspective to support the generation of plots. The matplotlib backend has nothing to do with other noteworthy backends such as databases, servers, messaging systems, or dispatchers of various sorts. The backend of matplotlib is an abstraction layer over various components that are capable of rendering a Figure. Such plots appear in desktop applications that are embedded in widgets or web pages; other plots are images in publications (digital and print). They can be generated with code, through user interfaces, or by deploying a combination of both. These plots might be the creation of a single user tweaking a widget or a batch processing job on a high-performance computing grid. All are supported by and require a matplotlib backend.

As you might have been able to deduce from the examples given in the previous sections, the backends in matplotlib can be divided into two functional categories:

- User interface backends (interactive)
- Hardcopy backends (noninteractive)

User interface backends include the following:

- GTK 2.x and GTK 3.x
- wxWidgets
- Tk
- Qt4 and Qt5
- Mac OS X Cocoa

The hardcopy backends comprise of the following:

- PS
- PDF
- SVG
- PNG

Hardcopy backends can be further divided based on the support of *raster graphics*, *vector graphics*, or both of these.

Furthermore, the user-interface and hardcopy backends are built upon some core abstractions. The base classes for these are as follows:

- `FigureCanvasBase` and `FigureManagerBase`
- `RendererBase` and `GraphicsContextBase`
- `Event`, `ShowBase`, and `Timer`

Examining these base classes brings us to the nuts and bolts of the matplotlib backend architecture.

FigureCanvasBase

The `FigureCanvasBase` class is a base class that is used by the user interface and hardcopy backends. It represents the canvas in which the Figure will render. Its responsibilities include the following:

- Holding a reference to the Figure
- Updating the Figure with a reference to the canvas
- Defining event methods that run registered
- Translating native toolkit events into the matplotlib event abstraction framework
- Defining draw methods to render the Figure
- Methods to start and stop non-GUI event loops

When used by hardcopy backends, the FigureCanvasBase classes can register the file types supported by hardcopy backends (for example, .tiff and .jpg). When used by the user interface backends, the FigureCanvasBase classes provide the means by which the matplotlib canvas is inserted into the native toolkit window (even when it is GTK, Mac OS X Cocoa, Qt, or Tk).

Additionally, there is a FigureManagerBase class that is used by matplotlib when running in pyplot mode. This class wraps FigureCanvasBase as well as various GUI toolkit methods for the easier rendering of figures and interfaces.

RendererBase

In matplotlib, the renderer handles the drawing operations. RendererBase was originally inspired by the GIMP drawing toolkit's Drawable class, and this is evident when one examines its drawing methods to render paths, images, Gouraud triangles, text, markers, path collections, and quad meshes.

Note that many of the render operations are handed off to an additional abstraction—GraphicsContextBase. This abstraction provides a clean separation for code that handles color, line styles, hatching styles, blending properties, and antialiasing options, among others.

Event

There are several aspects of the matplotlib backend that have to do with events, event loops, and timing. These responsibilities are divided across three base classes:

- Event: This is the base class for DrawEvent, MouseEvent, and KeyEvent, among others

- ShowBase: This is subclassed at the module level in the GUI backends

- TimerBase: This is the base class for TimerQT, TimerGTK3, and TimerWx, to name a few

As mentioned in a previous section, FigureCanvasBase defines event methods that are used when translating to and from native GUI toolkit events. These methods instantiate the Event classes and are connected to the callbacks stored in CallbackRegistry, which is itself stored as an attribute on FigureCanvasBase.

Depending on the nature of the event, it may need to track the data in the artist layer, work with renderers, and so on. As such, some of the Event classes carry references to more than just their event properties, allowing callback functions to easily access this data.

At the core of every GUI toolkit is an event loop. Every user interface backend that integrates with a toolkit needs to define a module-level Show class, subclassing ShowBase. Its mainloop method is what pyplot uses to start up the given toolkit's main loop. However, in order for this to work, matplotlib needs something to connect to the native toolkit's timer.

This is what implementations such as TimerQT, TimerGTK3, and TimerTornado provide. These classes have a callbacks attribute that is a simple list of (*function*, *args*, and *kwards*) tuples that get called upon by timer events. The TimerQT and TimerGTK3 classes integrate the GUI main loops, while the TimerTornado class integrates the I/O or event loop of the **Tornado** asynchronous networking library.

A practical example of how these can work together will include things such as a key press, a mouse click, or the picking of events. Key presses can be used to develop custom keyboard commands that change a plot based on the interactive input from the user. The ability to pick events allows the developers to support the interactive panning and zooming of their plots. All of these events are intercepted by the matplotlib event system and then forwarded to the native toolkits after the backend does the appropriate translation.

Visualizing the backend layer

The matplotlib backend components work together in order to provide a seamless experience regardless of:

- The GUI toolkit being used (if any)
- The type of output being produced (raster, vector, file type, and so on)
- Whether the events are being handled
- Whether the images are static or animated

We now have the information needed to visually summarize the backend layer. This information is portrayed in the following image:

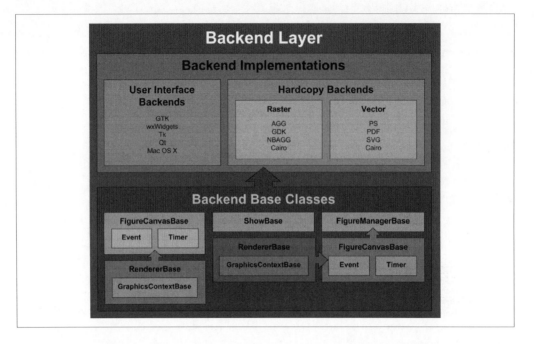

Note that in reality, the backend layer and its components are more complex than this graphic portrays. There are multiple relationships, as is exemplified by RendererBase and FigureCanvasBase appearing twice. The intent is to show the main backend base classes. The FigureManagerBase function has one of the other backend base classes as a supporting component (its canvas attribute).

This concludes our overview of matplotlib's backend layer. In the next section, we will move higher up the stack.

The artist layer

The artist layer constitutes the bulk of what matplotlib actually does—the generation of the plots for the purpose of display, manipulation, and publication. Most work in the artist layer is performed by a number of classes, most of which are derived from the Artist base class.

The artist layer is concerned with things such as the lines, shapes, axes, text, and so on. These are the subclasses of the `Artist` class that define things such as the following:

- A canvas-artist coordinate transformation
- Visibility
- A clip box that defines the paintable area
- Labels
- A callback registry instance to handle user interaction events

The `Artist` subclasses can be classified into one of the following two groups:

- Primitives
- Containers

The following two sections provide more details about these groups.

Primitives

The matplotlib artist primitives are classes of graphical objects that are supposed to be painted on a figure's canvas. These include, but are not limited to, the following:

- `Line2D`
- Shape (patch) classes such as `Rectangle`, `Polygon`, `Ellipse`, `Circle`, `ArcText`, `Annotation`, and `TextPath`
- `AxesImage` and `FigureImage`

Each of these primitive classes is a subclass of `Artist`, and as such have at their core the same definition of purpose—something that renders into an implementation of `FigureCanvasBase`.

Containers

This is another set of classes that subclass from `Artist` and which have additional responsibilities. They offer a useful abstraction to gather primitives. Examples of the containers include the following:

- `Figure`
- `XAxis` and `YAxis`
- `Axes`, `PolarAxes`, `HammerAxes`, `MollweideAxes`, and `LambertAxes`
- `Subplot`

Typically, a `Figure` would be instantiated and used to create one or more `Axes` or `Subplot` instances. The methods available for these objects would then be used to create the primitives as needed. Thus the user does not have to manually track the creation of the primitives and store them in the appropriate containers.

Of all the containers, the `Axes` class is one of the most important. It is the primary mover and shaker in the artist layer. The reason for this is simple—the `Axes` instances are where most of the matplotlib objects go (both primitives and other containers). In addition to the creation of primitives, the methods of this class can prepare the supplied data that is needed for the creation of primitives such as lines and shapes, add them to the appropriate containers, and draw them when called by some other objects.

Furthermore, the `Axes` objects set the coordinate system for the figure and track callbacks that can be connected to the `xlim_changed` and `ylim_changed` events. The callbacks will be called with the `Axes` instances as an argument.

Collections

Another component of the artist layer that we will touch on briefly is **collections**. These are the classes that provide for the efficient drawing of large numbers of similar objects. If you find yourself creating tens or hundreds of thousands of circles, polygons, lines, and so on, in most cases you will get much better performance from matplotlib if you put these in collections. The available classes include, but are not limited to `PathCollection`, `CircleCollection`, `PolyCollection`, `EllipseCollection`, `LineCollection`, and `EventCollection`.

A view of the artist layer

We now have enough additional information to create a diagram of the artist layer:

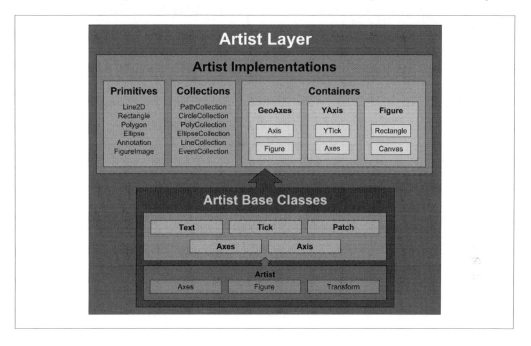

You may notice that a base class may paradoxically contain a parent class. This is really just a reference to a parent class that is often created at the time of creating the base class. Keeping this in mind is helpful when investigating matplotlib internals.

Like the logical backend diagram, the matplotlib internals is not intended to be comprehensive. However, it was meant to provide a conceptual aid for the visually oriented when thinking about how the bits fit together.

With this, we are brought to the final layer of the matplotlib architecture.

The scripting layer

While the backend layer focuses on providing a common interface to the toolkits and rendering the primitives and containers of the artist layer, the scripting layer is the user-facing interface that simplifies the task of working with other layers.

Programmers who integrate matplotlib with application servers will often find it more convenient to work directly with the backend and artist layers. However, for the scientists' daily use, data visualization, or exploratory interactions, pyplot — the scripting layer — is a better option. This is what we use in most of the IPython Notebooks in this book.

The pyplot interface is much less verbose; one can get insights into one's data in very few steps. Under the covers, pyplot uses module-level objects to track the state of the data so that the user does not have to create things like figures, axes, canvases, figure canvas managers, or preferred backends.

We will take a quick look at pyplot's internals later in this chapter (as well as again later in the book). However, for now, here are the important points that you need to know about pyplot:

- When imported, pyplot selects either the default backend for your system, or the one that you have previously configured

- After selecting a backend, pyplot calls a setup function which does the following:

  ◦ Creates a figure manager factory function, which when called will create a new figure manager appropriate for the selected backend

  ◦ Prepares the drawing function that should be used with the selected backend (taking into account whether the backend is a hardcopy or a user interface)

  ◦ Identifies the callable function that integrates with the backend mainloop function

  ◦ Provides the module for the selected backend

The pyplot interface defines a series of functions that depend on the components returned by the setup function. These include the following functions:

- plot(): This function calls the plot method in the current figure's Axes object and the figure canvas's draw* method (as identified in the preceding setup)
- title(): This function sets the title of the current figure's Axes instance
- savefig(): This function saves the current figure
- draw(): This function redraws the current figure
- gcf(): This function returns the current figure
- gca(): This function returns the Axes instance of the current figure
- get_current_fig_manager(): This returns the current figure manager
- figure(): This is a Figure factory function
- switch_backend(): This is a function that lets one easily change the selected backend

If one wishes to use the scripting layer, pyplot is the community-recommended approach. However, you may come across references to another scripting layer interface when digging through the source code or poking around in matplotlib's documentation, pylab.

The pylab interface is the procedural interface of matplotlib, and it was modeled after the commands that MATLAB provides. Many of the functions in pylab take their names from not only the MATLAB analogs, but also their function arguments. In support of this, pylab imports the mlab module as well as large chunks of NumPy. Additionally, pyplot is made available in the pylab namespace.

The pylab provided one of the most compelling features of matplotlib for scientists and students who wished to transition to an open source alternative, and it is given a lot of credit for matplotlib's initial adoption and success. However, note that pylab is deprecated and its use is discouraged by the community. Users should transition to pyplot for all of their scripting layer needs.

This overview provides us with sufficient information to create a logical diagram of the scripting layer's architecture:

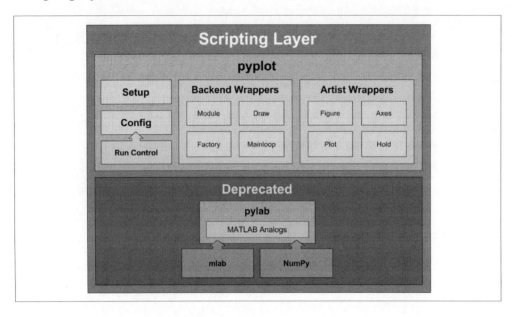

The supporting components of the matplotlib stack

In addition to the three major components of the matplotlib stack, there are supporting components. These include the following:

- Configuration support
- Utility modules and functions
- C extensions
- External libraries upon which matplotlib depends

We will touch on these in the coming chapters. They are related to the given topics at hand, but they do not impact the structure or nature of matplotlib's overall architecture.

Combining the details uncovered in the previous sections, the following diagram portrays a logical architecture for matplotlib that glosses over the finer details:

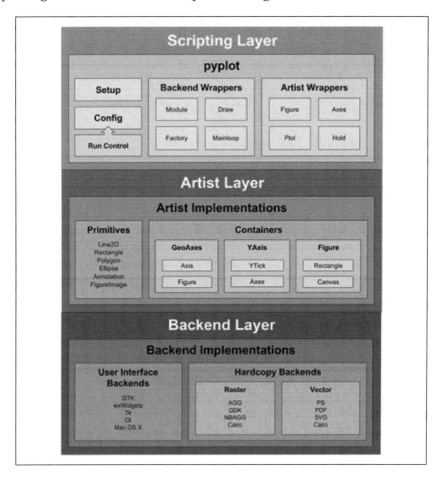

To make this more of a living reality, we will follow this high-level description with some more detailed examinations, which consist of the following:

- Learning about matplotlib modules and associated namespaces
- Creating a sample import graph
- Following the execution of the pyplot functions through the matplotlib stack

matplotlib modules

When discussing the architecture of software libraries, it is of great use to relate a conceptual overview to concrete software components. This not only increases the immediate knowledge with more definite context, but also provides a foundation for a quicker learning process during future explorations. Let's examine the modules in the matplotlib Python package.

Exploring the filesystem

Start by obtaining the IPython Notebook for this chapter, installing the dependencies, starting up the IPython server, and loading the notebook in your browser in the following way:

```
$ git clone https://github.com/masteringmatplotlib/architecture.git
$ cd architecture
$ make
```

Once the notebook is loaded, go ahead and run the initial setup commands:

```
In [1]: import matplotlib
        matplotlib.use('nbagg')
        %matplotlib inline
```

Now let's create two sets of imports, one for our dependencies and the other for modules that we've created specifically for this notebook:

```
In [2]: from glob import glob
        from modulefinder import Module
        from modulefinder import ModuleFinder
        from os.path import dirname
        from pprint import pprint
        import sys
        import trace
        import urllib.request

        import matplotlib.pyplot as plt
        from IPython.core.display import Image
```

```
             from pycallgraph import Config
             from pycallgraph import GlobbingFilter
             from pycallgraph import PyCallGraph
             from pycallgraph.output import GraphvizOutput
In [3]: sys.path.append("../lib")
             from modarch import matplotlib_groupings
             import modfind
             import modgraph
             from modutil import ls, rm
```

Next, let's take a look at matplotlib's top-level Python modules (output elided for compactness):

```
In [4]: libdir = "../.venv/lib/python3.4/site-packages/matplotlib"

             ls(libdir)
             ['matplotlib/__init__.py',
              'matplotlib/_cm.py',
              'matplotlib/_mathtext_data.py',
              'matplotlib/_pylab_helpers.py',
              'matplotlib/afm.py',
              'matplotlib/animation.py',
              'matplotlib/artist.py',
              ]
```

There are about 60 top-level modules in the resultant listing. This can be seen using the following command lines:

```
In [5]: toplevel = glob(libdir + "/*.py")
             modules = ["matplotlib" + x.split(libdir)[1]
                      for x in toplevel]
             len(modules)Out[5]: 59
```

Some of these modules should be pretty familiar to you now:

- `artist.py`
- `backend_bases.py`
- `figure.py`
- `lines.py`
- `pyplot.py`
- `text.py`

You can get a nicer display of these modules with the following:

```
In [6]: pprint(modules)
```

To see matplotlib's subpackages, run the following code:

```
In [7]: from os.path import dirname

        modfile = "/__init__.py"
        subs = [dirname(x) for x in glob(libdir + "/*" + modfile)]
        pprint(["matplotlib" + x.split(libdir)[1] for x in subs])

        ['matplotlib/axes',
         'matplotlib/backends',
         'matplotlib/compat',
         'matplotlib/delaunay',
         'matplotlib/projections',
         'matplotlib/sphinxext',
         'matplotlib/style',
         'matplotlib/testing',
         'matplotlib/tests',
         'matplotlib/tri']
```

The `backends` directory contains all the modules that support the user interface and hardcopy backends. The `axes` and `projections` directories form a crucial part of the artist layer. This brings up a point worth clarifying—there is no correlation in matplotlib code between the software (modules, subpackages, classes, and so on) and the architectural layers that we discussed. One is focused on the nuts and bolts of a plotting library and the other is concerned with helping us conceptually organize functional areas of the library.

That being said, there's no reason why we can't create a mapping. In fact, we did just that in the utility module for this notebook. If you execute the next set of commands in the IPython Notebook, you can see how we classified the matplotlib modules and subpackages (again, the output has been elided for compactness):

```
In [9]: pprint(matplotlib_groupings)

        {'artist layer': ['matplotlib.afm',
                           'matplotlib.animation',
                           'matplotlib.artist',
                           ...],
          'backend layer': ['matplotlib.backend',
                             'matplotlib.blocking',
                             'matplotlib.dviread',
                             ...],
          'configuration': ['matplotlib.rcsetup',
                             'matplotlib.style'],
          'scripting layer': ['matplotlib.mlab',
                              'matplotlib.pylab',
                              'matplotlib.pyplot'],
          'utilities': ['matplotlib.bezier',
                        'matplotlib.cbook',
                        'mpl_tool']}
```

Note that not all strings in the key/list pairs exactly match matplotlib's modules or subpackages. This is so because the strings in the preceding data structure are used to match the beginnings of the module names and subpackages. Their intended use is in a call, such as `x.startswith(mod_name_part)`.

We will use this data structure later in this section when building organized graphs of matplotlib imports. However for now, this offers additional insight into how one can view the Python modules that comprise matplotlib.

Exploring imports visually

The previous section showed us what the modules look like on the `filesystem` (as interpreted by Python, of course). Next we're going to see what happens when we import these modules and how this relates to the architecture of matplotlib.

Continuing with the same notebook session in your browser, execute the following command lines:

```
In [10]: #! /usr/bin/env python3.4
         import matplotlib.pyplot as plt


         def main () -> None:
             plt.plot([1,2,3,4])
             plt.ylabel('some numbers')
             plt.savefig('simple-line.png')


         if __name__ == '__main__':
             main()
```

These command lines are taken from the script in the repository saved in `scripts/simple-line.py`. As its name suggests (and as you will see when entering the preceding code into the IPython Notebook), this bit of matplotlib code draws a simple line on an axis. The idea here is to load a very simple matplotlib script so that we can examine matplotlib internals without distraction.

The first thing this script does is import the matplotlib scripting layer, and it's the import that we are interested in. So let's start digging.

ModuleFinder

The Python standard library provides an excellent tool to examine imports — the `modulefinder` module. Let's take the default finder for a spin in the same notebook session:

```
In [11]:  finder = ModuleFinder()
          finder.run_script('../scripts/simple-line.py')


In [12]: len(finder.modules)
Out[12]: 1068
```

Running the script for the first time and examining all the imports will take a few seconds. If you take a look at the data in `finder.modules`, you will see modules that are from not only matplotlib and NumPy, but also IPython, ZeroMQ, setuptools, Tornado, and the Python standard library.

We're only interested in matplotlib. So we need to create a custom finder that gives us just what we're looking for. Of course we did just that and saved it in the `modfind` module.

Skipping ahead a bit in the notebook, we will use our customer finder in exactly the same way as the one in the standard library:

```
In [16]: finder = modfind.CustomFinder()
         finder.run_script('../scripts/simple-line.py')
         len(finder.modules)
Out[16]: 62
```

That's much more manageable. One of the key things that the `ModuleFinder` does is keep track of which modules import which other modules. As such, once `finder` has run the given script, it has data on all the relationships between the modules that import other modules (and each other). This type of data is perfectly suited for graph data structures. It just so happens that this is something that matplotlib is able to work with as well, thanks to the NetworkX library and its matplotlib integration.

ModGrapher

In addition to `CustomFinder`, this notebook also has a class called `ModGrapher`. This module does the following:

- Creates an instance of `CustomFinder` and runs it
- Builds weight values for nodes based on the number of times a module is imported
- Colors nodes based on the similarity of names (more or less)
- Provides several ways to refine the relationships between imported modules
- Draws configured graphs using NetworkX and matplotlib

Due to the second bullet point, it is clear that the `ModGrapher` provides visualization for the usage and the extent to which one module is imported by another module.

Let's use `ModGrapher` to generate the import data (by using `CustomGrapher` behind the scenes) and then display a graph of the `import` relationships:

```
In [17]: grapher = modgraph.ModGrapher(
             source='../scripts/simple-line.py',
             layout='neato')
         grapher.render()
```

The following is the graph of the `import` relationships:

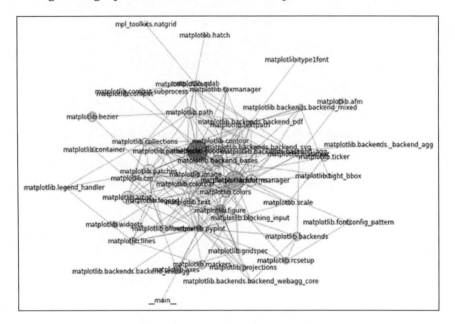

As you can see, the result looks somewhat chaotic. Even so, we are provided with useful meta information. A bit of a heads-up—when you start digging into the matplotlib code earnestly, you can expect the code in any given module to use classes and functions across the entire matplotlib code base.

However, it would be nice to see more structure in the relationships. This is where our use of the previously mentioned modarch.matplotlib_groupings comes in. We have at our disposal a data structure that maps the matplotlib modules to the various layers of the matplotlib architecture. There is a convenient function in modarch that does this, and the ModGrapher class uses this function in several of its methods to group imports according to the matplotlib architecture that we defined.

Let's try the simplest method first, re-rendering the graph with a different mode:

```
In [21]: grapher.render(mode="reduced-structure")
```

The following figure is the result of the preceding command:

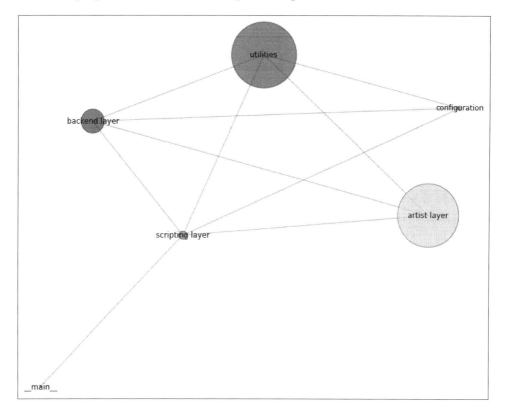

The chaos is gone, but so are the interesting features. What we need is a combination of the two—something that shows the various modules that are imported as well as the overall usage of the architectural elements. All that is required is that you ensure that the imports of any one area of matplotlib's architecture that go outside the group terminate inside the group instead of crossing into the other groups (otherwise, we'd end up with the same graph that we started with).

This too has been coded in our module, and we just need to use the appropriate mode to render it:

```
In [22]: grapher.render(layout="neato", labels=True,
                        mode="simple-structure")
```

The following figure is the result of the preceding command:

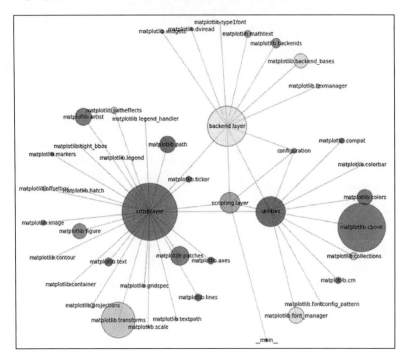

The code behind this graph does some additional simplification—it only goes two levels deep in the matplotlib namespace. For instance, `matplotlib.a.b.c` will be rolled up (with its weights contributing) into `matplotlib.a`. There is an additional mode, full-structure, which you can use to see all the imported matplotlib modules, as mapped to the architectural areas.

This brings us to the end of the our exploration of matplotlib's modules and module imports. Next, we will take a look at the architecture as reflected in the *running code*.

The execution flow

At the beginning of this chapter, we briefly sketched the flow of data from user creation to its display in a user interface. Having toured matplotlib's architecture, which included taking a side trip to the namespaces and dependency graphs, there is enough context to appreciate the flow of data through the code.

As we trace through our simple line example, remember that we used the `pyplot` interface. There are several other ways by which one may use matplotlib. For each of these ways, the code execution flow will be slightly different.

An overview of the script

As a refresher, here's our code from `simple-line.py`:

```python
#! /usr/bin/env python3.4
import matplotlib.pyplot as plt

def main () -> None:
    plt.plot([1,2,3,4])
    plt.ylabel('some numbers')
    plt.savefig('simple-line.png')

if __name__ == '__main__':
    main()
```

At the script level, here's what we've got:

1. Operating system shell executes the script.
2. Python 3.4 is invoked, which then runs the script.
3. `matplotlib` is imported.
4. A `main()` function is defined.
5. The script then executes the `main()` function.

Having reviewed familiar territory, let's jump into what matplotlib does in the script. Here's a brief summary of the trace:

- Using the `import matplotlib.pyplot` command line:
    1. Select the backend.
    2. Import and run `pylab_setup` from `matplotlib.backends`.

- Using the `pylab_setup` function:
    1. Import the previously selected backend.
    2. Get the figure manager factory function.
    3. Select the `show` instance that you want to use, which can be integrated with the selected backend's `mainloop` function.
    4. Return all of these.

- Plot the given data:
    1. Get the figure manager (or create one if it doesn't exist).
    2. Get its figure canvas.
    3. From this, get the figure object of the canvas.
    4. From the figure object, get the current axes object (or create it if it doesn't exist).
    5. Once the figure's axes object is available, call its `plot` function.
    6. The axes `plot` function clears the axes and creates some lines based on the provided data.
    7. Get the active figure manager.
    8. Call the figure manager's `canvas.draw()` function.

- Set the *y* axis label. This updates the `_text` attribute of the label object on the *y* axis.

- Save the plot as a `.png` image. This writes the file to `filesystem` by using the hardcopy backend, which correlates to the extension on the filename.

An interactive session

We can get a hands-on look at many of these via IPython either through an interactive shell in the terminal, or with this chapter's notebook in your browser. Note that if you run the following code in the notebook, you will get different results since a different backend is being used.

The following command in the terminal will ensure that you get an interactive IPython prompt, which has access to all the dependencies:

```
$ make repl
```

Let's examine some of the things that we covered in the execution flow outline in the preceding section. We'll start by importing pyplot and looking at the top-level setup that pyplot initiates after the import:

```
In [1]: import matplotlib.pyplot as plt
In [2]: plt.rcParams['backend']
Out[2]: 'MacOSX'
```

In some of the following calls, we will be able to access objects, methods, and so on that have been named according to the private Python naming convention. We will do this simply to explore some of the undocumented depths of matplotlib. The keyword here is *undocumented*. The private variables are subject to change without warning. So please do not use these in any projects.

```
In [3]: plt._backend_mod.__name__
Out[3]: 'matplotlib.backends.backend_macosx'


In [4]: plt._show
Out[4]: <matplotlib.backends.backend_macosx.Show at 0x1074bc940>
```

If we try to get a figure or its figure manager right now, nothing will be returned since one hasn't been created yet:

```
In [5]: plt._pylab_helpers.Gcf
Out[5]: matplotlib._pylab_helpers.Gcf


In [6]: plt._pylab_helpers.Gcf.get_active()
```

However, we can get the default figure manager in the following way:

```
In [7]: plt.get_current_fig_manager()
Out[7]: FigureManager object 0x106e1ea48 wrapping NSWindow 0x103e74e90
```

However, note that the figure manager too doesn't have a figure yet, this can be seen in the following way:

```
In [8]: plt.get_current_fig_manager().figure


---------------------------------------------------------------
AttributeError                     Traceback (most recent call last)
<ipython-input-8-a80f1a99bf26> in <module>()
----> 1 plt.get_current_fig_manager().figure


AttributeError: 'FigureManagerMac' object has no attribute 'figure'
```

Now, let's call the plot function and see what's available:

```
In [9]: plt.plot([1,2,3,4])
Out[9]: [<matplotlib.lines.Line2D at 0x1088367b8>]


In [10]: plt._pylab_helpers.Gcf.get_active()
Out[10]: FigureManager object 0x1074c4a88 wrapping NSWindow 0x107026030


In [11]: plt._pylab_helpers.Gcf.get_active().canvas
Out[11]: FigureCanvas object 0x1074c45c8 wrapping NSView 0x10761cd60


In [12]: plt._pylab_helpers.Gcf.get_active().canvas.figure
Out[12]: <matplotlib.figure.Figure at 0x1074b5898>
```

Depending upon the operating system and backend that you are currently using, you may get results (or no results) that are different from the ones in the preceding section.

Better yet, by using the API function and its attributes:

```
In [13]: plt.get_current_fig_manager()
Out[13]: FigureManager object 0x1074c4a88 wrapping NSWindow 0x107026030


In [14]: plt.get_current_fig_manager().canvas
Out[14]: FigureCanvas object 0x1074c45c8 wrapping NSView 0x10761cd60


In [15]: plt.get_current_fig_manager().canvas.figure
Out[15]: <matplotlib.figure.Figure at 0x1074b5898>


In [16]: plt.get_current_fig_manager().canvas.figure.axes
Out[16]: [<matplotlib.axes._subplots.AxesSubplot at 0x108826160>]


In [17]: plt.get_current_fig_manager().canvas.figure.axes[0].lines
Out[17]: [<matplotlib.lines.Line2D at 0x1088367b8>]
```

However, the most consistent results will be obtained when we use the `pyplot` utility functions in the following way:

```
In [18]: plt.gcf()
Out[18]: <matplotlib.figure.Figure at 0x1074b5898>


In [19]: plt.gca()
Out[19]: <matplotlib.axes._subplots.AxesSubplot at 0x108826160>


In [20]: plt.gca().lines
Out[20]: [<matplotlib.lines.Line2D at 0x1088367b8>]
```

The next step is to add a label in the following way:

```
In [21]: plt.gca().get_ylabel()
Out[21]: ''


In [22]: plt.ylabel('some numbers')
```

```
Out[22]: <matplotlib.text.Text at 0x1088464a8>


In [23]: plt.gca().get_ylabel()
Out[23]: 'some numbers'
```

Finally, we will save the image in the following way:

```
In [24]: ls -al *.png
ls: *.png: No such file or directory


In [25]: plt.savefig('simple-line.png')


In [26]: ls -al *.png
-rw-r--r--  1 oubiwann  staff  22473 Nov  9 15:49 simple-line.png
```

A note on tracing. What we did in the previous section is a bit like sightseeing—a quick overview, some interesting moments, and then we move on to the next thing. When you really want to dive deep into the execution flow of a program, script, or a function, you perform the operation of tracing. As you might expect, the Python standard library has a module for this as well—the `trace` module.

It's beyond the scope of this chapter to trace this script, but this is an excellent exercise for the motivated reader. Here is an example that illustrates the trace module's usage:

```
In [46]: def plotit():
             plt.plot([1,2,3,4])
             plt.ylabel('some numbers')
             plt.show()


         tracer = trace.Trace(countfuncs=1, countcallers=1)
         _ = tracer.runfunc(plotit)
```

This will take some time to run. When `runfunc()` completes, the tracing results will be stored in `tracer.results`, an instance of `trace.CoverageResults`:

```
In [47]: results = tracer.results()
         _ = results.write_results(show_missing=True, summary=True,
                                   coverdir=".")
```

Note that by enabling `countcallers`, our results will have the call relationship tracking data. With this information, you should be able to build some highly detailed graphs using NetworkX and matplotlib that visually reveal which functions in matplotlib call where and which layers of the architecture call the other layers.

The matplotlib architecture as it relates to this book

The previous sections covered some heavy material, and it can be sometimes difficult to remember the big picture when examining the details under the proverbial microscope. As a preventative measure, we'd like to bring the discussion back to a macroscopic scale as it relates to knowledge acquisition.

The three layers that we've talked about in matplotlib's architecture are the backend, artist, and the scripting layers. As an intermediate user of matplotlib, you've very likely used all the three layers. However, you've most probably spent a lot of of time on the scripting layer with `pyplot`. This is where most users of matplotlib not only start, but usually stay. The introductory material in this book focuses on getting the users up to speed with the scripting layer so that they can be as effective as possible. Intermediate materials (such as the books for reference mentioned earlier in the chapter) also focus on this.

An in-depth usage of the artist layer is usually required when tackling complex tasks in matplotlib that require a deeper understanding of the library as a whole. These tasks might include operations such as custom transforms, scaling axes in unique ways according to the requirements of the data sets, or creating new primitives that need to be rendered by matplotlib.

As for the backend layer, it is similar to the artist layer. Custom work on the backend will arise when you either need to integrate with a new or unsupported GUI toolkit, or have specialized requirements to generate files from the plots.

With regard to the architecture of matplotlib, this book will spend some time covering certain aspects of the scripting layer, but it will spend more time on the artist and backend layers. Finally, we will move beyond matplotlib's architecture.

Summary

In this chapter, we covered a lot of detailed material by starting with a high-level logical overview of matplotlib's structure. We then learned about the source code and examined how the matplotlib modules were laid out. We figured out the modules that were associated with different logical layers. Finally, we peered into the depths of matplotlib by tracing the function and method calls through the code. This was done by using a sample script in an interactive Python session.

One of the most commonly recommended practices for open source developers who want to improve is to read copious amounts of source code for the projects that you use the most and care about deeply. Similarly, as you develop your mastery of matplotlib, you will find yourself spending more and more time reading the source, exploring its depths, and ultimately making contributions to the project. This chapter is your first step in this direction.

The next step is learn more about the scripting layer and its best practices — the matplotlib APIs.

3
matplotlib APIs and Integrations

In the previous chapter, we examined the architecture of matplotlib by using the library itself to visualize some aspects of the structure of module imports, particularly the ones related to the scripting, artist, and backend layers of the matplotlib architecture. In this chapter, we are going to examine the developer interfaces against the backdrop of this architectural discussion.

The matplotlib module comes with what are essentially three different application programming interfaces:

- The pylab interface, a MATLAB analog (deprecated)
- The pyplot interface, which is synonymous with the scripting layer from the last chapter
- The matplotlib object-oriented interface

We will define these and talk more about them in the following sections. Since they are covered in great detail elsewhere, we won't spend much time going over each of the functions that is available in the API. Rather we will demonstrate typical good usage for each API type and the circumstances under which their use would be recommended. Afterwards we will take a look at how matplotlib is integrated with the other scientific computing and visualization libraries.

To follow along with this chapter's code, clone the notebook's repository and start up IPython by using the following commands:

```
$ git clone https://github.com/masteringmatplotlib/apis.git
$ cd apis
$ make
```

We're going to create some more libraries in this chapter, and we will use a custom color palette for our results. So, let's set them up now in the following way:

```
In [1]: import matplotlib
        matplotlib.use('nbagg')
        %matplotlib inline
In [2]: import numpy as np
        import matplotlib.pyplot as plt
        import matplotlib as mpl
        from matplotlib.backends import backend_agg
        from matplotlib.colors import LinearSegmentedColormap
        from matplotlib.gridspec import GridSpec
        import seaborn as sns
        from IPython.display import Image
In [3]: pallete_name = "husl"
        colors = sns.color_palette(pallete_name, 8)
        colors.reverse()
        cmap = mpl.colors.LinearSegmentedColormap.from_list(
            pallete_name, colors)
```

The procedural pylab API

The pylab API is a procedural interface to matplotlib's underlying object-oriented Python API. As mentioned in the previous chapter and stated in the matplotlib FAQ, the `pylab` module has been deprecated. The `pyplot` module is the preferred API for scripting. The original vision of pylab—to provide MATLAB users a nearly one-to-one mapping of the software they knew with that of an open source platform—has been accomplished. In the 12 years since its inception, matplotlib has become a household name in scientific computing circles, and as a result the need for pylab has decreased greatly.

The drawbacks of pylab include the following:

- It hides the workings (and thus, the deeper knowledge) of matplotlib, thus preventing the natural discovery of deeper feature sets that are available to the user through matplotlib objects.

- The additional development and maintenance of pylab are a burden for the matplotlib team in its continued efforts to provide the MATLAB functionality that wraps the already-existing functions from NumPy and matplotlib.

- The `import *` expression is used to pull pylab into the current namespace (thus, going against Python's philosophical tenet of *explicit is better than implicit*). The gains of simplicity in this are debatable. What's more, with `import *`, you don't know the module from which a function or an object comes.

Despite the reasons for not using pylab, there are some motivating factors for discussing this old API here:

- *Completeness*; pylab is still released with matplotlib
- A warning to the readers — don't base your new projects on it
- Most importantly, pylab introduces the means by which users may migrate from their MATLAB-based pylab projects to the preferred matplotlib API

It is the last point in particular that we are the most interested in — providing the recent matplotlib adopters with extensive knowledge of MATLAB and ways to utilize their old skills and apply them to the supported matplotlib APIs. First, let's have a quick overview of what pylab provides.

The pylab interface is comprised of functions that are categorized into the following areas:

- Plotting
- Event handling
- Matrices
- Probability
- Statistics
- Time series analysis
- Dates

It also includes a final *Other* category consisting of a handful of miscellaneous functions ranging from utility functions that save data to polynomial fitting. These functions are all actually defined elsewhere, though this defining is not done in the `pylab` module itself. Many of them are pulled from NumPy and the rest are imported from `matplotlib.mlab`.

To motivate notes on migration, let's start with a simple MATLAB example. Check out the following function:

$$z = xe^{-x^2 - y^2}$$

Now, let's plot the gradient for the preceding function. Here is the MATLAB code that accomplishes this:

```
[X,Y] = meshgrid(-2:.2:2);
Z = X.*exp(-X.^2 - Y.^2);
[DX,DY] = gradient(Z,.2,.2);
figure
contour(X,Y,Z)
hold on
quiver(X,Y,DX,DY)
hold off
```

Using the deprecated pylab interface, we can obtain the same result and in the process recognize the near isomorphism between MATLAB and pylab:

```
In [5]: from matplotlib.pylab import *

        (y, x) = mgrid[-2:2.1:0.2,-2:2.1:0.2]
        z = x * exp(-x ** 2 - y ** 2)
        (dy, dx) = gradient(z)

        quiver(x, y, dx, dy, z, cmap=cmap)
        hold(True)
        contour(x, y, z, 10, cmap=cmap)
        show()
```

From this, we will get the following plot, which is a nearly exact (arguably better looking) match of the graph presented in the MATLAB `quiver` documentation:

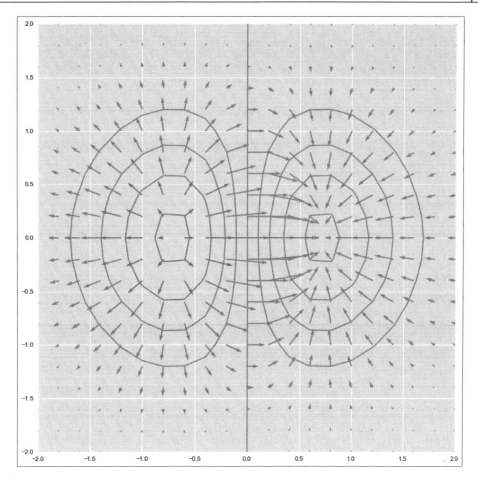

In the `pylab` code, we saw the following calls:

- `mgrid`, `exp`, and `gradient`
- `quiver`, `hold`, `contour`, and `show`

The first set of functions that are listed are from NumPy; the second set is from matplotlib. Knowing this will allow us to migrate from `pylab *` to `numpy.*` and `matplotlib.pyplot`. However, if you are unfamiliar with these libraries, how does one know where to look?

If you open the `pylab.py` file from a git clone repository of matplotlib or look at the files online, you will see that this module consists entirely of docstrings and imports and it has no actual function definitions. Most of the code comes from the following sources:

- `matplotlib.mlab`
- `matplotlib.pyplot`
- `matplotlib.cbook` (which is also known as a cookbook — a utility function module)
- `numpy`
- Various `numpy.*` modules

The following rules of thumb can be used to figure out whether you need to find your desired function in the matplotlib or NumPy code bases:

- If the function call has to deal directly with either the plotting, axes, figures, projections, and other transformations, or other visual elements of the plot, look for the function in matplotlib
- Likewise, if the function is concerned with the saving of images, the configuring of formats, the selecting of colors, and so on, look for it in matplotlib
- If the function is concerned with data, data types, mathematical operations, or transformations of data, search for the function in NumPy

To give you a better sense of the last item, some of the other NumPy functions imported by pylab are from the following modules:

- The **fast Fourier transform** (**FFT**) module
- The linear algebra module
- The masked array module

The other matplotlib libraries that were imported in pylab include the dates and finance modules.

All of these can represent many potential places that you can look at when trying to figure out how to use the recommended matplotlib API. Deducing the probable module from the function name should be enough most of the time. If your first guess doesn't locate the function's module, it might be a great idea to *grep* the source. When migrating from pylab to pyplot, you might want to keep a check on matplotlib and NumPy in the following way:

```
$ cd ~/lab
$ git clone https://github.com/numpy/numpy.git
$ git clone https://github.com/matplotlib/matplotlib.git
```

If you had assumed that `gradient` was in matplotlib and after a quick look in `matplotlib.mlab`, you didn't see it, you can then hop into the repository clone to locate the desired function by using the following commands:

```
$ git grep 'def gradient'
.../tests/test_triangulation.py:    def gradient_quad(x, y):
.../tri/triinterpolate.py:    def gradient(self, x, y):
.../tri/triinterpolate.py:    def gradient(self, x, y):
```

After taking a look at the content of these files, you'd realize that your desired gradient function wasn't present. Then you can try NumPy:

```
$ cd ../numpy
$ git grep 'def gradient'
numpy/lib/function_base.py:dezf gradient(f, *varargs, **kwargs):
```

Sure enough, this is more promising. Taking a look at `numpy.__init__`, which will then point you to `numpy.lib.__init__`, you will see that `function_base` gets pulled into the `numpy` namespace. This is the function that we were looking for. Now that we have gone through all these efforts, you should know about a shortcut that may provide you with insights when searching for the modules that house a given class or function. In an interactive Python session, you can use the `help` command. In addition to printing docstrings and function signatures, the `help` command will also indicate the module of the function or class in the very first line of the output. In our case, help(`gradient`) shows `numpy.lib.function_base` in the first line.

The place held by pylab is a venerable, even if an aging one; it has enormously helped the adoption of matplotlib, Python, and other general open source software in the world of scientific computing. Academia in many ways is the native home of open source and as such, matplotlib and Python are by now very much at home here. Now that matplotlib has secured its place in the scientific computing community along with the deprecation of pylab, it's time to use one of the two recommended methodologies to have an interface with the library.

The pyplot scripting API

Nearly all introductory matplotlib texts and a large portion of intermediate matplotlib material focuses on the pyplot scripting layer in matplotlib. The pyplot interface offers a highly flexible and convenient means to get data into the plots with no hassles. The `simple-line.py` script from the last chapter highlighted this. However, this can lead one to make an incorrect assessment of pyplot.

The pyplot API is not simply a tool for beginners, especially with the advanced use of data taking place in the object-oriented API. Rather, in pyplot's simplicity rests its power. It is the right tool to use when you need the following:

- One-off scripts
- Instant feedback for the visualization of newly obtained datasets
- The means to demonstrate plot features or workflow in an IPython matplotlib notebook
- Visualization and a manual check of data from laboratory experiments
- Ways to work through problems with a publication in a textbook or journal article, in graduate work, or for undergraduate classes
- A match for workflows that previously used the pylab API

Let's explore the pyplot API a bit with a real-world example that matches several of the use cases described in the preceding sections. The example is pertaining to the plotting of magnetic fields.

The following vector equation describes the magnetic field along an infinite wire by using cylindrical coordinates:

$$\vec{B} = \frac{\mu_0 I}{2\pi s}\hat{\theta}$$

This states that the magnetic vector $\vec{B}$ is defined as the product of the magnetic constant μ_0 and the current I in the wire divided by 2π and the distance from s to a point. This gives us the magnitude of the magnetic field. The direction off the cylindrical axis is indicated by the $\hat{\theta}$ component, thus giving us a cylindrical vector.

To convert this to the Cartesian coordinates ($\hat{x}$ and $\hat{y}$ components instead of a $\hat{\theta}$ component) that can be used in this example, we can use trigonometry to make the following substitution:

$$\vec{B} = \frac{\mu_0 I}{2\pi s}(-\sin\theta\hat{x} + \cos\theta\hat{y}) = \left(\frac{\mu_0 I}{2\pi}\right)\frac{1}{s}\left(-\frac{y}{s}\hat{x} + \frac{x}{s}\hat{y}\right) = \left(\frac{\mu_0 I}{2\pi}\right)\left(-\frac{y}{s^2}\hat{x} + \frac{x}{s^2}\hat{y}\right)$$

In the preceding equation, $s^2 = x^2 + y^2$. Due to the defined value of the magnetic s constant, we can reduce our equation to the following:

$$\vec{B} = \mu I\left(-\frac{y}{s^2}\hat{x} + \frac{x}{s^2}\hat{y}\right)$$

In the preceding equation, the value of μ is 2×10^{-7} volt seconds per ampere meters. For this problem, we're interested in looking at an x-y plane cross-section of a wire in the z axis carrying a current of 50 A (positive direction). We will calculate the numerical solutions for an area of 4 square meters.

Let's set our initial values:

```
In [10]: u = 2.0e-7
         I = 50
         (xmin, xmax, _) = xrange = (-2.0, 2.0, 30)
         (ymin, ymax, _) = yrange = (-2.0, 2.0, 30)
```

The last value of each tuple represents the number of points that we want to define along each axis. We won't use these values individually (only as a part of the xrange and yrange variables). So, we will assign them to the *ignore* variable, the underscore. We can now create a 30 × 30 grid (evenly spaced throughout the 4 square meters) and from this grid, we can calculate the squared distance values in the following way:

```
In [11]: x, y = np.meshgrid(
             np.linspace(*xrange),
             np.linspace(*yrange))
         s2 = (x ** 2) + (y ** 2)
```

Since we are not using pylab anymore, we will need to access NumPy functions from their own namespace. We've imported and aliased these functions to `np` according to the community convention. In this case, we've used the `linspace` function to provide us with a range of values which take as arguments a minimum for the range, a maximum, and the total number of values to generate between these two. The resulting arrays are then given as an input for the `meshgrid` function. The `meshgrid` function returns the coordinate matrices, which are used for the evaluations of vector fields over a grid defined by the inputs. In other words, this is how we perform n-dimensional vector field computations in NumPy.

Lastly, we will create another grid that represents the squared values for each coordinate in our grid.

Now that we have the x and y components for the coordinates over the given range as well as the squared distance s^2, we can obtain the vector components of the magnetic field and use each of these to create the final equation for the complete magnetic field for the chosen values, that is, the vector components sum:

```
In [12]: Bx = u * I * (-y / s²)

         By = u * I * (x / s²)

         B = Bx + By
```

Step by step, we have converted the magnetic field equation in Cartesian coordinates to a set of numerical values that can be accepted by matplotlib. In this section, we will use the scripting layer. So, all the calls will be through the `pyplot` module, which is imported as `plt`.

Let's feed pyplot:

```
In [13]: plt.figure(figsize=(12,10))

         plt.quiver(x, y, Bx, By, B, cmap=cmap)

         plt.axis(ranges=1, aspect=1)

         plt.title('Magnetic Field of a Wire with I=50 A',

                 fontsize=20)

         plt.xlabel('$x \mathrm{(m)}$', fontsize=16)

         plt.ylabel('$y \mathrm{(m)}$', fontsize=16)

         plt.colorbar(orientation='vertical')

         plt.show()
```

The following plot is the result of the preceding command:

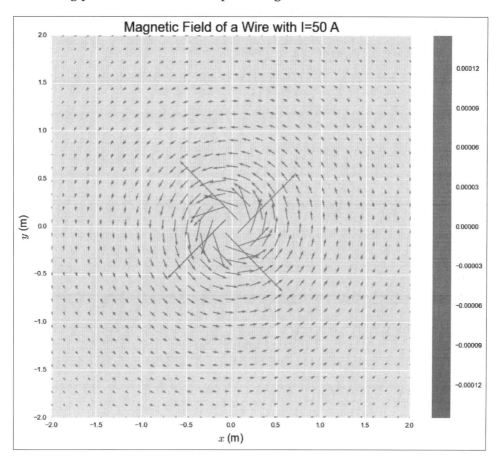

Most of the preceding `plt.*` calls should be familiar to you owing to your experience with matplotlib. The one thing that may be new for you is the use of the in-lined **LaTeX** for the x and y labels.

Let's zoom in on the magnetic field and overlay our vectors on an image generated from the continuous values in our previously defined range:

```
In [14]: figure, axes = plt.subplots(figsize=(12,10))
         im = axes.imshow(B, extent=ranges,
                          cmap=sns.dark_palette("#666666",
                          as_cmap=True))
```

```
q = axes.quiver(x, y, Bx, By, B, cmap=cmap)
figure.colorbar(q, shrink=0.96)
plt.axis([-0.5, 0.5, -0.5, 0.5], aspect=1)
plt.title('Magnetic Field of a Wire with I=50 A',
          fontsize=20)
plt.xlabel('$x \mathrm{(m)}$', fontsize=16)
plt.ylabel('$y \mathrm{(m)}$', fontsize=16)
plt.show()
```

The following plot is the result of the preceding command:

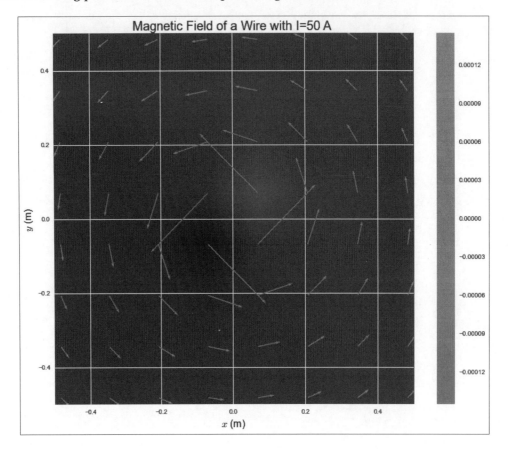

As you know, the zooming of the magnetic field plot is accomplished by defining new limits on the axes. With this plot, we are able to see not only the vectors (the magnitude and direction) of the selected grid and the evenly distributed coordinates, but also the smooth and continuous magnitude of the magnetic field, which appears in shades of grey.

 Note that even though we are defining objects in this example, we are still doing so using only the pyplot interface.

We have seen some use cases that are a good fit for the pyplot API, and we have gone through an example. The next question that you may naturally ask is: when should we not use pyplot? All the examples in the bullet list at the beginning of this section have one thing in common—they imply that one or more individuals are working on problems in a simple, manual workflow. There are other workflows.

If you're going to generate huge numbers of plots, process vast quantities of data, or have particular needs for highly customized plots, you'll want to skip the scripting layer and work directly with the artist or backend layers.

The matplotlib object-oriented API

Before we begin, a caveat about the terminology is in order. We use the phrase *matplotlib object-oriented API* to refer to a direct access to matplotlib's artist and backend layers. The pyplot scripting layer is also object-oriented in that it is composed of functions and instances that are object-oriented by design. The pyplot interface is built upon the OOP methodologies utilized by matplotlib. The distinction that we attempt to make in this section is that we will be creating these objects directly instead of using a scripting layer that does the same for us.

As with the previous section, we acknowledge that the object-oriented API for matplotlib has been covered in great detail in other materials and we will therefore simply provide an overview of the interface via an example, much like with the pyplot API overview.

Of the many circumstances that require fine-grained control over the elements of a plot or the customized use of the backend, a very clear use case to directly access the object-oriented matplotlib API is a noninteractive, programmatic generation of plots.

Let's assume that you have just received an enormous amount of data from some experiments that measured magnetic fields under varying conditions, and you need to generate plots for all the interesting datasets, which happen to number in the hundreds. Unless you are a very unlucky grad student (who doesn't have this book), this is a task for which you will have to create specialized code. This is not something that you would want to do manually, creating one image file at a time. You might even run your new code on a cluster, splitting the plotting tasks up across many machines, allowing your results to be viewed much more quickly.

Let's get started by refactoring one of the pylab examples from the notebook—magnetic fields that are generated due to the current that flows through two wires. We will need to accomplish the following:

- Convert the pyplot procedural-style definition of values to functions that return values
- Create an object that wraps the experimental data
- Create an object that wraps the configuration data that is needed by our plots
- Create an object that manages the matplotlib instances that we need for our plot
- Create some experiments and have their plots saved in separate files

The first three points represent the work that has to be done in support of our use of matplotlib; the last two points are the focus of the following section. Let's get started.

Equations

This is another magnetic field example, but to keep things interesting, we are going to use a different equation. We will use the equation that describes the magnetic field that is generated due to the current passing through two wires in opposite directions (again, in the z axis). Here's the equation that represents this, and which we will solve:

$$\vec{\mathbf{B}} = \mu\left(-\left(\frac{I_1 s_2^2 + I_2 s_1^2}{s_1^2 s_2^2} y \right)\hat{x} + \left(\frac{I_1 s_2^2 x_1 + I_2 s_1^2 x_2}{s_1^2 s_2^2} \right)\hat{y} \right)$$

 A note for the curious reader—if you are following along in the IPython Notebook for this chapter, you will see a link in the section where this equation is presented. This link will take you to another notebook accompanying this chapter, which guides you through the preceding derivation.

Let's convert this to a function. The following code should look very familiar after the last section—one function is responsible for the building of the vectors that will feed the `quiver` plot function, and the other for doing the hard work of computing the vectors of the magnetic field:

```
In [35]: def get_grid_values(xrange: tuple, yrange:tuple) -> tuple:
             return np.meshgrid(np.linspace(*xrange),
                                np.linspace(*yrange))


         def get_field_components(distance: float, currents: tuple,
                                  magconst: float, xrange: tuple,
                                  yrange:tuple) -> tuple:
             (x, y) = get_grid_values(xrange, yrange)
             x1 = x - distance
             x2 = x + distance
             s12 = x1 ** 2 + y ** 2
             s22 = x2 ** 2 + y ** 2
             (I1, I2) = currents
             const = magconst / (s12 * s22)
             Bx = const * -y * ((I1 * s22) + (I2 * s12))
             By = const * ((I1 * s22 * x1) + (I2 * s12 * x2))
             return (Bx, By)
```

Helper classes

As mentioned at the beginning of the preceding section, we are going to create some classes that will make our code cleaner. The code will be easier to read six months from now, and it will be easier to troubleshoot it should something go wrong. There are two areas that need to be addressed:

- A class that is used to organize experimental data
- A class that is used to configure data

The `Experiment` class just needs to accept experimental data in its constructor and then provide access to this data via the attributes. As such, only a single method is needed—its constructor:

```
In [36]: class Experiment:
             def __init__(self, d: float, Is: tuple,
                          xrange, yrange, m: float=2.0e-7):
```

```
        self.distance = d
        self.magconst = m
        (self.current1, self.current2) = Is
        self.xrange = xrange
        (self.xmin, self.xmax, _) = xrange
        self.yrange = yrange
        (self.ymin, self.ymax, _) = yrange
        (self.x, self.y) = get_grid_values(xrange, yrange)
        self.ranges = [self.xmin, self.xmax,
                        self.ymin, self.ymax]
        (self.Bx, self.By) = get_field_components(
            self.distance, Is, self.magconst,
            self.xrange, self.yrange)
        self.B = self.Bx + self.By
```

Next, let's create a configuration class. This will hold everything the artist and backend layers need to create the plots:

```
In [37]: from matplotlib.colors import LinearSegmentedColormap


class ExperimentPlotConfig:
    def __init__(self, size: tuple, title_size: int=14,
                    label_size: int=10,
                    bgcolor: str="#aaaaaa", num_colors: int=8,
                    colorbar_adjust: float=1.0,
                    aspect_ratio=1.0):
        self.size = size
        self.title_size = title_size
        self.label_size = label_size
        self.bgcolor = bgcolor
        self.num_colors = num_colors
        self.colorbar_adjust = colorbar_adjust
        self.aspect_ratio = aspect_ratio

    def fg_cmap(self, palette_name="husl"):
        colors = sns.color_palette(
```

```
            pallete_name, self.num_colors)
        colors.reverse()
        return LinearSegmentedColormap.from_list(
            pallete_name, colors)


    def bg_cmap(self):
        return sns.dark_palette(self.bgcolor, as_cmap=True)
```

The Plotter class

We've arrived at the point where we need to create the most significant bit of functionality in our task. This code will serve the same purpose as pyplot in matplotlib. In our particular case, it will batch jobs via matplotlib's object-oriented interface.

From your previous reading (as well as this book's chapter on the matplotlib architecture), you'll remember that the Plotter class needs to do the following tasks:

- Create a figure manager
- Provide access to the managed figure instance
- Create and configure the axes
- Plot the data
- Save the plot to a file

In our case, we will have two plots—one representing the magnitude of the vector field at any given point (this will be a background image), on top of which will be the second plot, which is a quiver plot of the vectors from the grid of coordinates.

Here's the Plotter class, which demonstrates the object-oriented API of matplotlib:

```
In [38]: class Plotter:
        def __init__(self, index, plot_config, experiment):
            self.cfg = plot_config
            self.data = experiment
            self.figure_manager = backend_agg.new_figure_manager(
                index, figsize=self.cfg.size)
            self.figure = self.figure_manager.canvas.figure


        def get_axes(self):
```

```python
        gs = GridSpec(1, 1)
        return self.figure.add_subplot(gs[0, 0])

    def update_axes(self, axes):
        tmpl = ('Magnetic Field for Two Wires\n'
                '$I_1$={} A, $I_2$={} A, at d={} m')
        title = tmpl.format(self.data.current1,
                            self.data.current2,
                            self.data.distance)
        axes.set_title(
            title, fontsize=self.cfg.title_size)
        axes.set_xlabel(
            '$x$ m', fontsize=self.cfg.label_size)
        axes.set_ylabel(
            '$y$ m', fontsize=self.cfg.label_size)
        axes.axis(
            self.data.ranges,
            aspect=self.cfg.aspect_ratio)
        return axes

    def make_background(self, axes):
        return axes.imshow(
            self.data.B, extent=self.data.ranges,
            cmap=self.cfg.bg_cmap())

    def make_quiver(self, axes):
        return axes.quiver(
            self.data.x, self.data.y,
            self.data.Bx, self.data.By,
            self.data.B, cmap=self.cfg.fore_cmap())

    def make_colorbar(self, figure, quiver):
        return self.figure.colorbar(
```

```
                    quiver, shrink=self.cfg.colorbar_adjust)


    def save(self, filename, **kwargs):
        axes = self.update_axes(self.get_axes())
        back = self.make_background(axes)
        quiver = self.make_quiver(axes)
        colorbar = self.make_colorbar(self.figure, quiver)
        self.figure.savefig(filename, **kwargs)
        print("Saved {}.".format(filename))
```

Take a look at the creation of the figure manager in the constructor method of the `Plotter` class—we directly interfaced with the backend layer. Likewise, when we obtain the figure reference from the canvas, this is the domain of the backend layer.

Most of the remaining code interfaces with the artist layer of the matplotlib architecture. There are some points worth making in some of this code:

- We named the axes-generating method intuitively. It is not obvious, however, that the `Figure.add_subplot` method returns an `Axes` instance.

- The `Axes.imshow` method may not be immediately obvious either. It is named `show` and the docstring says that it *displays*, but what it really does is create an `AxesImage` instance from the given data and add the image to the `Axes` instance (returning the `AxesImage` instance).

- We used the `shrink` keyword in the `Figure.colorbar` call for an aesthetic purpose. It balanced the relative size of the colorbar with the plot.

The last bit that touches the backend layer is done indirectly through the artist layer—via the call to `savefig`. Under the hood, what really happens here is that the backend layer's particular canvas instance (in our case, `FigureCanvasAgg`) calls its `print_figure` method (which, in turn, calls a method appropriate for the given output format).

Running the jobs

To bring all of these together, we need some code to perform the following tasks:

- Create a configuration instance that the `Plotter` class can use

- Create a list of the `Experiment` instances, complete with the data that has to be plotted

- Iterate through each of these instances, saving the plots to a file

Here's the code for this:

```
In [39]: plot_config = ExperimentPlotConfig(
            size=(12,10),
            title_size=20,
            label_size=16,
            bgcolor="#666666",
            colorbar_adjust=0.96)


         experiments = [
            Experiment(d=0.04, Is=(1,1),
                       xrange=(-0.1, 0.1, 20),
                       yrange=(-0.1, 0.1, 20)),
            Experiment(d=2.0, Is=(10,20),
                       xrange=(-1.2, 1.2, 70),
                       yrange=(-1.2, 1.2, 70)),
            Experiment(d=4.0, Is=(45,15),
                       xrange=(-5.3, 5.3, 60),
                       yrange=(-5.3, 5.3, 60)),
            Experiment(d=2.0, Is=(1,2),
                       xrange=(-8.0, 8.0, 50),
                       yrange=(-8.0, 8.0, 50))]


         for (index, experiment) in enumerate(experiments):
            filename = "expmt_{}.png".format(index)
            Plotter(index,
                    plot_config,
                    experiment).save(filename)
```

When you press the *Shift + Enter* keys for the cell in the IPython Notebook, you will see whether the output for each file that it saves is printed or not. You can also verify the same with the following code:

```
In [40]: ls -1 expmt*.png
         expmt_0.png
         expmt_1.png
```

```
expmt_2.png
expmt_3.png
```

If you would like to view the files in the notebook, you can import the image display class from IPython in the following way:

```
In [41]: Image("expmt_1.png")
```

The following plot is the result of the preceding command:

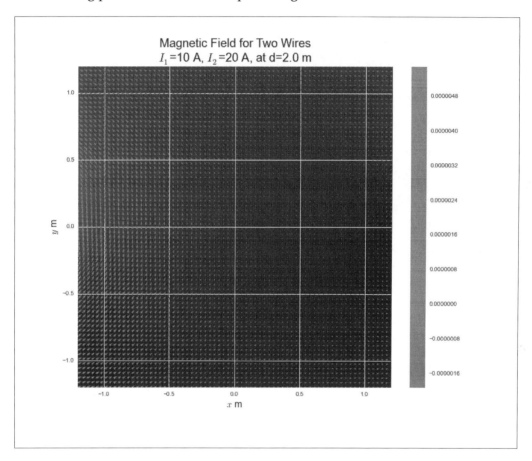

```
In [42]: Image("expmt_2.png")
```

The following plot is the result of the preceding command:

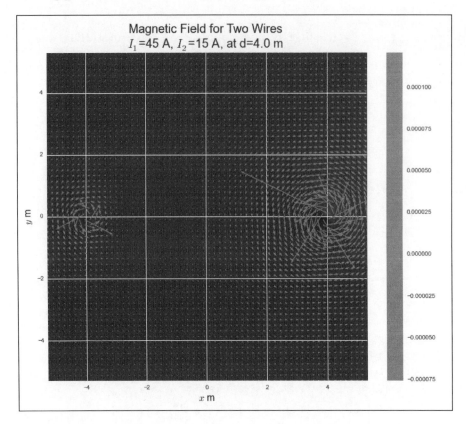

This brings the review of the object-oriented matplotlib API to a close. However, before we finish the chapter, we will take a look at how the other libraries use matplotlib.

matplotlib in other frameworks

In general, third-party libraries that depend on or provide support to the process of interfacing with matplotlib do so mostly through the scripting layer. Here is a quick summary of a few libraries that use matplotlib:

- **Seaborn**: This library uses all the `matplotlib.pyplot` functions.

- **NetworkX**: This library essentially uses all the `matplotlib.pyplot` functions, with the only exception being some backend and artist layer interfacing that is used to generate the project's gallery (which is another good example of the programmatic approach for batched jobs).

- **Pandas**: This library mostly uses `matplotlib.pyplot`, but it sometimes also uses the deprecated pylab interface. It also has some custom transforms and tickers in its time series converter code.

- **scikit-learn**: This library mostly uses `matplotlib.pyplot` along with some custom use of the font manager and color mapping. It also takes advantage of the collections, finance, and `mpl_toolkits` modules, among others. Additionally, this library performs some custom backend tweaking.

This is just a partial sampling of the respectable scientific computing libraries available that use matplotlib. The overwhelming impression that one is left with is twofold:

- The matplotlib module has been put to some very impressive use.

- The pyplot API in matplotlib is extensively used by every project in the community. Respect.

An important note on IPython

While discussing matplotlib in other frameworks, I would be remiss if the following was not mentioned. As of April 2014, IPython no longer supports starting with the -pylab flag. This is a *big change*, and many tutorials, books, and open source documents need to be updated with new best practices to start up IPython along with matplotlib. The preferred way of using matplotlib in the IPython Notebooks is demonstrated in the following code:

```
In [1]: %matplotlib inline
        import numpy as np
        import matplotlib.pyplot as plt
```

This change in IPython came as a result of the project's expansive growth in non-Python communities. With the ongoing development in the support of Julia and Haskell, their architecture is becoming language-agnostic. In fact, the project now has a new, more inclusive name (with a nice nod to its Python roots) — Jupyter.

Summary

As indicated, this chapter is connected to the previous one by the virtue of the relationship between matplotlib's architecture and the software library's APIs. While material for various matplotlib APIs is available online and in other books, we strove to view these from a different perspective. Firstly, in sources that cover matplotlib APIs exhaustively, one can be exposed to too many use cases. This can lead to a slight confusion on the part of the reader who is attempting to gain mastery over the subject area (matplotlib). Instead, we aimed for an overview approach that focused on some real-world examples in order to keep the story clear.

Secondly, we wanted to emphasize that there are many advanced users of matplotlib whose sole experience with regard to the library is via its deprecated compatibility layer with MATLAB. We wanted to provide useful material for those who wish to make the leap into the land of matplotlib.

Finally, it almost goes without saying that this chapter's work of the APIs builds upon our efforts in the previous chapter. Having just read about matplotlib's architecture and internals, our study of its APIs and integrations has us with additional insight, giving us a deeper understanding of how it all fits together.

This chapter brings to a close our exploration of the big picture. From here on out, we will engage with very specific advanced topics that are accompanied by in-depth exercises. Our first stop on the next leg of the journey will be event handling and interactive plots.

4

Event Handling and Interactive Plots

This chapter marks the beginning of our transition into specialized topics. While we will continue making references to the preceding overview, the subsequent chapters will focus on taking you deeper into the domain of advanced matplotlib usage.

In this chapter, we will delve into matplotlib events and interactive plots and cover the following topics:

- A general overview of event-based systems
- The anatomy of an event loop
- The GUI toolkit event loop basics
- Event loops in IPython and matplotlib
- Event handling in matplotlib
- Events for mouse, keyboard, axes, figures, and picking
- Compound events

The material presented here will be pulled from matplotlib's artist and backend layers, and it should provide a nice starting point for the vast world of user interaction in data visualization.

To follow along with this chapter's code, clone the notebook's repository and start up IPython by using the following code:

```
$ git clone https://github.com/masteringmatplotlib/interaction.git
$ cd interaction
$ make
```

Since we will be using the IPython Notebook backend—which is also known as nbagg—for interactive plots, we will not enter the usual %matplotlib inline command:

```
In [1]: import matplotlib
        matplotlib.use('nbagg')
```

We'll use the regular imports as well as a few other imports in the following examples:

```
In [2]: import random
        import sys
        import time
        import numpy as np
        import matplotlib as mpl
        import matplotlib.pyplot as plt
        import seaborn as sns
        from IPython.display import Image
        from typecheck import typecheck

        sys.path.append("../lib")
        import topo
```

Event loops in matplotlib

In the chapter on matplotlib architecture, we mentioned the event loops that the GUI toolkits use and which are integrated with matplotlib. As you dig through the matplotlib libraries, you will eventually come across several mentions with regard to the event loops that are not from the GUI toolkits. So that we can better understand the difference between these and, more importantly, the event handling and user interaction with plots, we're going to spend some time learning more about these event loops in matplotlib.

Event-based systems

In general, event loops are part of a recurring set of patterns that are used together in various computing frameworks. Often, they comprise of the following:

- An incoming event
- A mechanism that is used to respond to an event
- A looping construct (for example, the while loop, listener, and the message dispatch mechanism)

Event-based systems are typically asynchronous in nature, allowing events to be sent to the system and then responded to in any order without the slower operations preventing the faster ones from being executed sooner. It is this characteristic that makes the event-based systems such a compelling option for software architects and developers. When used properly, asynchronous programming can lead to significant improvements in the perceived performance of an application.

Event-based systems take many forms. Some common examples for the same include the following:

- Asynchronous networking libraries
- Toolkits that are used to build graphical user interfaces
- Enterprise messaging systems
- Game engines

It is a combination of the first two examples with which we will occupy ourselves in this chapter. Before we tackle this though, let's take a look at the basic workings of event-based systems, and in particular, the event loop.

The event loop

So, what did we mean previously when we said *a looping construct*? Well, the simplest loop that you can create in Python is the following:

```
while True:
    pass
```

This will just run forever until you press the *Ctrl* + *C* keys or the power goes out. However, this particular loop does nothing useful. Here's another loop that will run until its event fires a change of a value from `True` to `False`:

```
In [4]: x = True
        while x:
            time.sleep(1)
            if random.random() < 0.1:
                x = False
```

So, what relation do these simple loops have with the loops that power toolkits, such as GTK and Qt, or frameworks, such as Twisted and Tornado, possess? Usually, the event systems have the following:

- A way to start the event loop
- A way to stop the event loop
- Means to register events
- Means to respond to events

During each run, a loop will usually check a data structure to see whether there are any new events that occurred since the last time it looped. In a network event system, each loop will check to see whether any file descriptors are ready to read or write. In a GUI toolkit, each loop will check to see whether any clicks or button presses occurred.

Given the preceding simple criteria, let's explore another slightly more sophisticated and minimally demonstrative event loop. To keep this small, we are not going to integrate with socket or GUI events. The event that our loop will respond to will be quite minimal indeed—a keyboard interrupt:

```
In [5]: class EventLoop:
            def __init__(self):
                self.command = None
                self.status = None
                self.handlers = {"interrupt": self.handle_interrupt}
                self.resolution = 0.1

            def loop(self):
                self.command = "loop"
```

```
        while self.command != "stop":
            self.status = "running"
            time.sleep(self.resolution)

    def start(self):
        self.command = "run"
        try:
            self.loop()
        except KeyboardInterrupt:
            self.handle_event("interrupt")

    def stop(self):
        self.command = "stop"

    @typecheck
    def add_handler(self, fn: callable, event: str):
        self.handlers[event] = fn

    @typecheck
    def handle_event(self, event: str):
        self.handlers[event]()

    def handle_interrupt(self):
        print("Stopping event loop ...")
        self.stop()
```

Here's what we did:

- We created a class that maintains a data structure for event handlers
- We added a default handler for the `interrupt` event
- We also created a `loop` method
- We created methods to start and stop the loop via an attribute change
- In the start method, we checked for an interrupt signal and fired off an interrupt handler for the signal
- We created a method to add event handlers to the handler data structure (should we want to add more)

Now, you can run this loop in the notebook by using the following code:

```
In [*]: el = EventLoop()
        el.start()
```

When you evaluate this cell, IPython will display the usual indicator that a cell is running, in other words, the `In [*]` cell. When you're satisfied that the loop is merrily looping, go to the IPython Notebook menu and navigate to `Kernel | Interrupt`. The cell with a loop in it will finish, and the asterisk will be replaced by the input number. The interrupt handler will be printed out as a status message as well:

```
In [6]: el = EventLoop()
        el.start()
Stopping event loop ...
```

Though this event loop is fairly different from the power networking libraries or GUI toolkits, it's *very close* (both in nature as well as the code) to the default event loops matplotlib provides for its canvas objects. As such, this is a perfect starting place if you want to have a deeper understanding of matplotlib. To continue in this vein, reading the matplotlib backend source code will serve you well.

The preceding practical background information should be enough for you to more fully appreciate the following few sections.

GUI toolkit main loops

How are the main loops in the GUI toolkits different from the preceding ones? Well, for one, the GTK and Qt event systems aren't written in Python. The GTK main loop is written in C, and it is a part of one of the libraries underlying GTK — `GLib`. More importantly, the GUI toolkits are designed to respond to the user input from many types of devices, and sometimes, at a very fine-grained level. The loop demonstrated previously is a simple, generic loop that allows one to define any sort of event, which can also be connected to a callback.

However, even with all the differences, they can still be mapped to each other. The GLib event loop documentation provides the following diagram:

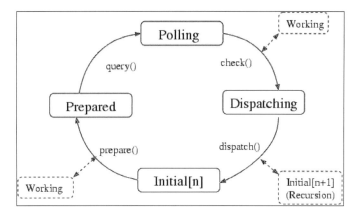

In the simple EventLoop class, setting the initial value of the handlers attribute is similar to what GLib can do in a prepare() or query() call. Our version of the check() call is really just a part of the Python control flow; we took the easy route with a try/except method wrapped around the loop call. The only way the class can monitor the outside world for events is through a KeyboardInterrupt exception. Our dispatch() is the call to the registered handler for the interrupt event. Hence, despite the simplicity of our example, one can see how it relates to the fully featured, real-world event systems.

An in-depth exploration of the GUI main loops is well beyond the scope of this book, but before we leave the topic entirely behind, let's look at what's running under IPython's bonnet.

IPython Notebook event loops

IPython originally started as an advanced **read-eval-print loop** (**REPL**) for Python. After about a decade of becoming a powerful tool for Python scientific computing, using NumPy and matplotlib, and providing parallel computing features, IPython added support for HTML notebooks. Since then, the popularity of IPython Notebook and the user-created content that runs on it has exploded. The matplotlib development community has responded with a matplotlib backend that enables interaction in the browser, which is similar to what users might expect when running a GTK or Qt backend.

The IPython Notebook requires two main components—an HTTP server and a web client, such as your browser. The functionality of a websocket-enabled HTTP server is provided by Tornado, a Python web framework, and an asynchronous networking library. Your browser provides the infrastructure necessary to support the websocket communications with the web server. Through ZeroMQ, IPython provides the means to send the data it receives over websockets to the rest of the components in the IPython architecture.

Some of these components have their own event loops. They include the following:

- The browser's event loop
- Tornado's HTTP Server event loop
- IPython's PyZMQ event loops (for instance, pollers)

However, what this picture is missing is how this relates to matplotlib. In order for a web-based matplotlib backend to work, it needs the following:

- A means to send data and receive results for display
- A figure manager that establishes two-way communications with IPython
- A figure canvas with its own event loop
- A timer class to get events to the Tornado `ioloop` in IPython Notebook app
- An event loop for each canvas

matplotlib event loops

The last bullet item may cause confusion. So, it is important to make this clear—the event loops that matplotlib uses for its canvases are completely different and quite separate from the GUI event loops. In fact, the default figure canvas event loop is very similar to the loop method in the `EventLoop` class from the previous section.

The GUI and matplotlib event loops have different code. Yet, they are still connected. In the case of an IPython Notebook app, the web browser's JavaScript events and websockets ultimately communicate with the IPython kernel, which in turn communicates with the instances of matplotlib figure managers, figures, and canvases.

Understanding how these pieces work together and communicate is the key to mastering the matplotlib events, both for the creation of more advanced plots, as well as the inevitable debugging that they will need. The best resource for a deeper understanding of these events is the matplotlib source code. Spend time getting to know how figures and canvases respond to events, messages get sent from one class to another, how matplotlib generalizes the event experience across the GUI toolkits, and how this affects the toolkit of your choice.

Event handling

We now have a good background for some practical work with matplotlib events. We are now ready to explore the nitty-gritty. Let's begin with the list of events that matplotlib supports:

Event name	Class	Description
button_press_event	MouseEvent	The mouse button is pressed
button_release_event	MouseEvent	The mouse button is released
draw_event	DrawEvent	The canvas draw occurs
key_press_event	KeyEvent	A key is pressed
key_release_event	KeyEvent	A key is released
motion_notify_event	MouseEvent	Motion of the mouse
pick_event	PickEvent	An object in the canvas is selected
resize_event	ResizeEvent	The figure canvas is resized
scroll_event	MouseEvent	The scroll wheel of the mouse is rolled
figure_enter_event	LocationEvent	The mouse enters a figure
figure_leave_event	LocationEvent	The mouse leaves a figure
axes_enter_event	LocationEvent	The mouse enters an axes object
axes_leave_event	LocationEvent	The mouse leaves an axes object

Note that the classes listed in the preceding events table are defined in `matplotlib.backend_bases`.

The perceptual field of matplotlib is the canvas object—this is where the events take place, and this is the object that provides the interface to connect the code to the events. The canvas object has an `mpl_connect` method, which must be called if you want to provide custom user interaction features along with your plots. This method just takes the following two arguments:

- A string value for the event, which can be any of the values listed in the `Event Name` column of the preceding table
- A callback function or method

We will demonstrate some ways to use `mpl_connect` in the subsequent examples.

Mouse events

In matplotlib, the mouse events may be any of the following:

- `button_press_event`: This event involves a mouse button press
- `button_release_event`: This event involves a mouse button release
- `scroll_event`: This event involves scrolling of the mouse
- `motion_notify_event`: This event involves a notification pertaining to the mouse movement

The notebook for this chapter has a section on mouse events, which shows several examples. We will take a look at one of these in particular; it demonstrates the press and release events, and it does so with an almost tactile feedback mechanism. These are the tasks that it does:

- It connects a callback for mouse press and mouse release
- It records the time of the click
- It records the time of the release
- It draws a circle at the coordinates of the click
- It draws another partially transparent circle whose size is determined by the amount of time that passed between the click and the release

Let's take a look at the code so that you can clearly see how to implement each of the aforementioned things:

```
In [8]: class Callbacks:
            def __init__(self):
```

```python
        (figure, axes) = plt.subplots()
        axes.set_aspect(1)
        figure.canvas.mpl_connect(
            'button_press_event', self.press)
        figure.canvas.mpl_connect(
            'button_release_event', self.release)

    def start(self):
        plt.show()

    def press(self, event):
        self.start_time = time.time()

    def release(self, event):
        self.end_time = time.time()
        self.draw_click(event)

    def draw_click(self, event):
        size = 4 * (self.end_time - self.start_time) ** 2
        c1 = plt.Circle(
            [event.xdata, event.ydata], 0.002,)
        c2 = plt.Circle(
            [event.xdata, event.ydata], 0.02 * size,
            alpha=0.2)
        event.canvas.figure.gca().add_artist(c1)
        event.canvas.figure.gca().add_artist(c2)
        event.canvas.figure.show()

cbs = Callbacks()
cbs.start()
```

Here, we saw the aforementioned `mpl_connect` method in action. The constructor in our class sets up the figure's canvas instance with two callbacks. One will be fired when the canvas detects `button_press_event`, and the other will be fired when the canvas detects `button_release_event`.

When you run the preceding code in the notebook and click on the resulting graph, you will see something like this (depending on where you click and how long you hold down the mouse button):

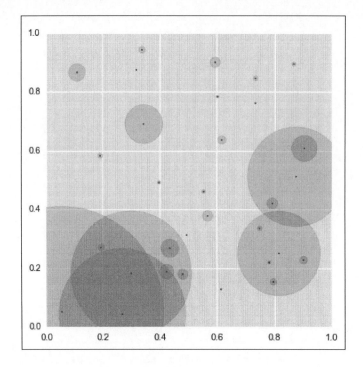

There are a few things worth highlighting here:

- We don't need to store any references to the canvas or the figure in this object; we utilize the constructor merely to set up the callbacks for the two events

- We utilized the canvas' `mpl_connect` method to register callbacks, as previously discussed

- The event object not only provides access to event-specific attributes such as the coordinates of the mouse click, but also has references to useful objects, such as the canvas instance and therefore, the figure instance as well

Keyboard events

Keyboard events are similar to the mouse events, though there are only two of them:

- `key_press_event`
- `key_release_event`

These are used in the same way as the corresponding mouse button events, though they provide an interesting opportunity for the ergonomically sensitive user.

As of matplotlib version 1.4 and IPython version 2.3, keyboard events for plots are not supported in the `nbagg` backend. Therefore, we will use IPython from the terminal for this section.

In the following section, we're going to take a look at an example that may give you some ideas with regard to the customization of your own plots. We're going to make a simple data viewer. Before we look at the code, let's describe what we want to do:

- We want to easily navigate through large datasets with simple keyboard commands
- Given a large dataset, we would like to have each subset displayed in its own plots
- In the GUI, we would like to navigate forwards and backwards through the datasets, visualizing the plot of each set on the fly
- We would like to return to the beginning of the datasets with a key press

This is pretty straightforward, and it an excellent use case for keyboard events. We'll have to build some pieces for this, though. Here's what we will need:

- A function that returns each member of our large dataset one after the other
- A class that lets us move forwards and backwards through our dataset (by making use of the preceding function)
- A class that performs the basic configuration and setup
- Additional support functions to create and update the plots

In a terminal IPython session, we can perform the initial imports and run the *color map* setup in the following way:

```
In [1]: import numpy as np
In [2]: import matplotlib as mpl
In [3]: from matplotlib import pyplot as plt
In [4]: import seaborn as sns


In [5]: pallete_name = "husl"
In [6]: colors = sns.color_palette(pallete_name, 8)
In [7]: colors.reverse()
In [8]: cmap = mpl.colors.LinearSegmentedColormap.from_list(
            pallete_name, colors)
```

Next, we need a function that can act as a given dataset as well as another function that will act as the very large dataset (infinite, in this case). The second function is a good fit if you wish to use a generator:

```
In [9]: def make_data(n, c):
            r = 4 * c * np.random.rand(n) ** 2
            theta = 2 * np.pi * np.random.rand(n)
            area = 200 * r**2 * np.random.rand(n)
            return (r, area, theta)


In [10]: def generate_data(n, c):
            while True:
                yield make_data(n, c)
```

We've now received an endless number of datasets that can be used in our viewer. Now, let's create the data `Carousel` class. It's needs to perform the following tasks:

- Maintain a reference to the data
- Move to the next data in the set, putting the viewed data into a queue
- Move back to the previous data items, pushing the ones it passes onto a separate queue while it takes them off the other queue
- Provide a callback for `key_press_event` and then dispatch to the other functions, depending on the pressed key
- Provide an initial plot as well as the event-handling functions for specific keys

Here's what the data `Carousel` class looks like:

```
In [13]: class Carousel:
             def __init__(self, data):
                 (self.left, self.right) = ([], [])
                 self.gen = data
                 self.last_key = None
             def start(self, axes):
                 make_plot(*self.next(), axes=axes)
             def prev(self):
                 if not self.left:
                     return []
                 data = self.left.pop()
                 self.right.insert(0, data)
                 return data
             def next(self):
                 if self.right:
                     data = self.right.pop(0)
                 else:
                     data = next(self.gen)
                 self.left.append(data)
                 return data
             def reset(self):
                 self.right = self.left + self.right
                 self.left = []
             def dispatch(self, event):
                 if event.key == "right":
                     self.handle_right(event)
                 elif event.key == "left":
                     self.handle_left(event)
                 elif event.key == "r":
                     self.handle_reset(event)
             def handle_right(self, event):
                 print("Got right key ...")
                 if self.last_key == "left":
                     self.next()
```

```
                  update_plot(*self.next(), event=event)
                  self.last_key = event.key
          def handle_left(self, event):
              print("Got left key ...")
              if self.last_key == "right":
                  self.prev()
              data = self.prev()
              if data:
                  update_plot(*data, event=event)
              self.last_key = event.key
          def handle_reset(self, event):
              print("Got reset key ...")
              self.reset()
              update_plot(*self.next(), event=event)
              self.last_key = event.key

In [14]: %paste
```

The class that will perform the setup and configuration duties, including the connecting of key_press_event to the callback and the instantiating of the Carousel object, is as follows:

```
In [15]: class CarouselManager:
              def __init__(self, density=300, multiplier=1):
                  (figure, self.axes) = plt.subplots(
                      figsize=(12,12), subplot_kw={"polar": "True"})
                  self.axes.hold(False)
                  data = generate_data(density, multiplier)
                  self.carousel = Carousel(data)
                  _ = figure.canvas.mpl_connect(
                      'key_press_event', self.carousel.dispatch)
              def start(self):
                  self.carousel.start(self.axes)
                  plt.show()

In [16]: %paste
```

Note that after pasting the code for each class, IPython will need you to use the %paste command so that it can accurately parse what was pasted.

And with this, we're ready to navigate through our data visually. We'll make the displayed circles larger than the default size by setting the multiplier to a higher number in the following way:

```
In [17]: cm = CarouselManager(multiplier=2)
In [18]: cm.start()
```

This will make a GUI window pop up on the screen with an image that looks like this:

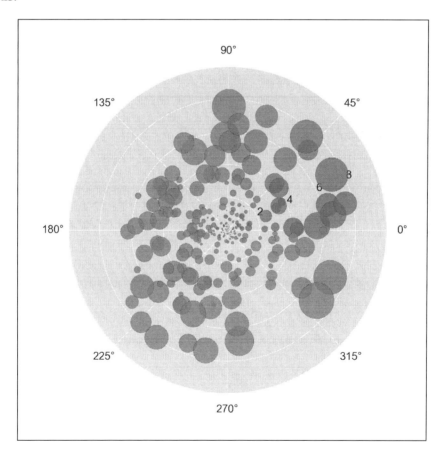

Now try pressing the right and left arrows of your keyboard to view the different (randomly generated) datasets. As coded in the `Carousel` class, pressing *R* will return us to the beginning of the data.

 Depending on the web browser that you are using, you may see different results, experience poor performance, or find out that some actions don't work at all. We have found out that the best user experience with regard to a browser for matplotlib is with the Firefox and Chrome browsers.

The most practical understanding that you can take away, which you can use in your own projects, is that you need to write a dispatch method or function for every key (or key combination) press and release event. The simplicity of the matplotlib interface of providing a single key press event for all the keys ensures that the matplotlib code stays compact while keeping the options open for the developers. The flip side is that you need to implement the individual key handling yourself for whichever keys your particular use case has a need of.

Axes and figure events

We can execute callbacks when the mouse enters and leaves figures or axes in a way that is similar to the connection of the keyboard and mouse events. This can be helpful if you have complex plots with many subplots. It will allow you to provide a visual feedback to the user regarding the subplot that is our focus or even expose a larger view of the focused plot. The IPython Notebook for this chapter covers an example of this.

Object picking

The next event that we will mention is a special one—the event of an object being *picked*. Object picking is one of the greatest, although unsung, features of matplotlib as it allows one to essentially create a custom data browser that is capable of revealing the details in the deeply nested or rich data across large scales.

Every `Artist` instance (naturally including subclasses of `Artist`) has an attribute called `picker`. The setting of this attribute is what enables object picking in matplotlib.

The definition of *picked* can vary, depending on the context. For instance, setting `Artist.picker` can have the following results:

- If the result is `True`, picking is enabled for the artist object and `pick_event` will be fired every time a mouse event occurs over the artist object in the figure.

- If the result is a number (for instance, `float` or `int`), the value is interpreted as a *tolerance*. If the event's data (such as the x and y values) is within the value of this *tolerance*, `pick_event` will be fired.

- If the result is a callable, then the provided function or method returns a boolean value, which determines whether `pick_event` is fired.

- If the result is `None`, picking is disabled.

The object picking feature provides the means by which a programmer can create dynamic views on data. This feature is rivaled only by expensive proprietary software. Thanks to this capability, in conjunction with matplotlib's custom styles, one can easily create beautiful, compelling data visualization applications that are tailored for the needs of the user.

The IPython Notebook in this chapter covers an example of this, and it should serve as a source of inspiration for a great number of use cases.

Compound event handling

This section discusses the combining of multiple events or other sources of data in order to provide a more highly customized user experience for visual plot updates, the preparation of data, the setting of object properties, or the updating of widgets. The multiple events or decisions that are made based on multiple or cascading events is what we will refer to as **compound events**.

The navigation toolbar

The first example of compound events that we will touch upon are those managed by a backend widget for interactive navigation. This widget is available for all backends (including the `nbagg` backend for IPython when it is not in the `inline` mode). The navigation toolbar widget has multiple buttons, each with a specific function. In brief, the functionality associated with each button is as follows:

- **Home**: This button returns the figure to its originally rendered state.

- **Previous**: This returns to the previous view in the plot's history.

- **Next**: This moves to the next view in the plot's history.
- **Pan/Zoom**: You can pan across the plot by clicking and holding the left mouse button. You can zoom by clicking and holding the right mouse button (behavior differs between the Cartesian and Polar plots).
- **Zoom-to-Rectangle**: You can zoom in on a selected portion of the plot by using this button.
- **Subplot Configuration**: With this button, you can configure the display of subplots via a pop-up widget with various parameters.
- **Save**: This button will save the plot in its currently displayed state to a file.

Furthermore, when a toolbar action is engaged, the `toolbar` instance sets the toolbar's current mode. For instance, when the **Zoom-to-Rectangle** button is clicked, the mode will be set to zoom rect. When in **Pan/Zoom**, the mode will be set to pan/zoom. These can be used in conjunction with the supported events to fire callbacks in response to the toolbar activity.

As a matter of fact, the `matplotlib.backend_bases.NavigationToolbar2` toolbar class is an excellent place to look for examples of compound events. Let's examine the **Pan/Zoom** button. The class tracks the following via the attributes that can be set:

- The connection ID for a `press` event
- The connection ID for a `release` event
- The connection ID for a `mouse move` event (this is correlated to a mouse drag later in the code)
- Whether the toolbar is active
- The `toolbar` mode
- The `zoom` mode

During the toolbar setup, the toolbar button events are connected to callbacks. When these buttons are pressed and the callbacks are fired, old events are disconnected and the new ones are connected. In this way, a chain of events may be set up with a particular sequence of events firing only a particular set of callbacks in a particular order.

Specialized events

The code in `NavigationToolbar2` is a great starting place if you want some ideas on how you can combine events in your own projects. You can have a workflow that requires responses to plot updates only if a series of other events have taken place first. You can accomplish this by connecting the events to and disconnecting them from various callbacks.

Interactive panning and zooming

Let's utilize a combination of the `toolbar` mode and a mouse button release for a practical example that demonstrates the creation of a compound event.

The problem that we want to address is this—when a user pans or zooms out of the range of the previously computed data in a plotted area, the user is presented with parts of an empty grid with no visualization in the newly exposed area. It would be nice if we could put our newfound event callback skills to use in order to solve this issue.

One possible example where it would be useful to refresh the plot figure when it has been panned is a plot for a *topographic* map. We're going to do a few things with this example:

- Add a custom `cmap` (matplotlib's *color map*) method to give the altitudes the look of a physical map
- Provide the altitude in meters and the distance in kilometers
- Create a class that can update the map via a method call

The custom color map and the equations to generate a topographical map have been saved to `./lib/topo.py` in this chapter's IPython Notebook repository. We imported this module at the beginning of the notebook. So it's ready to use. The first class that we will define is `TopoFlowMap`, a wrapper class that will be used to update the plot when we pan:

```
In [21]: class TopoFlowMap:
            def __init__(self, xrange=None, yrange=None, seed=1):
                self.xrange = xrange or (0,1)
                self.yrange = yrange or (0,1)
                self.seed = seed
                (self.figure, self.axes) = plt.subplots(
```

```python
            figsize=(12,8))
        self.axes.set_aspect(1)
        self.colorbar = None
        self.update()

    def get_ranges(self, xrange, yrange):
        if xrange:
            self.xrange = xrange
        if yrange:
            self.yrange = yrange
        return (xrange, yrange)

    def get_colorbar_axes(self):
        colorbar_axes = None
        if self.colorbar:
            colorbar_axes = self.colorbar.ax
            colorbar_axes.clear()
        return colorbar_axes

    def get_filled_contours(self, coords):
        return self.axes.contourf(
            cmap=topo.land_cmap, *coords.values())

    def update_contour_lines(self, filled_contours):
        contours = self.axes.contour(
            filled_contours, colors="black", linewidths=2)
        self.axes.clabel(
            contours, fmt="%d", colors="#330000")

    def update_water_flow(self, coords, gradient):
        self.axes.streamplot(
            coords.get("x")[:,0],
            coords.get("y")[0,:],
```

```
                    gradient.get("dx"),
                    gradient.get("dy"),
                    color="0.6",
                    density=1,
                    arrowsize=2)

    def update_labels(self):
        self.colorbar.set_label("Altitude (m)")
        self.axes.set_title(
            "Water Flow across Land Gradients", fontsize=20)
        self.axes.set_xlabel("$x$ (km)")
        self.axes.set_ylabel("$y$ (km)")

    def update(self, xrange=None, yrange=None):
        (xrange, yrange) = self.get_ranges(xrange, yrange)
        (coords, grad) = topo.make_land_map(
            self.xrange, self.yrange, self.seed)
        self.axes.clear()
        colorbar_axes = self.get_colorbar_axes()
        filled_contours = self.get_filled_contours(coords)
        self.update_contour_lines(filled_contours)
        self.update_water_flow(coords, grad)
        self.colorbar = self.figure.colorbar(
            filled_contours, cax=colorbar_axes)
        self.update_labels()
```

The notebook returns to the IPython backend to display the graph (previously using a different backend for other examples):

```
In [22]: plt.switch_backend('nbAgg')
In [23]: tfm = TopoFlowMap(
             xrange=(0,1.5), yrange=(0,1.5), seed=1732)
         plt.show()
```

The preceding code gives us the following plot:

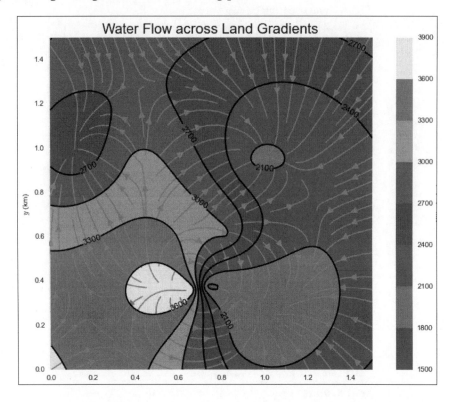

If you click on the **Pan/Zoom** button in the navigation toolbar and then drag the plotted data about, you will see that the empty grid contains the data that hasn't been plotted (the area that was outside the axes prior to the panning action).

Since we do want to redraw and there is no pan event to connect to, what are our options? Well, two come to mind:

- Piggyback on `draw_event`, which fires each time the canvas is moved
- Use `button_release_event`, which will fire when the panning is complete

If our figure was easy to draw with simple equations, the first option would probably be fine. However, we're performing some multivariate calculus on our simulated topography. As you might have noticed, our plot does not render immediately. So, let's go with the second option.

To make our lives easier, we will take advantage of the mode attribute of `NavigationTool2`, which will let us know when one of the events that we care about, `pan/zoom`, has taken place.

Here's the manager class for the *plot-refresh* feature:

```
In [24]: class TopoFlowMapManager:
             def __init__(self, xrange=None, yrange=None, seed=1):
                 self.map = TopoFlowMap(xrange, yrange, seed)
                 _ = self.map.figure.canvas.mpl_connect(
                     'button_release_event',
                     self.handle_pan_zoom_release)

             def start(self):
                 plt.show()

             def handle_pan_zoom_release(self, event):
                 if event.canvas.toolbar.mode != "pan/zoom":
                     return
                 self.map.update(event.inaxes.get_xlim(),
                                 event.inaxes.get_ylim())
                 event.canvas.draw()
```

As with the other examples, we used the constructor to set up the event callback for a mouse button release. The callback will be fired for every button click. However, the code will not execute past the conditional if we are not in the `pan/zoom` mode. In our case, the callback does two crucial things for our feature:

- It recalculates the ranges of the *x* and *y* axes
- It calls the `update` method on the `TopoFlowMap` instance, which changes the range for the NumPy `mgrid` function and recalculates the gradients for this new range

You can test this out with the following code:

```
In [25]: tfmm = TopoFlowMapManager(
             xrange=(0,1.5), yrange=(0,1.5), seed=1732)
         tfmm.start()
```

This particular plot is fairly involved, and hence, it is potentially similar to some real-world examples that you may come across. However, keep in mind that if you have simple data to display with little or no calculation, firing your callback on `draw_event` instead of `button_release_event` will render the update as you move the mouse.

Summary

In this chapter, we covered details on event systems, event loops, and how these relate to matplotlib. We also covered details on event types in matplotlib and ways to employ them to build interactive plots

The first area comprised of the background, which helped us appreciate the inner workings of matplotlib's event system. It also armed us with the knowledge that avoids confusion between the GUI toolkit event loops that matplotlib ties to and the matplotlib event loops that power the ability of the canvas to respond to the events on plots.

There are even more examples of plot interaction in the notebook for this chapter. So, be sure to check out the repository for extra goodies.

In the next chapter, we will take a new direction. Instead of low-level internals, we will focus on high-level operations and data analysis.

5

High-level Plotting and Data Analysis

A significant aspect of gaining matplotlib mastery is familiarizing oneself with the use of the other Python tools in the scientific programming ecosystem. Libraries such as **NumPy**, **SciPy**, **Pandas**, or **SymPy** are just the beginning. The tools available in the community cover an enormous amount of ground, entailing the spectrum of many fields and subspecialties. Projects such as **scikit-learn**, **AstroPy**, **h5py**, and so on, build upon the foundations provided by others, thus being able to provide more functionality quicker than, if they had to start from scratch themselves.

Those who may want to look more deeply into these and other tools may benefit from a guided tour into one area that could serve as a template for future exploration into many other areas. This is our mission in this chapter, with our entry points for further examination being the following:

- A background and overview of high-level plotting
- Practical high-level plotting, using a data analysis example

We will use the term *high-level plotting* to describe things such as wrapping matplotlib functionality for use in new contexts, combining different libraries for particular plots that are not available in matplotlib, and visualization of complex datasets using wrapper functions, classes, and libraries.

The following high-level plotting topics will be covered in this chapter:

- Historical background
- matplotlib libraries, and high-level plotting
- An introduction to the grammar of graphics
- Libraries inspired by the grammar of graphics

When speaking of *data analysis*, our focus will be on the pragmatic aspects of parsing, grouping, filtering, applying computational workflows to, and subjecting to statistical methods to various sources of data, all in the context of high-level data visualization. The topics we will cover in this area will include:

- Selected functions and methods from Pandas, SciPy, and NumPy

- Examination and manipulation of a Pandas dataset

- A tour of the various plots that are useful to have at one's fingertips when performing visualization tasks of a statistical nature

We have another IPython Notebook for you to work with while reading this chapter. You can clone the repository and run it with the following:

```
$ git clone https://github.com/masteringmatplotlib/high-level.git
$ cd high-level
$ make
```

> Some of the examples in this chapter use **Pygraphviz**, which needs the graphviz C header files that are present on the system. This is usually accomplished by installing graphviz and its development libraries, although you may need to upset Pygraphviz's setup.py, to point to the location of the graphviz header files.

High-level plotting

In this book, when we mention *high-level*, we are referring not to some assessment of value or improvement over something, but rather to layers of abstraction, or more precisely, layers of interaction. When engaged in *high-level plotting*, we expect that users and developers will be creating visualizations of complex data with fewer commands or steps required than by using matplotlib's basic functionality directly. This is a result of complex tasks wrapping a greater number of smaller, simpler tasks.

Plotting itself is a high-level activity: raw data and often calculations on that data are combined, processed, some more in anticipation of user consumption, arranged or grouped in ways suitable for conveying the desired information, and then applied to some medium in ways that one hopes will render greater insight. By our definition, each activity upon that original raw data is, in some way, *high-level*.

Before we look at examples of modern high-level plotting, let us gain some perspective through examining the historical context by which we arrived at matplotlib and its ecosystem of related libraries.

Historical background

In 2005, Princeton Alum and Professor of Psychology, Michael Friendly, published the paper, *Milestones in the History of Data Visualization: A Case Study in Statistical Historiography*, which provided an excellent overview of data visualization and perhaps the first comprehensive summary of *the entire development of visual thinking and the visual representation of data*. Dr. Friendly's paper and his related, and extraordinary, work on the Milestones Timeline are the sources used for the background presented in this section.

Flemish astronomer Michael Florent van Langren is credited with the first visual representation of statistical data in a 1644 graph of 12 contemporary estimates for the distance between Toledo and Rome.

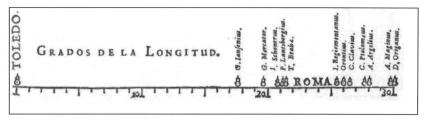

Visual representation of statistical data of distances by Michael Florent van Langren, 1644

In 1669, Christiaan Huygens created the first graph of a continuous distribution function. A few years later, in 1686, Edmond Halley created a plot predicting barometric pressure versus altitude, which was derived from experimental observation.

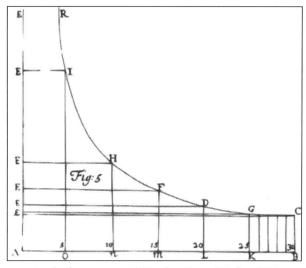

Graph of pressure prediction by Edmond Halley, 1686

The first line graph and bar chart came in 1786, with the pie chart and circle graph following in 1801, both due to noted Scottish engineer and political economist William Playfair. This is commonly considered to be the birth of modern graphical methods in statistics:

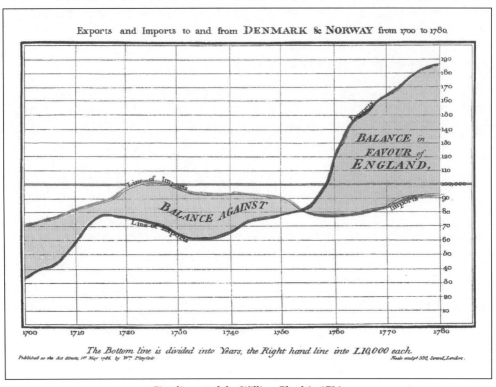

First line graph by William Playfair, 1786

Though the intervening years did bring advances in visual representation, it wasn't until the mid-20th century that significant strides were made, both in the deeper understanding of visual methods themselves as well as a growing set of tools via the rise of computing science. In 1968, the **Macsyma** (short for **Mac's Symbolic Manipulator**) project was started at **MIT** (short for **Massachusetts Institute of Technology**). Written in Lisp, this was the first comprehensive symbolic mathematics system created, many of whose ideas were later adopted by software programs such as Mathematica and Maple. In 1976, the S programming language was invented at Bell Labs. It was from this language that the R programming language was derived, since then gaining fame as a highly respected platform for data analysis and visualization. In 1979, Chris Cole and Stephen Wolfram created the computer algebra system SMP, often considered *version 0* of Mathematica. 1980 saw the first release of the Maple computer algebra system, with MATLAB arriving on the scene in 1984, and Mathematica in 1988.

It is this heritage to which matplotlib owes its existence: both the historical work done with ink and paper, as well as the advances made in the software. At the time of matplotlib's genesis, the Python programming language was beginning to establish itself in the world of high-level languages, already seeing adoption in applications of the scientific computing field. As we can see, the plotting that we do now has a richer and more diverse background that we might have initially imagined, and provides the foundation for the lofty aspirations of high-level plotting.

matplotlib

As we have discussed, matplotlib provides *mid-level* access to the mechanics plotting using the programmatic, object-oriented API of the backend and artist layers. One could then make the argument that the scripting layer, as represented by pyplot or the deprecated pylab, provides APIs for high-level plotting. A better example would be if there was any use of pyplot in matplotlib itself, employed as a means of providing a simple interface for a complex plotting task. It turns out that there is an example of this in the codebase, and it occurs in the `sankey.py` file.

The Sankey diagram is named after Captain Matthew Henry Phineas Riall Sankey, who used it in 1898 to visually depict the thermal efficiency of steam engines. Sankey diagrams in matplotlib have been supported since 2010 when the `matplotlib.sankey` module was contributed by Yannick Copin and Kevin Davies. The following diagram is that of a Rankine power cycle, another example of Sankey diagrams:

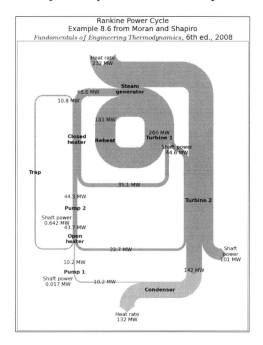

Though named after Captain Sankey, the first such diagram was created years earlier by French civil engineer Charles Joseph Minard.

In this module, `pyplot` is imported and used simply to generate a figure and an axes object. However, the impressive demo image is only fully appreciated when the contents of `sankey.py` are examined and one sees the extensive logic used, to render these flow diagrams in matplotlib. The module not only uses `pyplot`, but also combines paths, patches, and transforms to give users the ability to generate plots containing these extraordinary diagrams — an excellent and concise example of high-level plotting.

For the rest of the chapter, we will look at other libraries offering similar examples of wrapping matplotlib plotting functionality. Each of these accomplish a great deal with considerably less effort that would be exerted than if we were left to our own devices and had to use only matplotlib to produce the desired effect.

NetworkX

In *Chapter 2, The matplotlib Architecture*, we encountered the graph library **NetworkX** and used it in conjunction with matplotlib, something that NetworkX supports directly. Let us take a deeper look at this library from the perspective of our high-level plotting topic.

We'll start with a commented code sample and plot, and then go into more details. The following example is adapted from one in the NetworkX gallery by Aric Hagberg of Los Alamos National Laboratory:

```
In [5]: import sys
        sys.path.append("../lib")
        import lanl

        # Set up the plot's figure instance
        plt.figure(figsize=(14,14))

        # Generate the data graph structure representing
        # the route relationships
        G = lanl.get_routes_graph(debug=True)

        # Perform the high-level plotting operations in
        # NetworkX
```

```
pos = nx.graphviz_layout(G, prog="twopi", root=0)
nx.draw(G, pos,
        node_color=[G.rtt[v] for v in G],
        with_labels=False,
        alpha=0.5,
        node_size=50,
        cmap=cmap)

# Update the ranges
xmax = 1.02 * max(xx for xx, _ in pos.values())
ymax = 1.02 * max(yy for _, yy in pos.values())

# Final matplotlib tweaks and rendering
plt.xlim(0, xmax)
plt.ylim(0, ymax)
plt.show()
```

The following plot is the result of the preceding code:

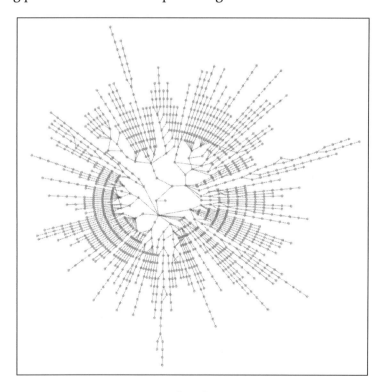

In *Chapter 2, The matplotlib Architecture*, we needed to employ some custom logic to refine graph relationships, which accounted for both the structure of the modules and the conceptual architecture of matplotlib. Dr. Hagberg had to do something similar when rendering the Internet routes from Los Alamos National Laboratory. We've put this code in the `lanl` module for this notebook repository; that is where all the logic is defined for converting the route data to graph relationships.

We can see clearly from the code comments where the high-level plotting occurs:

- The call to `nx.graphviz_layout`
- The call to `nx.draw`

We can learn how NetworkX acts as a high-level plotting library by taking a look at these, starting with the `layout` function.

NetworkX provides several possible graph library backends, and to do so in a manner that makes it easier for the end user, some of the imports can be quite obscured. Let us get the location of the `graphviz_layout` function the easy way:

```
In [6]: nx.graphviz_layout
```

```
Out [6]: <function networkx.drawing.nx_agraph.graphviz_layout>
```

If you open that file (either in your virtual environment's site-packages or on GitHub), you can see that `graphviz_layout` wraps the `pygraphviz_layout` function. From there, we see that NetworkX is converting pygraphviz's node data structure to something general, which can be used for all NetworkX backends. At this point, we're already several layers deep in NetworkX's high-level API internals. Let us continue:

```
In [7]: nx.draw
```

```
Out [7]: <function networkx.drawing.nx_pylab.draw>
```

`nx_pylab` gives us a nice hint that we're getting closer to matplotlib itself. In fact, the `draw` function makes direct use of `matplotlib.pyplot` in order to achieve the following:

- Get the current figure from `pyplot`
- Or, if it exists, from the axes object
- Hold and un-hold the matplotlib figures
- Call a matplotlib `draw` function

It also makes a subsequent call to the NetworkX graph backend to draw the actual edges and nodes. Theses additional calls get node, edge, and label data and make further calls to matplotlib `draw` functions. None of which we have to do; we simply call `nx.draw` (with appropriate parameters). Thus the benefits of high-level plotting!

Pandas

The following example is from a library whose purpose is to provide Python users and developers extensive support for high-level data analysis. Pandas offers several high performant data structures for this purpose, in a large part, built around the NumPy scientific computing library.

How does this relate to a high-level plotting? In addition to providing such things as its `Series`, `DataFrame`, and `Panel` data structures, Pandas incorporate a plotting functionality into some of these as well.

Let us take a look at an example, where we generate some random data and then utilize the `plot` function made available on the `DataFrame` object. We'll start with generating some random data samples:

```
In [8]: from scipy.stats import norm, rayleigh


        a = rayleigh.rvs(loc=5, scale=2, size=1000) + 1
        b = rayleigh.rvs(loc=5, scale=2, size=1000)
        c = rayleigh.rvs(loc=5, scale=2, size=1000) - 1
```

With these, we can populate our Pandas data structure:

```
In [9]: data = pd.DataFrame(
            {"a": a, "b": b, "c": c},
            columns=["a", "b", "c"])
```

And then, view it via a call in IPython:

```
In [10]: data.plot(
            kind="hist", stacked=True, bins=30,
            figsize=(16, 8))
         axes.set_title("Fabricated Wind Speed Data",
            fontsize=20)
```

```
axes.set_xlabel("Mean Hourly Wind Speed (km/hr)",
    fontsize=16)
_ = axes.set_ylabel("Velocity Counts", fontsize=16)
```

The following plot is the result of the preceding code:

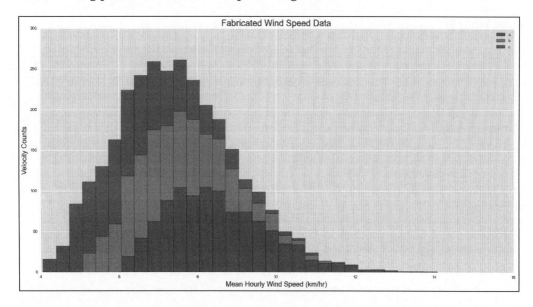

Let us go spelunking in the Pandas source, to get a better understanding of how Pandas is doing this. In the Pandas source code directory, open the file `pandas/core/frame.py`. This is where the `DataFrame` object is defined. If you search for `DataFrame.plot`, you will see that plot is actually an attribute of `DataFrame`, not a defined method. Furthermore, the code for the plot implementation is in `pandas.tools.plotting.plot_frame`.

After opening that module's file, search for `def plot_frame`. What we see here is a short chain of functions that are handing all sorts of configuration and options for us, allowing us to easily use a plot method on the data structure. The Pandas developers have very kindly returned the matplotlib result of the `plot` call (the top-level axes object) so that we may work with it in the same way as other matplotlib results.

We're going to shift gears a bit now, and take a new look at high-level plotting. It is what many consider to be the future of data visualization: the grammar of graphics.

The grammar of graphics

In the section, where we covered the historical background of plotting, we briefly made reference to the rebirth of data visualization in the mid-20th century. One of the prominent works of this time was by famed French cartographer Jacques Bertin, author of the *Semiologie Graphique*. Published in 1967, this was the first significant work dedicated to identifying the theoretical underpinnings of visualized information. In 1977, the American mathematician known for creating of one of the most common FFT algorithms, John Tukey, published the book *Exploratory Data Analysis, Sage Publications*, in which he introduced the world to the box plot. The method of data analysis described in this work inspired development in the S programming language, which later carried over to the R programming language. This work allowed statisticians to better identify trends and recognize patterns in large datasets. Dr. Tukey set the data visualization world on its current course by advocating for the examination of data itself, to lead to insights. The next big leap in the visualization of data for statistical analysis came with the 1985 publication of the book, *The Elements of Graphing Data, William S. Cleveland, Hobart Press*, representing 20 years of work in active research and scientific journal article publication.

32 years after Jacques Bertin's seminal work, during which time leaders of the field had been pursuing meta-graphical concepts, Leland Wilkinson published the book, *The Grammar of Graphics, Springer Publishing*, which, as had been the case with Dr. Cleveland, was the culmination from a combined background of academic research and teaching with professional experience of developing statistical software platforms. The first software implementation that was inspired by this book was SPSS's **nViZn** (pronounced as *envision*). This was followed by R's **ggplot2**, and in the Python world, **Bokeh**, among others.

But what *is* this grammar? What did three decades of intensive research and reflection reveal about the nature of data visualization and plotting of statistical results? In essence, the **grammar of graphics** did for the world of statistical data plotting and visualization what **design patterns** did for a subset of programming, and **a pattern language** did for architecture and urban design. The grammar of graphics explores the space of data, its graphical representation, the human minds that view these, and the ways in which these are connected, both obviously and subtly. The book provides a conceptual framework for the cognitive analysis of our statistical tools and how we can make them better, allowing us to ultimately create visualizations that are more clear, meaningful, and reveal more of the underlying problem space.

A grammar such as this is not only helpful in providing a consistent framework for concisely describing and discussing plots, but it is of an inestimable value for developers who wish to create a well thought-out and logically structured plotting library. The grammar of graphics provides a means by which we can clearly organize components such as geometric objects, scales, or coordinate systems while relating this to both the data they will represent (including related statistical use cases) and a well-defined visual aesthetic.

Bokeh

One of the first Python libraries to explore the space of the grammar of graphics was the Bokeh project. In many ways, Bokeh views itself as a natural successor to matplotlib, offering their view of improvements in the overall architecture, scalability of problem datasets, APIs, and usability. However, in contrast to matplotlib, Bokeh focuses its attention on the web browser.

Since this is a matplotlib book, and not a Bokeh book, we won't go into too much detail, but it is definitely worth mentioning, that Bokeh provides a matplotlib compatibility layer. It doesn't cover the complete matplotlib API usage a given project may entail, but enough so that one should be able to very easily incorporate Bokeh into existing matplotlib projects.

The ŷhat ggplot

A few years ago, the **ŷhat** company open-sourced a project of theirs: a clone of R's ggplot2 for Python. The developers at ŷhat wanted to have a Python API that matched ggplot2 so that they could move easily between the two.

A quick view of the project's web site shows the similarity with ggplot2:

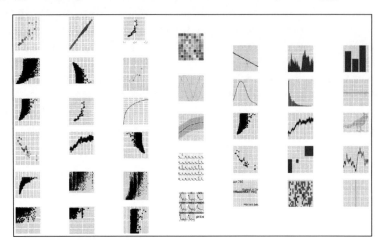

The comparison of the following two code samples shows the extraordinary similarity between R's ggplot2 and Python's ggplot. The code for R's ggplot2 is as follows:

```
library(ggplot2)

ggplot(movie_data, aes(year, budget)) +
  geom_line(colour='red') +
  scale_x_date(breaks=date_breaks('7 years') +
  scale_y_continuous(labels=comma)
```

And the code for Python's ggplot:

```
from ggplot import *

ggplot(movie_data, aes('year','budget')) + \
    geom_line(color='red') + \
    scale_x_date(breaks=date_breaks('7 years')) + \
    scale_y_continuous(labels='comma')
```

A demonstration of how the Python ggplot provides a high-level experience for the developer is given, when examining the matplotlib code necessary, to duplicate the preceding ggplot code:

```
import matplotlib.pyplot as plt
from matplotlib.dates import YearLocator

tick_every_n = YearLocator(7)
x = movie_data.date
y = movie_data.budget
fig, ax = plt.subplots()
ax.plot(x, y, 'red')
ax.xaxis.set_major_locator(tick_every_n)
plt.show()
```

Here's an example of ggplot usage from the IPython Notebook for this chapter:

```
In [12]: import ggplot
         from ggplot import components, geoms, scales, stats
         from ggplot import exampledata


In [13]: data = exampledata.movies
         aesthetics = components.aes(x='year', y='budget')

         (ggplot.ggplot(aesthetics, data=data) +
```

```
        stats.stat_smooth(span=.15, color='red', se=True) +
        geoms.ggtitle("Movie Budgets over Time") +
        geoms.xlab("Year") +
        geoms.ylab("Dollars"))
```

Out[13]:

The following plot is the result of the preceding code:

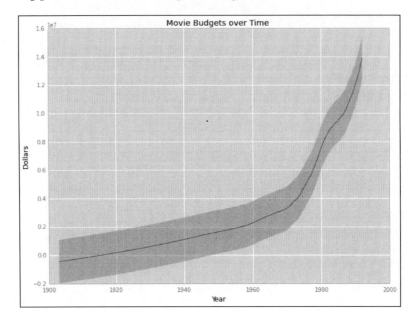

New styles in matplotlib

Not to be left behind, matplotlib has embraced the sensibilities of the ggplot world and has supported the ggplot style since its 1.4 release. You can view the available styles in matplotlib with the following:

```
In [20]: plt.style.available
Out[20]: ['ggplot', 'fivethirtyeight', 'dark_background',
          'grayscale', 'bmh']
```

To enable the ggplot style, simply do this:

```
In [21]: plt.style.use('ggplot')
```

Here's a comparison of several plots before and after enabling; the plots on the right are the ones using the ggplot style:

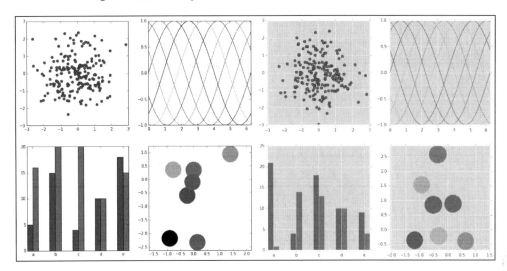

Seaborn

The development of Seaborn has been greatly inspired by the grammar of graphics, and R's ggplot in particular. The original goals of Seaborn were twofold: to make computationally-based research more reproducible, and to improve the visual presentation of statistical results.

This is further emphasized in the introductory material on the project site, with Seaborn's stated aims being to make visualization a central part of exploring and understanding data. Its goals are similar to those of R's ggplot2, though Seaborn takes a different approach: it uses a combined imperative and object-oriented approach with a focus on easy, straight-forward construction of sophisticated plots.

The fact that Seaborn has accomplished undeniable success in these aims is evident by looking at the impressive example plots that it provides, which are generated by relatively few lines of code. The notebook for this chapter shows several examples; we'll highlight just one here, the facet grid plot.

When you want to split up a dataset by one or more variables and then group subplots of these separated variables, you will probably want to use a facet grid. Another use case for the facet grid plot is when you need to examine repeated runs of an experiment to reveal potentially conditional relationships between variables. Below is a concocted instance of the latter from the Seaborn examples. It displays data from a generated dataset, simulating repeated observations of a walking behavior, examining positions of each step of a multi-step walk.

The following demo assumes that you have previously performed the following imports in the notebook, to add this chapter's library to the Python's search path:

```
In [18]: import sys
         sys.path.append("../lib")
         import mplggplot
```

With that done, let us run the demo:

```
In [25]: import seademo

         sns.set(style="ticks")
         data = seademo.get_data_set()
         grid = sns.FacetGrid(data, col="walk", hue="walk",
                              col_wrap=5, size=2)
         grid.map(plt.axhline, y=0, ls=":", c=".5")
         grid.map(plt.plot, "step", "position", marker="o", ms=4)
         grid.set(xticks=np.arange(5), yticks=[-3, 3],
                  xlim=(-.5, 4.5), ylim=(-3.5, 3.5))
         grid.fig.tight_layout(w_pad=1)
```

The following plot is the result of the preceding code:

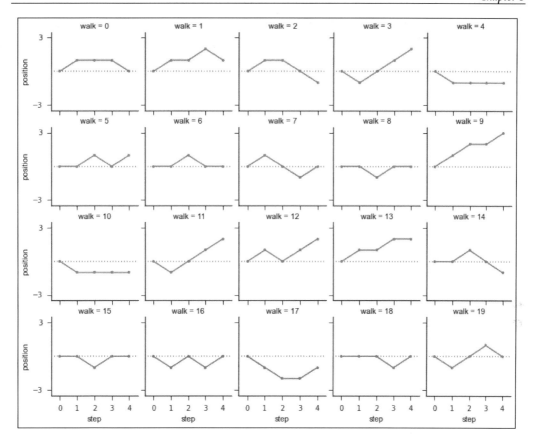

There will be more Seaborn examples in the hands-on part of this chapter, where we will save huge amounts of time by using several very high-level Seaborn functions for creating sophisticated plots.

With this, we conclude our overview of high-level plotting with regard to the topic of the grammar of graphics in the Python (particularly matplotlib) world. Next, we will look at high-level plotting examples in the context of a particular dataset and various methods for analyzing trends in that data.

Data analysis

The following is the definition of data analysis given by Wikipedia:

> *"Analysis of data is a process of inspecting, cleaning, transforming, and modeling data with the goal of discovering useful information, suggesting conclusions, and supporting decision-making."*

In the Python scientific computing community, the definition tends to lean away from the software business applications and more towards a statistical analysis. In this section, while we will see a little math, our purpose is not to engage in a rigorous exploration of mathematical analysis, but rather provide a plausible context for using various tools in the matplotlib ecosystem that assist in high-level plotting and various related activities.

Pandas, SciPy, and Seaborn

We've just learned more about Seaborn, and we'll be working more with it in this section. We've used Pandas a bit, but haven't formally introduced it, nor SciPy.

The Pandas project describes generic Python as a great tool for data managing and preparation, but not much strong in the areas of data analysis and modeling. This is the area that Pandas was envisioned to focus upon, filling a much-needed gap in the suite of available libraries, and allowing one to carry out the entire data analysis workflows in Python without having to switch to tools like R or SPSS.

The `scipy` library is one of the core packages, that make up the SciPy *stack*, providing many user-friendly and efficient numerical calculation routines such as those for numerical integration, clustering, signal processing, and statistics, among others.

We have imported `pandas` as `pd` and will import `stats` from `scipy`. The `seaborn` module is already imported in our chapter notebook as `sns`. As you see these various module aliases, note that we are taking an advantage of these high-level libraries: to great effect, as you will soon see.

Examining and shaping a dataset

For demonstration purposes in this chapter, we requested the mean monthly temperatures (in Fahrenheit) and mean monthly precipitation (in inches) for the century ranging from 1894 to 2013, in the small farming town of Saint Francis, Kansas from the **United States Historical Climatology Network** (**USHCN**). Our goal is to select a dataset amenable to statistical analysis and explore the various ways in which the data (raw and analyzed) may be presented to reveal patterns, which may be more easily uncovered using the tools of high-level plotting in matplotlib.

Let us do some more imports and then use Pandas to read this CSV data and instantiate a `DataFrame` object with it:

```
In [27]: import calendar

        from scipy import stats

        sns.set(style="darkgrid")
```

```
In [28]: data_file = "../data/KS147093_0563_data_only.csv"
         data = pd.read_csv(data_file)
```

As part of creating the `DataFrame` object, the headers of the CSV file are converted to column names, by which we can refer to the data later:

```
In [29]: data.columns
Out[29]: Index(['State ID', 'Year', 'Month',
                'Precipitation (in)',
                'Mean Temperature (F)'],
                dtype='object')
```

As a quick sanity check on our data loading, we can view the first few lines of the set with this command:

```
In [30]: data.head()
Out[30]:
```

The following table is the result of the preceding command:

	State ID	Year	Month	Precipitation (in)	Mean temperature (F)
0	'147093'	1894	1	0.43	25.4
1	'147093'	1894	2	0.69	22.5
2	'147093'	1894	3	0.45	42.1
3	'147093'	1894	4	0.62	53.7
4	'147093'	1894	5	0.64	62.9

The months in our dataset are numbers; that's exactly what we want for some calculations; for others (and for display purposes) we will sometimes need these as names. In fact, we will need month names, month numbers, and a lookup dictionary with both. Let us do that now:

```
month_nums = list(range(1, 13))
month_lookup = {x: calendar.month_name[x] for x in month_nums}
month_names = [x[1] for x in sorted(month_lookup.items())]
```

We can use the lookup to edit our data in-place with the following:

```
data["Month"] = data["Month"].map(month_lookup)
```

If you run `data.head()`, you will see that the month numbers have been replaced with the month names that we defined in the lookup dictionary.

Since we have changed our dataset now, let us reload the CSV for the cases when want to use the raw data as is with its month numbers:

```
data_raw = pd.read_csv(data_file)
```

For the purposes of keeping the example code clear, we'll define some more variables as well, and then confirm that we have data that makes sense.

```
In [32]: years = data["Year"].values
         temps_degrees = data["Mean Temperature (F)"].values
         precips_inches = data["Precipitation (in)"].values
In [33]: years_min = data.get("Year").min()
         years_min
Out[33]: 1894
In [34]: years_max = data.get("Year").max()
         years_max
Out[34]: 2013
In [35]: temp_max = data.get("Mean Temperature (F)").max()
         temp_max
Out[35]: 81.799999999999997
In [36]: temp_min = data.get("Mean Temperature (F)").min()
         temp_min
Out[36]: 13.199999999999999
In [37]: precip_max = data.get("Precipitation (in)").max()
         precip_max
Out[37]: 11.31
In [38]: precip_min = data.get("Precipitation (in)").min()
         precip_min
Out[38]: 0.0
```

Next, we are going to create a Pandas pivot table. This spreadsheet-like feature of Pandas allows one to create new views of old data, creating new indices, limiting columns, and so on. The `DataFrame` object we obtained when reading the CSV data provided us with an automatic, incremented index and all the data from our file, in columns. We're going to need a view of the data, where the rows are months and the columns are years. Our first pivot table will give us a `DataFrame` object with just that setup:

```
In [39]: temps = data_raw.pivot(
```

```
             "Month", "Year", "Mean Temperature (F)")
      temps.index = [calendar.month_name[x] for x in temps.index]
```

Typing `temps` by itself in the notebook will render an elided table of values, showing you what the shape of this new `DataFrame` is.

Let us do the same thing with the precipitation data in our dataset:

```
In [40]: precips = data_raw.pivot(
             "Month", "Year", "Precipitation (in)")
      precips.index = [
          calendar.month_name[x] for x in precips.index]
```

We've just taken the necessary steps of preparing our data for analysis and plotting, which we're going to be doing for the rest of this chapter.

Analysis of temperature

We will be utilizing the temperature portion of our dataset (for the period of 1894-2013) in this section, to demonstrate functionality in Pandas, SciPy, and Seaborn, as it relates to the use of these for the purpose of high-level plotting and associated data analysis.

Throughout the rest of the chapter, do keep in mind that this analysis is done to provide examples of usage of libraries. It is not meant to provide deep insights into the nature of climatology or to draw conclusions about the state of our environment. To that point, this dataset is for a single small farming town in the American High Plains. There's not enough data in this set to do much science, but there's plenty to explore.

Since we will be discussing temperature, we should create a palette of colors that intuitively translates to the range of temperatures we will be examining. After some experimentation, we have settled on the following:

```
In [41]: temps_colors = ["#FCF8D4", "#FAEAB9", "#FAD873",
                          "#FFA500", "#FF8C00", "#B22222"]

      sns.palplot(temps_colors)
```

The following set of colors forming a palette is the result of the preceding code:

Next, let us convert this list of colors to a color map that can be used by matplotlib:

```
In [42]: temps_cmap = mpl.colors.LinearSegmentedColormap.from_list(
              "temp colors", temps_colors)
```

That being said and done, our first plot won't actually use color. We first need to build some intuition about our raw data. Let us see what it looks like. Keep in mind that our temperature data points represent the mean temperature for every month, from 1894 through the end of 2013. Given that these are discrete data points, a scatter plot is a good choice for a first view of the data, as it will quickly reveal any obvious patterns such as clustering. The scatter plot is created as follows:

```
In [43]: sns.set(style="ticks")

         (figure, axes) = plt.subplots(figsize=(18,6))
         scatter = axes.scatter(
             years, temps_degrees, s=100, color="0.5",
             alpha=0.5)
         axes.set_xlim([years_min, years_max])
         axes.set_ylim([temp_min - 5, temp_max + 5])
         axes.set_title(
             ("Mean Monthly Temperatures from 1894-2013\n"
              "Saint Francis, KS, USA"),
             fontsize=20)
         axes.set_xlabel("Years", fontsize=16)
         _ = axes.set_ylabel(
             "Temperature (F)", fontsize=16)
```

The following scatter plot is the result of the preceding code:

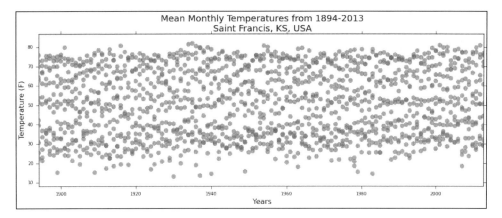

We've seen code like this before, so there are no surprises. The one bit that may be new is the Seaborn style that we set at the beginning. Some of the plots we'll be generating look better with ticks, with white backgrounds, with darker backgrounds, and so on. As such, you will notice that we occasionally make calls to Seaborn's styling functions.

Something else you might have noticed was that we assigned the last call to the *don't care* variable. Sometimes we want IPython to print its results and sometimes we don't. We've decided to enable output by default, so if we're not interested in seeing the output of a function call (in this case it would have been a Python object's representation), we simply assign it to a variable.

There are a few things that we might notice upon first seeing this data rendered as a scatter plot:

- There appears to be a banding at the minimum and maximum temperatures
- The banding in the minimum temperatures looks like it might be a bit wider
- It appears that the mean temperatures are trending slightly upward
- The lower temperatures seem to trend upward more than the higher temperatures

The first point, we can address immediately with a logical inference: we are examining data that is cyclic in nature (due primarily to the axial tilt of the planet, and thus the corresponding temperatures). Cyclic processes can be described with trigonometric functions such as the sine or cosine of a scalar value. If we were to sample points from a continuous trigonometric and scatter plot them on a Cartesian coordinate system, we'd see a familiar banding pattern: as the *y* values reach the maximum level, the density of points appears greater, due to the fact that the same vertical space is being used to plot the increase to and then the decrease from the maximum.

For our dataset, we can expect that mean temperatures increase during the summer months, typically hold there for a month or two, and then decrease towards the minimum, where the same pattern will apply for the winter months.

As for the other three points of observation, we will need to do some analysis to discern whether those observations are valid or not. Where should we start? How about the following:

1. Let us get the minimum and maximum values for every year.
2. Then, find the line that describes those values across the century.
3. Examine the slopes of the minimum and maximum lines.
4. Then, compare the slopes with each other.

Our first bullet is actually a matter of performing a linear regression on the maximum and minimum values. SciPy has just the thing for us: `scipy.stats.linregress`. We'll use the results from that function to create a Pandas data **Series**, with which we can run calculations. We'll define a quick little function to make that a bit easier, and then use it:

```
In [44]: def get_fit(series, m, b):
             x = series.index
             y = m * x + b
             return pd.Series(y, x)

         temps_max_x = temps.max().index
         temps_max_y = temps.max().values
         temps_min_x = temps.min().index
         temps_min_y = temps.min().values

         (temps_max_slope,
```

```
    temps_max_intercept,
    _, _, _) = stats.linregress(temps_max_x, temps_max_y)
temps_max_fit = get_fit(
    temps.max(), temps_max_slope, temps_max_intercept)


(temps_min_slope,
 temps_min_intercept,
    _, _, _) = stats.linregress(temps_min_x, temps_min_y)
temps_min_fit = get_fit(
    temps.min(), temps_min_slope, temps_min_intercept)
```

The `linregress` function returns the slope of the regression line, its intercept, the correlation coefficient, and the p-value. For our purposes, we're just interested in this slope and intercept; so we ignore the other values. Let us look at the results:

```
In [45]: (temps_max_slope, temps_min_slope)
Out[45]: (0.015674352385582326, 0.04552191124383638)
```

So what does this mean? Let us do a quick refresher: the slope m is defined as the change in y values over the change in x values:

$$m = \frac{\Delta y}{\Delta x} = \frac{\text{vertical change}}{\text{horizontal change}}$$

In our case, the y values are the minimum and maximum mean monthly temperatures in degrees Fahrenheit; the x values are the years these measurements were taken.

The slope for the minimum mean monthly temperatures over the last 120 years is about three times greater than that of the maximum mean monthly temperatures:

```
In [46]: temps_min_slope/temps_max_slope
Out[46]: 2.9042291588205336
```

Let us go back to our scatter plot and superimpose our linear fits for the maximum and minimum annual means:

```
In [47]: (figure, axes) = plt.subplots(figsize=(18,6))
         scatter = axes.scatter(
             years, temps_degrees, s=100, color="0.5", alpha=0.5)
```

```
temps_max_fit.plot(
    ax=axes, lw=5, color=temps_colors[5], alpha=0.7)
temps_min_fit.plot(
    ax=axes, lw=5, color=temps_colors[3], alpha=0.7)
axes.set_xlim([years_min, years_max])
axes.set_ylim([temp_min - 5, temp_max + 5])
axes.set_title(("Mean Monthly Temperatures from 1894-2013\n"
               "Saint Francis, KS, USA\n"
               "(with max and min fit)"), fontsize=20)
axes.set_xlabel("Years", fontsize=16)
_ = axes.set_ylabel("Temperature (F)",
fontsize=16)
```

The following scatter plot is the result of the preceding code:

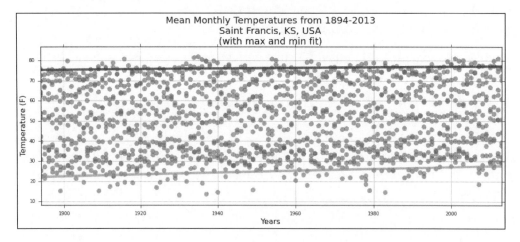

It still looks like there is a greater rise in the minimum mean temperatures than the maximums. We can get a better visual by superimposing the two lines. Let us remove the vertical distance and compare:

```
In [48]: diff_1894 = temps_max_fit.iloc[0] - temps_min_fit.iloc[0]
```

```
        diff_2013 = temps_max_fit.iloc[-1] - temps_min_fit.iloc[-1]
        (diff_1894, diff_2013)
Out[48]: (53.125096418732781, 49.573236914600542)
```

Note that, we have used the `iloc` attribute on our Pandas Series objects. The `iloc` attribute allows one to extract elements in a Series based on integer indices.

With this, we have the difference between high and low in 1894 and then the same difference in 2013, the latter being a smaller difference by a few degrees. We can overlay our two linear regression lines by shifting one of them downwards, so that they converge on the same point (this is done solely for comparison reasons):

```
In [49]: vert_shift = temps_max_fit - diff_2013

        (figure, axes) = plt.subplots(figsize=(18,6))
        vert_shift.plot(
            ax=axes, lw=5, color=temps_colors[5], alpha=0.7)
        temps_min_fit.plot(
            ax=axes, lw=5, color=temps_colors[3], alpha=0.7)
        axes.set_xlim([years_min, years_max])
        axes.set_ylim([vert_shift.min() - 5, vert_shift.max() + 1])
        axes.set_title(("Mean Monthly Temperature Difference "
                        "from 1894-2013\nSaint Francis, KS, USA\n"
                        "(vertical offset adjusted to "
                        "converge at 2013)"),
                       fontsize=20)
        axes.set_xlabel("Years", fontsize=16)
        _ = axes.set_ylabel(
            "Temperature\nDifference (F)", fontsize=16)
```

The following plot is the result of the preceding code:

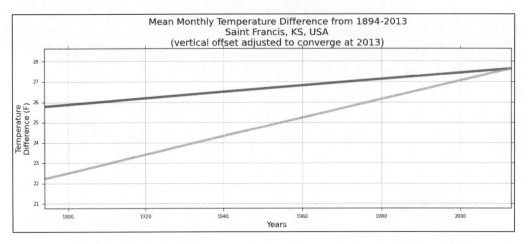

Now, we can *really* see the difference and can confirm that the rise in minimum mean temperatures is greater than the rise in maximum means.

Let us take a big jump from scatter plots and liner regressions to the `heatmap` functionality that Seaborn provides. Despite the name, heat maps don't have any intrinsic relationship with temperatures. The idea behind heat maps is to present a dataset in a matrix where each value in the matrix is encoded as a color, thus allowing one to easily see patterns of values across an entire dataset. Creating a heat map in matplotlib directly can be a rather complicated affair, although Seaborn makes this very easy for us, as shown in the following manner:

```
In [50]: sns.set(style="darkgrid")
In [51]: (figure, axes) = plt.subplots(figsize=(17,9))
         axes.set_title(("Heat Map\nMean Monthly Temperatures, "
                         "1894-2013\nSaint Francis, KS, USA"),
                        fontsize=20)

         sns.heatmap(
             temps, cmap=temps_cmap,
             cbar_kws={"label": "Temperature (F)"})
         figure.tight_layout()
```

The following heat map is the result of the preceding code:

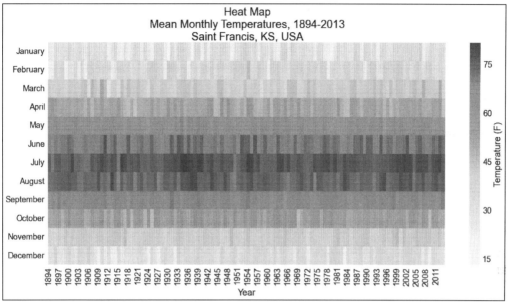

Given that this is a town in the Northern hemisphere near to the 40th parallel, we don't see any surprises:

- Highest temperatures are in the summer
- Lowest temperatures are in the winter

There is some interesting summer banding in the 1930s, which indicates several years of hotter-than-normal summers. We see something similar for a few years, starting around 1998 and 1999. There also seems to be a wide band of cold Decembers from 1907 through to about 1932.

Next, we're going to look at Seaborn's `clustermap` functionality. Cluster maps of this sort are very useful in sorting out data that may have hidden (or not) hierarchical structure. We don't expect that with this dataset, so this is more of a demonstration of the plot than anything. However, it might have a few insights for us. We shall see.

Due to the fact that this is a composite plot, we'll need to access subplot axes, as provided by the `clustermap` class:

```
In [53]:clustermap = sns.clustermap(
        temps, figsize=(19, 12),
```

```
cbar_kws={"label": "Temperature\n(F)"},
cmap=temps_cmap)
_ = clustermap.ax_col_dendrogram.set_title(
    ("Cluster Map\nMean Monthly Temperatures, 1894-2013\n"
    "Saint Francis, KS, USA"),
    fontsize=20)
```

The following heat map is the result of the preceding code:

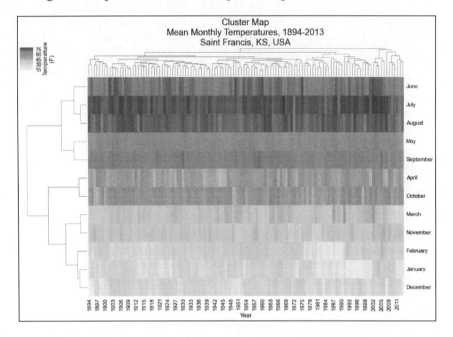

You've probably noticed that everything got rearranged; here's what happened: while keeping the temperatures for each year together, the *x* (years) and *y* (months) values have been sorted/grouped to be close to those with which it shares the most similarity. Here's what we can discern from the graph with regard to our current dataset:

- The century's temperature patterns each year can be viewed in two groups: higher and lower temperatures

- **January** and **December** share similar low-temperature patterns, with the next closest being **February**

- The next grouping of similar temperature patterns are **November** and **March**, sibling to the **January/December/February** grouping

- The last grouping of the low-temperature months is the **April/October** pairing

A similar analysis (with no surprises) can be done for the high-temperature months.

Looking across the *x* axis, we can view patterns/groupings by year. With careful tracing (ideally with a larger rendering of the cluster map), one could identify similar temperature patterns in various years. Though this doesn't reveal anything intrinsically, it could assist in additional analysis (for example, pointing towards the historical records to examine the possibility, trends may be discovered).

In the preceding cluster map, we passed a value for the color map to use, the one we defined at the beginning of this section. If we leave that out, Seaborn will do something quite nice: it will normalize our data and then select a color map that highlights values above and below the mean:

```
In [53]: clustermap = sns.clustermap(
    temps, z_score=1, figsize=(19, 12),
    cbar_kws={"label": "Normalized\nTemperature (F)"})
_ = clustermap.ax_col_dendrogram.set_title(
        ("Normalized Cluster Map\nMean Monthly Temperatures, "
        "1894-2013\nSaint Francis, KS, USA"),
        fontsize=20)
```

The following normalized cluster map is the result:

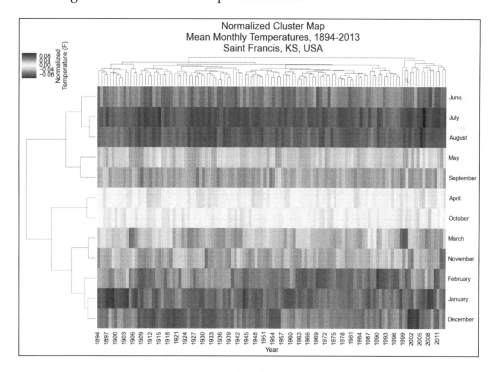

Note that we get the same grouping as in the previous heat map; the internal values at each coordinate of the map (and the associated color) are all that have changed. This view offers great insight for statistical data: not only do we see the large and obvious grouping between the above and below the mean, but the colors give obvious insights as to how far any given point is from the overall mean.

With the following plot, we're going to return two previous plots:

- The temperature heat map
- The scatter plot for our temperature data

Seaborn has an option for heat maps to display a histogram above them. We will see this usage when we examine the precipitation. However, for the temperatures, counts for a year isn't quite as meaningful as the actual values for each month of that year. As such, we will replace the standard histogram with our scatter plot:

```
In [54]: figure = plt.figure(figsize=(18,13))
         grid_spec = plt.GridSpec(2, 2,
                                  width_ratios=[50, 1],
                                  height_ratios=[1, 3],
                                  wspace=0.05, hspace=0.05)
         scatter_axes = figure.add_subplot(grid_spec[0])
         cluster_axes = figure.add_subplot(grid_spec[2])
         colorbar_axes = figure.add_subplot(grid_spec[3])

         scatter_axes.scatter(years,
                              temps_degrees,
                              s=40,
                              c="0.3",
                              alpha=0.5)
         scatter_axes.set(xticks=[], ylabel="Yearly. Temp. (F)")
         scatter_axes.set_xlim([years_min, years_max])
         scatter_axes.set_title(
             ("Heat Map with Scatter Plot\nMean Monthly "
             "Temperatures, 1894-2013\nSaint Francis, KS, USA"),
             fontsize=20)
         sns.heatmap(temps,
                     cmap=temps_cmap,
                     ax=cluster_axes,
                     cbar_ax=colorbar_axes,
```

```
            cbar_kws={"orientation": "vertical"})
    _ = colorbar_axes.set(xlabel="Temperature\n(F)")
```

The following scatter plot and heat map are the result:

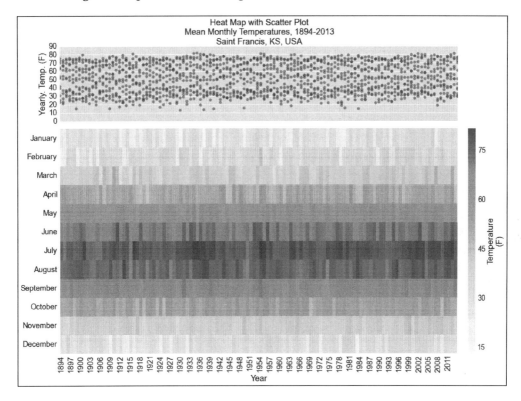

Next, we're going to take a closer look at the average monthly temperatures by month using a histogram matrix. To do this, we'll need a new pivot. Our first one created a pivot with the *Month* data being the index; now, we want to index by *Year*. We'll do the same trick of keeping the data in the correct month order by converting the month numbers to names *after* we create the pivot table, however, in the case of the histogram matrix plot, that won't actually help us: to keep the sorting correct, we'll need to pre-pend the zero-filled month number:

```
In [55]: temps2 = data_raw.pivot(
            "Year", "Month", "Mean Temperature (F)")
        temps2.columns = [
            str(x).zfill(2) + " - " + calendar.month_name[x]
            for x in temps2.columns]
        monthly_means = temps2.mean()
```

We'll use the histogram provided by Pandas for this. Unfortunately, Pandas does not return the figure and axes that it creates with its `hist` wrapper. Instead, it returns a NumPy array of subplots. As such, we're left with fewer options than we might like for further tweaking of the plot. Our use of `plt.text` is a quick hack (of trial and error) that lets us label the overall figure (instead of the enclosing axes, as we'd prefer).

```
In [56]: axes = temps2.hist(figsize=(16,12))
         plt.text(-20, -10, "Temperatures (F)", fontsize=16)
         plt.text(-74, 77, "Counts", rotation="vertical", fontsize=16)
         _ = plt.suptitle(
             ("Temperatue Counts by Month, 1894-2013\n"
             "Saint Francis, KS, USA"),
             fontsize=20)
```

The following plots are the result of the preceding code:

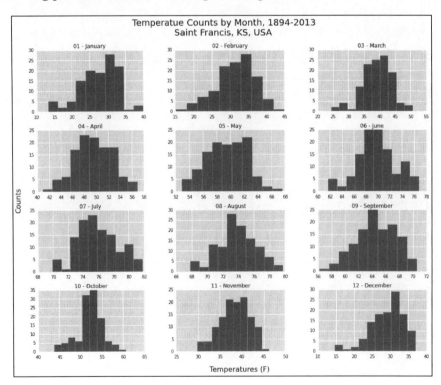

This provides a nice view on the number of occurrences for temperature ranges in each month over the course of the century. For the most part, these have roughly normal distributions, as we would expect.

Now what we'd like to do is:

- Look at the mean temperature for *all* months over the century
- Show the constituent data that generated that mean
- Trace the maximum, mean, and minimum temperatures

Let us tackle that last one, first. The minimum, maximum, and means are discrete values in our case, one for each month. What we'd like to do is see what a smooth curve through those points might look like (as a visual aid more than anything). At first, one might think of using NumPy's or Pandas' histogram and distribution plotting capabilities. That would be perfect if we were just binning data. That is not what we are doing, though: we are not generating counts for data that falls in a given range. We are looking at temperatures in a given range. The next thought might be to use the 2D histogram capabilities of NumPy, and while that does work, it's a rather different type of a plot than what we want.

Instead of trying to fit our needs into the tools, what data do we have and what work could we do on that with the tools at hand? We already have our maximums, means, and minimums. We have temperatures per month over the course of the century. We just need to connect our discrete points with a smooth, continuous line.

SciPy provides just the thing: **spline interpolation**. This will give us a smooth curve for our discrete values:

```
In [57]: from scipy.interpolate import UnivariateSpline

         smooth_mean = UnivariateSpline(
             month_nums, list(monthly_means), s=0.5)
         means_xs = np.linspace(0, 13, 2000)
         means_ys = smooth_mean(means_xs)

         smooth_maxs = UnivariateSpline(
             month_nums, list(temps2.max()), s=0)
         maxs_xs = np.linspace(0, 13, 2000)
```

```
maxs_ys = smooth_maxs(maxs_xs)


smooth_mins = UnivariateSpline(
    month_nums, list(temps2.min()), s=0)
mins_xs = np.linspace(0, 13, 2000)
mins_ys = smooth_mins(mins_xs)
```

We'll use the raw data from the beginning of this section, since we'll be doing interpolation on our *x* values (month numbers):

```
In [58]: temps3 = data_raw[["Month", "Mean Temperature (F)"]]
```

Now we can plot our means for all months, a scatter plot (with data points as lines, in this case) for each month superimposed over each mean, and finally our maximum / mean / minimum interpolations:

```
In [59]: (figure, axes) = plt.subplots(figsize=(18,10))
         axes.bar(
             month_nums, monthly_means, width=0.96, align="center",
             alpha=0.6)
         axes.scatter(
             temps3["Month"], temps3["Mean Temperature (F)"],
             s=2000, marker="_", alpha=0.6)
         axes.plot(means_xs, means_ys, "b", linewidth=6, alpha=0.6)
         axes.plot(maxs_xs, maxs_ys, "r", linewidth=6, alpha=0.2)
         axes.plot(mins_xs, mins_ys, "y", linewidth=6, alpha=0.5)
         axes.axis(
             (0.5, 12.5,
             temps_degrees.min() - 5, temps_degrees.max() + 5))
         axes.set_title(
             ("Mean Monthly Temperatures from 1894-2013\n"
              "Saint Francis, KS, USA",
             fontsize=20)
         axes.set_xticks(month_nums)
         axes.set_xticklabels(month_names)
         _ = axes.set_ylabel("Temperature (F)", fontsize=16)
```

The following plot is the result of the preceding code:

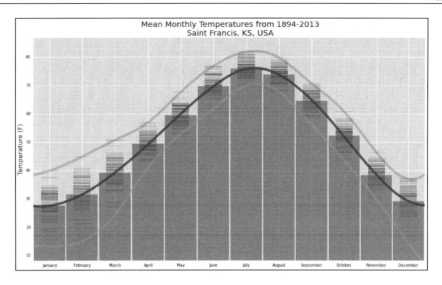

You may have noticed that these plot components have echoes of the box plot in them. They do, in fact, share some basic qualities in common with the box plot. The box plot was invented by the famous statistical mathematician John Tukey.

 The inventor of many important concepts, John Tukey is often forgotten as the person who coined the term *bit*. A term which now permeates multiple industries and has made its way into the vocabularies of non-specialists, too.

Box plots concisely and visually convey the following *bits* (couldn't resist) of information:

- **Upper part of the box**: approximate distribution, 75th percentile
- **Line across box**: median
- **Lower part of the box**: approximate distribution, 25th percentile
- **Height of the box**: fourth spread
- **Upper line out of box**: greatest non-outlying value
- **Lower line out of box**: smallest non-outlying value
- **Dots above and below**: outliers

Sometimes, you will see box plots of different width; the width indicates the relative size of the datasets.

The box plot allows one to view data without making any assumptions about it; the basic statistics are there to view, in plain sight.

The following plot will overlay a box plot on our bar chart of medians (and line scatter plot of values):

```
In [64]: (figure, axes) = plt.subplots(figsize=(18,10))
         axes.bar(
             month_nums, monthly_means, width=0.96, align="center",
             alpha=0.6)
         axes.scatter(
             temps3["Month"], temps3["Mean Temperature (F)"],
             s=2000, marker="_", alpha=0.6)
         sns.boxplot(temps2, ax=axes)
         axes.axis(
             (0.5, 12.5,
              temps_degrees.min() - 5, temps_degrees.max() + 5))
         axes.set_title(
             ("Mean Monthly Temperatures, 1894-2013\n"
              "Saint Francis, KS, USA"),
             fontsize=20)
         axes.set_xticks(month_nums)
         axes.set_xticklabels(month_names)
         _ = axes.set_ylabel("Temperature (F)", fontsize=16)
```

The following plot is the result of the preceding code:

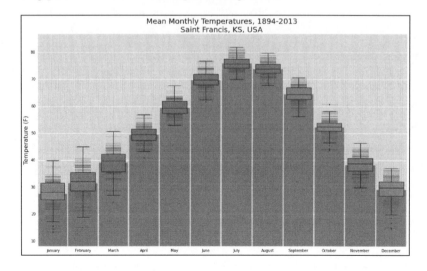

Now, we can easily identify the spread, the outliers, the area that contains half of the distribution, and so on. Though pretty, the color of the box plots merely represents relative closeness of values to that of its neighbors and as such holds no significant sources for insight.

A variation on the box plot that focuses on the probability distribution rather than quartiles is the violin plot, an example of which we saw earlier in the introduction to Seaborn. We will configure a violin plot to show our data points as lines (the `stick` option), thus combining our use of the line-scatter plot above with the box plot:

```
In [65]: sns.set(style="whitegrid")
In [66]: (figure, axes) = plt.subplots(figsize=(18, 10))
         sns.violinplot(temps2, bw=0.2, lw=1, inner="stick")
         axes.set_title(
             ("Violin Plots\nMean Monthly Temperatures, 1894-2013\n"
              "Saint Francis, KS, USA"),
             fontsize=20)
         axes.set_xticks(month_nums)
         axes.set_xticklabels(month_names)
         _ = axes.set_ylabel("Temperature (F)", fontsize=16)
```

The following violin plot is the result of the preceding code:

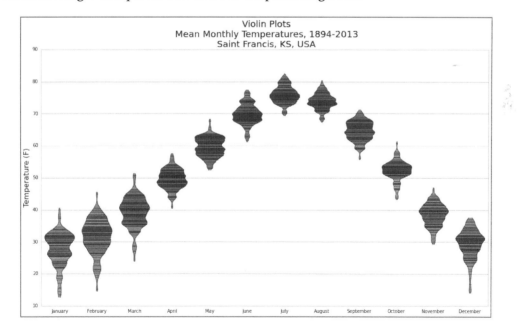

In the violin plot, the outliers are part of the probability distribution, though they are just as easy to identify as they are in the box plot due to the thinning of the distribution at these points.

For our final plot of this section, we will dip back into mathematics and finish up with a feature from the Pandas library with a plot of *Andrews' curves*. Andrews' curves can be useful when attempting to uncover a hidden structure in datasets of higher dimensions. As such, it may be a bit forced in our case; we're essentially looking at just two dimensions: the temperature and the time of year. That being said, it is such a useful tool that it's worth covering, if only on a toy example.

Andrews' curves are groups of lines where each line represents a point in the input dataset, and the line is a transformation of that point. In fact, the line is a plot of a finite Fourier series, and is defined as follows:

$$f_x(t) = \frac{x_1}{\sqrt{2}} + x_2 \sin(t) + x_3 \cos(t) + x_4 \sin(2t) + x_5 \cos(2t) + \dots$$

This function is then plotted for the interval from $-\pi < t < \pi$. Thus, each data point may be viewed as a line between $-\pi$ and π. The following formula can be thought of as the projection of the data point onto the vector:

$$\left(\frac{1}{\sqrt{2}}, \sin(t), \cos(t), \sin(2t), \cos(2t), \dots \right)$$

Let us see it in action:

```
In [67]: months_cmap = sns.cubehelix_palette(
             8, start=-0.5, rot=0.75, as_cmap=True)

         (figure, axes) = plt.subplots(figsize=(18, 10))
         temps4 = data_raw[["Mean Temperature (F)", "Month"]]
         axes.set_xticks([-np.pi, -np.pi/2, 0, np.pi/2, np.pi])
         axes.set_xticklabels(
             [r"$-{\pi}$", r"$-\frac{\pi}{2}$",
              r"$0$", r"$\frac{\pi}{2}$", r"${\pi}$"])
         axes.set_title(
             ("Andrews Curves for\nMean Monthly Temperatures,
              "1894-2013\nSaint Francis, KS, USA"),
             fontsize=20)
         axes.set_xlabel(
```

```
        (r"Data points mapped to lines in the range "
          "$[-{\pi},{\pi}]$"),
        fontsize=16)
    axes.set_ylabel(r"$f_{x}(t)$", fontsize=16)
    pd.tools.plotting.andrews_curves(
        temps4, class_column="Month", ax=axes,
        colormap=months_cmap)
    axes.axis(
        [-np.pi, np.pi] + [x * 1.025 for x in axes.axis()[2:]])
    _ = axes.legend(labels=month_names, loc=(0, 0.67))
```

The following plot is the result of the preceding code:

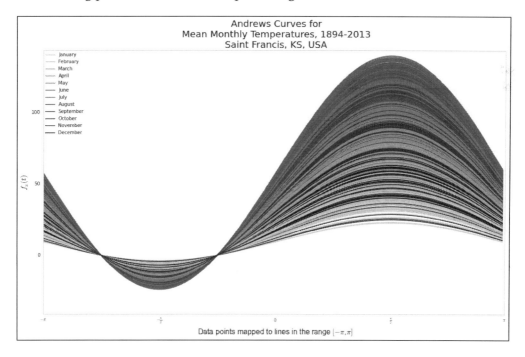

If we examine the rendered curves, we see the same patterns that we identified in the cluster map plots:

- The temperatures of **January** and **December** are similar (thus the light and dark banding, staying close together)
- Likewise for the temperatures during the summer months

- The alternate banding of colors represent the same relationship that we saw in the cluster map, where months of similar temperature patterns (though at different times of year) were paired together

Notice that the curves preserve the distance between the high and low temperatures. This is another property of Andrews' curves. Others include the following:

- The mean is preserved
- Linear relationships are preserved
- The variance is preserved

Things to keep in mind when using Andrews' curves in your projects:

- The order of the variables matters; changing that order will result in different curves
- The lower frequencies show up better; as such, put the variables you feel to be more important first

For example, if we *did* have a dataset with more variables that contributed to the temperature, such as atmospheric pressure or wind speed, we might have defined our Pandas `DataFrame` with the columns in this order:

```
temps4 = data_raw[
    ["Mean Temperature (F)", "Wind Speed (kn)",
    "Pressure (Pa)", "Month"]]
```

Analysis of precipitation

In the *Analysis of precipitation* section of the IPython Notebook for this chapter, all the graphs that are explored in the *temperature* section are also created for the precipitation data. We will leave that review as an exercise for the interested reader. However, it is worth noting a few of the differences between the two aspects of the datasets, so we will highlight those here.

Our setup for the precipitation colors are as follows:

```
In [68]: sns.set(style="darkgrid")
In [69]: precips_colors = ["#f2d98f", "#f8ed39", "#a7cf38",
                          "#7fc242", "#4680c2", "#3a53a3",
                          "#6e4a98"]

         sns.palplot(precips_colors)
```

The following graph is obtained as the result of the preceding code:

The first precipitation graph will be the one we had mentioned before: a combination of the precipitation amount heat map and a histogram of the total counts for the corresponding year:

```
In [72]: figure = plt.figure(figsize=(18, 13))
         grid_spec = plt.GridSpec(2, 2,
                                   width_ratios=[50, 1],
                                   height_ratios=[1, 3],
                                   wspace=0.05, hspace=0.05)
         hist_axes = figure.add_subplot(grid_spec[0])
         cluster_axes = figure.add_subplot(grid_spec[2])
         colorbar_axes = figure.add_subplot(grid_spec[3])

         precips_sum = precips.sum(axis=0)
         years_unique = data["Year"].unique()
         hist_axes.bar(years_unique, precips_sum, 1,
                      ec="w", lw=2, color="0.5", alpha=0.5)
         hist_axes.set(
             xticks=[], ylabel="Total Yearly\nPrecip. (in)")
         hist_axes.set_xlim([years_min, years_max])
         hist_axes.set_title(
             ("Heat Map with Histogram\nMean Monthly Precipitation,"
             "1894-2013\nSaint Francis, KS, USA"),
             fontsize=20)

         sns.heatmap(precips,
                    cmap=precips_cmap,
                    ax=cluster_axes,
                    cbar_ax=colorbar_axes,
                    cbar_kws={"orientation": "vertical"})
         _ = colorbar_axes.set(xlabel="Precipitation\n(in)")
```

The following plot is the result of the preceding code:

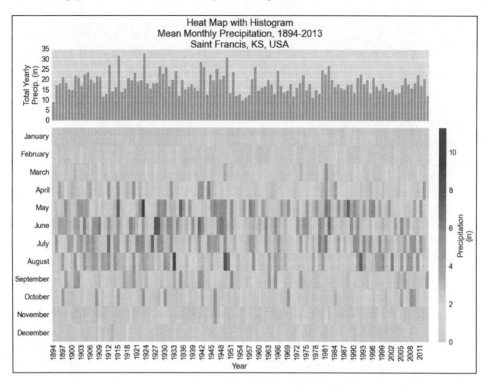

This plot very nicely allows us to scan the heat map and then trace upwards to the histogram for a quick summary for any year we find interesting. In point of fact, we notice the *purple* month of **May** in **1923** right away. The histogram confirms for us that this was the rainiest year of the century for **Saint Francis, KS**. A quick search on the Internet for kansas rain 1923 yields a USGS page discussing major floods along the Arkansas River where they mention "flood stages on the Ninnescah [river] were the highest known."

In contrast to the temperature data, we can see that the precipitation is highly irregular. This is confirmed when rendering the histogram for the months of the century: few or no normal distributions. The cluster map does bear more examination, however, the clustering of the years could reveal stretches of drought.

The other plot we will include in this section, is the precipitation box plot, as there are some pretty significant outliers:

```
In [84]: (figure, axes) = plt.subplots(figsize=(18,10))

         axes.bar(

             month_nums, monthly_means, width=0.99, align="center",
```

```
        alpha=0.6)
axes.scatter(
        precips3["Month"], precips3["Precipitation (in)"],
        s=2000, marker="_", alpha=0.6)
axes.boxplot(precips2, ax=axes)
axes.axis(
        (0.5, 12.5,
         precips_inches.min(), precips_inches.max() + 0.25))
axes.set_title(
        ("Mean Monthly Precipitation from 1894-2013\n"
         "Saint Francis, KS, USA"),
        fontsize=20)
axes.set_xticks(month_nums)
axes.set_xticklabels(month_names)
_ = axes.set_ylabel("Precipitation (in)", fontsize=16)
```

The following plot is the result of the preceding code:

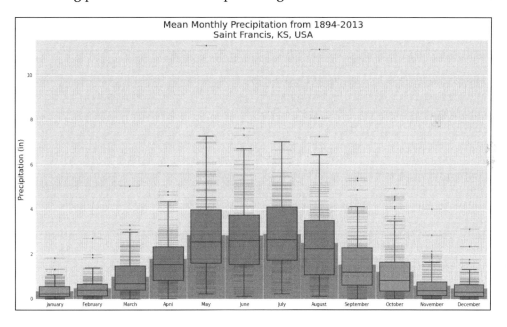

The greatest amount of rain we saw was in **May** of 1923, and there is its outlying data point in the plot. We see another one almost as high in **August**. Referencing our precipitation heat map, we easily locate the other *purple* month corresponding to the heaviest rains, and sure enough: it's in **August** (1933).

Summary

In this chapter, we covered a great deal of material:

- A quick review of the evolution of high-level plotting
- An examination of third-party libraries, which wrap matplotlib functionality for high-level plotting results
- An overview of the grammar of graphics and the implementations available in the Python world
- A tour of a one town's data climate over a century, and the ways in which this might be rendered in various high-level plots

Our goal was to not only provide more context into the world of data visualization where each layer builds upon one before it, but to also demonstrate practical usage on a real-world dataset, identifying the ways in which one might need to modify the collected or supplied data, and then apply various methods to gain deeper insights about the data. Sometimes those insights come as a result of simply highlighting different relationships within a dataset; other times they come when supplementing a dataset with new calculations.

It is our hope that having walked with us through this valley of high-level plotting and data analysis, you are better prepared to strike out on your own adventures in the high-plains of the vast datasets and analysis that await you.

6
Customization and Configuration

This chapter marks a conceptual dividing line for the book. We've focused on topics such as matplotlib internals and APIs, plot interaction, high-level plotting, and the use of third-party libraries. We will continue in that vein in the first part of this chapter as we discuss advanced customization techniques for matplotlib. We will finish the chapter by discussing the elements of the advanced and lesser-known matplotlib configuration. The configuration theme will continue into the next chapter and then go beyond that into the realm of deployment. As such, this chapter will mark a transition to our exploration of matplotlib in the real world and its usage in computationally intensive tasks.

This chapter will provide an overview of the following, giving you enough confidence to tackle these in more depth at your own pace:

- Customization
    - matplotlib styles
    - Subplots
    - Further exploration

- Configuration
    - The matplotlib run control
    - Options in IPython

To follow along with this chapter's code, clone the notebook's repository and start up IPython in the following way:

```
$ git clone https://github.com/masteringmatplotlib/custom-and-config.git
$ cd custom-and-config
$ make
```

Customization

On the journey through the lands of matplotlib, one of the signposts for intermediate territories is an increased need for fine-grained control over the libraries in the ecosystem. In our case, this means being able to tweak matplotlib for particular use cases such as specialty scales or projections, complex layouts, or a custom look and feel.

Creating a custom style

The first customization topic that we will cover is that of the new style support introduced in matplotlib 1.4. In the previous notebook, we saw how to get a list of the available styles:

```
In [2]: print(plt.style.available)
        ['bmh', 'ggplot', 'fivethirtyeight', 'dark_background',
        'grayscale']
```

Now, we're going to see how we can create and use one of our own custom styles.

You can create custom styles and use them by calling `style.use` with the path or URL to the style sheet. Alternatively, if you save the `<style-name>.mplstyle` file to the `~/.matplotlib/stylelib` directory (you may need to create it), you can reuse your custom style sheet with a call to `style.use(<style-name>)`. Note that a custom style sheet in `~/.matplotlib/stylelib` will override a style sheet defined by matplotlib if the styles have the same name.

There is a custom matplotlib style sheet included in this chapter's IPython Notebook `git` repository, but before we go further, let's create a function that will generate a demo plot for us. We'll then render it by using the default style in the following way, thus having a baseline to compare our work to:

```
In [3]: def make_plot ():
            x = np.random.randn(5000, 6)
            (figure, axes) = plt.subplots(figsize=(16,10))
```

```
        (n, bins, patches) = axes.hist(
            x, 12, normed=1, histtype='bar',
            label=['Color 1', 'Color 2', 'Color 3',
                'Color 4', 'Color 5', 'Color 6'])
    axes.set_title(
        "Histogram\nfor a\nNormal Distribution", fontsize=24)
    axes.set_xlabel("Data Points", fontsize=16)
    axes.set_ylabel("Counts", fontsize=16)
    axes.legend()
    plt.show()
In [4]: make_plot()
```

The following is the sample plot obtained as result of the preceding code:

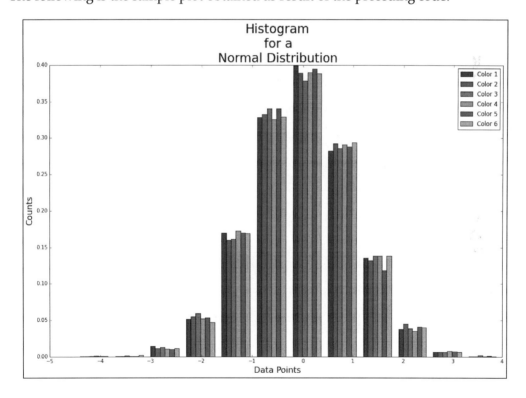

The preceding plot is the default style for matplotlib plots. Let's do something fun by copying the style of Thomas Park's *Superhero* Bootstrap theme. It's a darker theme with muted blues and desaturated accent colors. There is a screenshot of a demo website in the IPython Notebook for this chapter.

There are two styles provided, which differ only in the coloring of the text:

```
In [6]: ls -l ../styles
total 16
-rw-r--r--  1 u  g  473 Feb  4 14:54 superheroine-1.mplstyle
-rw-r--r--  1 u  g  473 Feb  4 14:53 superheroine-2.mplstyle
```

Let's take a look at the second one's contents, which show the hexadecimal colors that we copied from the Bootstrap theme:

```
In [7]: cat ../styles/superheroine-2.mplstyle
lines.color: 4e5d6c
patch.edgecolor: 4e5d6c

text.color: df691b

axes.facecolor: 2b3e50
axes.edgecolor: 4e5d6c
axes.labelcolor: df691b
axes.color_cycle: df691b, 5cb85c, 5bc0de, f0ad4e, d9534f, 4e5d6c
axes.axisbelow: True

xtick.color: 8c949d
ytick.color: 8c949d

grid.color: 4e5d6c

figure.facecolor: 2b3e50
figure.edgecolor: 2b3e50

savefig.facecolor: 2b3e50
savefig.edgecolor: 2b3e50

legend.fancybox: True
legend.shadow: True
legend.frameon: True
legend.framealpha: 0.6
```

The idea behind the matplotlib styles is wonderfully simple—don't reinvent anything, just offer an option for easy organization of data. If the preceding code looks familiar, it's because it is also available in the matplotlib `run` control configuration file, `matplotlibrc`, which will be discussed at the end of the chapter. Let's see how our custom style overrides the default color definitions:

```
In [8]: plt.style.use("../styles/superheroine-2.mplstyle")
```

```
In [9]: make_plot()
```

The following is the plot obtained as result of the preceding code:

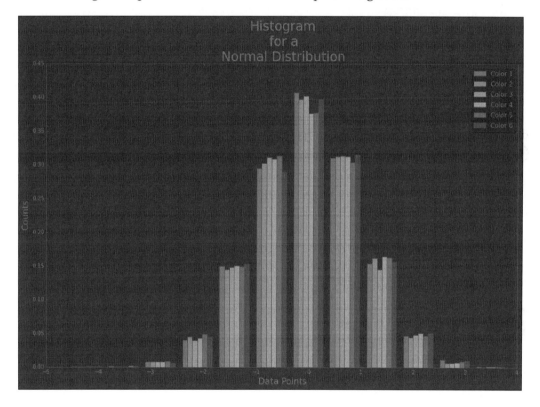

For a tiny bit of an effort, we have a significantly different visual impact. We'll continue using this style for the remainder of the chapter. In particular, we'll see what it looks like in the following section, when we assemble a collection of subplots.

Subplots

In this section, we'll create a sophisticated subplot to give you a sense of matplotlib's plot layout capabilities. The system is flexible enough to accommodate everything from simple adjustments to the creation of dashboards in a single plot.

For this section, we have chosen to ingest data from the well-**known UCI Machine Learning Repository**. In particular, we'll use the 1985 **Automobile Data Set**. It serves as an example of data that can be used to assess the insurance risks for different vehicles. We will use it in an effort to compare 21 automobile manufacturers (using the 1985 data) along the following dimensions:

- Mean price
- Mean city MPG
- Mean highway MPG
- Mean horsepower
- Mean curb weight
- Mean relative average loss payment
- Mean insurance riskiness

We will limit ourselves to automobile manufacturers that have data for losses, as well as six or more rows of data. Our subplot will comprise of the following sections:

- An overall title
- Line plots for maximum, mean, and minimum prices
- A stacked bar chart for combined riskiness or losses
- A stacked bar chart for riskiness
- A stacked bar chart for losses
- Radar charts for each automobile manufacturer
- A combined scatterplot for the city and highway MPG

These will be composed as subplots in the following manner:

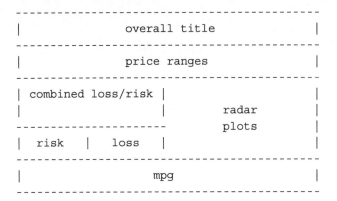

Revisiting Pandas

We've going to use a set of demonstration libraries that we included with this notebook to extract and manipulate the automobile maker data. Like we did before, we will take advantage of the power provided by the Pandas statistical analysis library. Let's load our modules by using the following code:

```
In [10]: import sys
         sys.path.append("../lib")
         import demodata, demoplot
```

As you can see in the IPython Notebook, there's more data there than what we need for the subplotting tasks. Let's created a limited set by using the following code:

```
In [11]: limited_data = demodata.get_limited_data()
         limited_data.head()
Out[11]:
```

The following table is obtained as a result of the preceding command:

	make	price	city mpg	highway mpg	horsepower	weight	riskiness	losses
0	audi	13950	24	30	102	2337	2	164
1	audi	17450	18	22	115	2824	2	164
2	audi	17710	19	25	110	2844	1	158
3	audi	23875	17	20	140	3086	1	158
4	bmw	16430	23	29	101	2395	2	192

This has provided us with the full set of data minus the columns that we don't care about right now. However, we want to apply an additional constraint—we want to exclude auto manufacturers that have fewer than six rows in our dataset. We will do so with the help of the following command:

```
In [16]: data = demodata.get_limited_data(lower_bound=6)
```

We've got the data that we want, but we still have some preparations left to do. In particular, how are we going to compare data of different scales and relationships? Normalization seems like the obvious answer, but we want to make sure that the normalized values compare appropriately. High losses and a high riskiness factor are less favorable, while a higher number of miles per gallon is more favorable. All this is taken care of by the following code:

```
In [19]: normed_data = data.copy()
         normed_data.rename(
             columns={"horsepower": "power"}, inplace=True)
In [20]: demodata.norm_columns(
             ["city mpg", "highway mpg", "power"], normed_data)
In [21]: demodata.invert_norm_columns(
             ["price", "weight", "riskiness", "losses"],
             normed_data)
```

What we did in the preceding code was make a copy of the limited data that we've established as our starting point, and then we updated the copied set by calling two functions—the first function normalized the given columns whose values are more favorable when higher, and the other function inverted the normalized values to match the first normalization (as their pre-inverted values are more favorable when lower). We now have a normalized dataset in which all the values are more favorable when higher.

If you would like to have more exposure to Pandas in action, be sure to view the functions in the demodata module. There are several useful tricks that are employed there to manipulate data.

Individual plots

Before jumping into subplots, let's take a look at a few individual plots for our dataset that will be included as subplots. The first one that we will generate is for the automobile price ranges:

```
In [22]: figure = plt.figure(figsize=(15, 5))
         prices_gs = mpl.gridspec.GridSpec(1, 1)
         prices_axes = demoplot.make_autos_price_plot(
             figure, prices_gs, data)
         plt.show()
```

Note that we didn't use the usual approach that we had taken, in which we get the figure and axes objects from a call to `plt.subplots`. Instead, we opted to use the `GridSpec` class to generate our axes (in the `make_autos_price_plot` function). We've done this because later, we wish to use `GridSpec` to create our subplots.

Here is the output that is generated from the call to `plt.show()`:

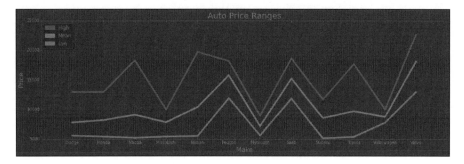

Keep in mind that the preceding plot is a bit contrived (there's no inherent meaning in connecting manufacturer maximum, mean, and minimum values). Its sole purpose is to simply provide some eye candy for the subplot that we will be creating. As you can see from the instantiation of `GridSpec`, this plot has one set of axes that takes up the entire plot. Most of our individual plots will have the same geometry. The one exception to this is the radar plot that we will be creating.

Radar plots are useful when you wish to compare normalized data to multiple variables and populations. Radar plots are capable of providing visual cues that reveal insights instantly. For example, consider the following figure:

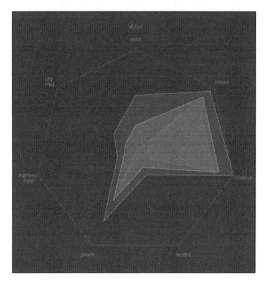

The preceding figure shows the data that was consolidated from several 1985 Volvo models across the dimensions of price, inverse losses to insurers, inverse riskiness, weight, horsepower, and the highway and city miles per gallon. Since the data has been normalized for the highest values as the most positive, the best scenario would be for a manufacturer to have colored polygons at the limits of the axes. The conclusions that we can draw from this is this—relative to the other manufacturers in the dataset, the 1985 Volvos are heavy, expensive, and have a pretty good horsepower. However, where they really shine is in the safety for insurance companies—low losses and a very low risk (again, the values that are larger are better). Even Volvo's minimum values are high in these categories. That's one manufacturer. Let's look at the whole group:

```
In [27]: figure = plt.figure(figsize=(15, 5))
         radar_gs = mpl.gridspec.GridSpec(
             3, 7, height_ratios=[1, 10, 10], wspace=0.50,
             hspace=0.60, top=0.95, bottom=0.25)
         radar_axes = demoplot.make_autos_radar_plot(
             figure, radar_gs, normed_data)
         plt.show()
```

The following table is obtained as a result of the preceding code:

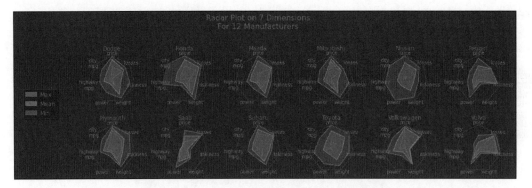

There are interesting conclusions to the graph from this view of the data, but we will focus on the code that generated it. In particular, note the geometry of the grid—three by seven. What does this mean and how are we going to use it? We have two rows of six manufacturers. However, we added an extra row for an empty (and hidden) axis. This is used at the top for the overall title. We then added an extra column for the legend, which spans two rows. This brings us from a grid of two by six to a grid of three by seven. The remaining 12 axes in the grid are populated with a highly customized polar plot, giving us the radar plots for each of the manufacturers.

This example was included not only because it's visually compelling, but also because it will show how flexible the grid specification system for matplotlib is when we put them together. We have the ability to place plots within plots.

Bringing everything together

We've seen a small aspect of the `GridSpec` usage. This has been a tiny warm-up exercise compared to what's coming! Let's refresh with the ASCII sketch of the subplots that we wanted to create. Flip back to that page and look at the layout. We have three axes that will be stretching all the way across the title, price ranges, and the MPG data at the bottom. The three riskiness or losses plots will then be placed on the left-hand side in the middle of the page, and the radar plots will take the other half of that part of the plot on the right-hand side.

We can plot what this will look like before adding any of the data, just by creating the grid and subplot specification objects. The following may look a bit hairy, but keep in mind that when splicing the subplot specs, you're using the same technique that was used when splicing the NumPy array data:

```
In [28]: figure = plt.figure(figsize=(10, 8))
         gs_master = mpl.gridspec.GridSpec(
             4, 2, height_ratios=[1, 2, 8, 2])
         # Layer 1 - Title
         gs_1 = mpl.gridspec.GridSpecFromSubplotSpec(
             1, 1, subplot_spec=gs_master[0, :])
         title_axes = figure.add_subplot(gs_1[0])
         # Layer 2 - Price
         gs_2 = mpl.gridspec.GridSpecFromSubplotSpec(
             1, 1, subplot_spec=gs_master[1, :])
         price_axes = figure.add_subplot(gs_2[0])
         # Layer 3 - Risks & Radar
         gs_31 = mpl.gridspec.GridSpecFromSubplotSpec(
             2, 2, height_ratios=[2, 1],
             subplot_spec=gs_master[2, :1])
         risk_and_loss_axes = figure.add_subplot(gs_31[0, :])
         risk_axes = figure.add_subplot(gs_31[1, :1])
         loss_axes = figure.add_subplot(gs_31[1:, 1])
         gs_32 = mpl.gridspec.GridSpecFromSubplotSpec(
             1, 1, subplot_spec=gs_master[2, 1])
```

```
radar_axes = figure.add_subplot(gs_32[0])
# Layer 4 - MPG
gs_4 = mpl.gridspec.GridSpecFromSubplotSpec(
    1, 1, subplot_spec=gs_master[3, :])
mpg_axes = figure.add_subplot(gs_4[0])
# Tidy up
gs_master.tight_layout(figure)
plt.show()
```

In the preceding code, when we instantiated `GridSpec`, we provided a geometry of four rows and two columns. We then passed the data for the height ratios so that each row will have an appropriate size that is relative to the others. In the section at the middle, for the `risk` and `radar` plots, we gave a geometry of two rows and two columns, and again passed the height ratios that provide the proportions we desire. This code results in the following plot:

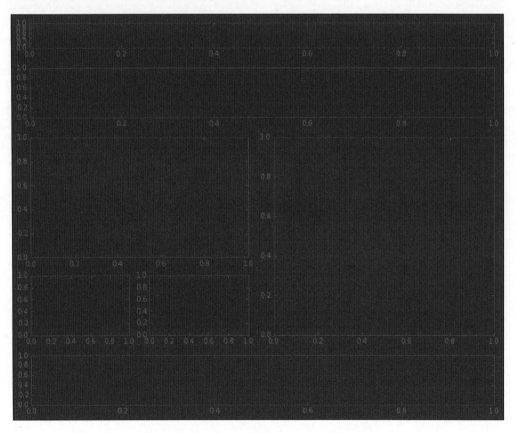

That's exactly what we were aiming for. Now, we're ready to start adding individual plots. The code that generated the preceding skeleton plot differs from the final result in the following three key ways:

- The axes that are created will now get passed to the plot functions
- The plot functions will update the axes with their results (and thus no longer be empty)
- The skeleton radar plot had a one-by-one geometry; the real version will instead have a five-by-three geometry in the same area

Here is the code that inserts all the individual plots into their own subplots:

```
In [29]: figure = plt.figure(figsize=(15, 15))
         gs_master = mpl.gridspec.GridSpec(
             4, 2, height_ratios=[1, 24, 128, 32], hspace=0,
             wspace=0)

         # Layer 1 - Title
         gs_1 = mpl.gridspec.GridSpecFromSubplotSpec(
             1, 1, subplot_spec=gs_master[0, :])
         title_axes = figure.add_subplot(gs_1[0])
         title_axes.set_title(
             "Demo Plots for 1985 Auto Maker Data",
             fontsize=30, color="#cdced1")
         demoplot.hide_axes(title_axes)

         # Layer 2 - Price
         gs_2 = mpl.gridspec.GridSpecFromSubplotSpec(
             1, 1, subplot_spec=gs_master[1, :])
         price_axes = figure.add_subplot(gs_2[0])
         demoplot.make_autos_price_plot(
```

```
        figure, pddata=data, axes=price_axes)


# Layer 3, Part I - Risks
gs_31 = mpl.gridspec.GridSpecFromSubplotSpec(
    2, 2, height_ratios=[2, 1], hspace=0.4,
    subplot_spec=gs_master[2, :1])
risk_and_loss_axes = figure.add_subplot(gs_31[0, :])
demoplot.make_autos_loss_and_risk_plot(
    figure, pddata=normed_data,
    axes=risk_and_loss_axes, x_label=False,
    rotate_ticks=True)
risk_axes = figure.add_subplot(gs_31[1, :1])
demoplot.make_autos_riskiness_plot(
    figure, pddata=normed_data, axes=risk_axes,
    legend=False, labels=False)
loss_axes = figure.add_subplot(gs_31[1:, 1])
demoplot.make_autos_losses_plot(
    figure, pddata=normed_data, axes=loss_axes,
    legend=False, labels=False)


# Layer 3, Part II - Radar
gs_32 = mpl.gridspec.GridSpecFromSubplotSpec(
    5, 3, height_ratios=[1, 20, 20, 20, 20],
    hspace=0.6, wspace=0,
    subplot_spec=gs_master[2, 1])
(rows, cols) = geometry = gs_32.get_geometry()
title_axes = figure.add_subplot(gs_32[0, :])
inner_axes = []
projection = radar.RadarAxes(spoke_count=len(
    normed_data.groupby("make").mean().columns))
```

```
[inner_axes.append(figure.add_subplot(
    m, projection=projection))
    for m in [n for n in gs_32][cols:]]
demoplot.make_autos_radar_plot(
    figure, pddata=normed_data,
    title_axes=title_axes, inner_axes=inner_axes,
    legend_axes=False, geometry=geometry)


# Layer 4 - MPG
gs_4 = mpl.gridspec.GridSpecFromSubplotSpec(
    1, 1, subplot_spec=gs_master[3, :])
mpg_axes = figure.add_subplot(gs_4[0])
demoplot.make_autos_mpg_plot(
    figure, pddata=data, axes=mpg_axes)


# Tidy up
gs_master.tight_layout(figure)
plt.show()
```

Though there is a lot of code here, keep in mind that it's essentially the same as the skeleton of subplots that we created. For most of the plots, all we had to do was make a call to the function that creates the desired plot, passing the axes that we created by splicing a part of the spec and adding a subplot for that splice to the figure. The one that wasn't so straightforward was the radar plot collection. This is due to the fact that we not only needed to define the projection for each radar plot, but also needed to create the 12 axes needed for each manufacturer. Despite this complication, the use of `GridSpec` and `GridSpecFromSubplotSpec` clearly demonstrates the ease with which complicated visual data can be assembled to provide all the power and convenience of a typical dashboard view.

The following plot is the result of the preceding code:

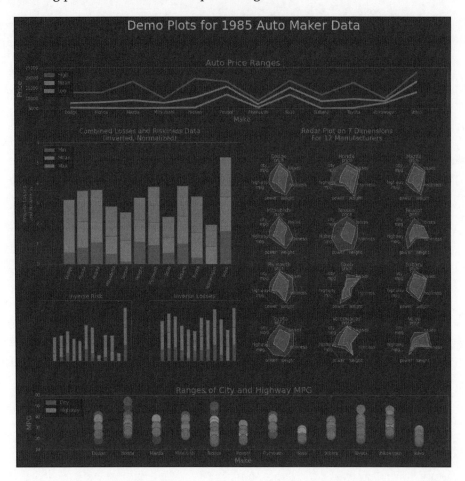

The creation of complex subplots in matplotlib can be perceived as a daunting task. However, the following basic practices can help you make it a painless process of creating visual goodness:

1. Write down an explicit plan for what you want to present, which data you want to combine, where you will use the stacked data and means, and so on.

2. Sketch out on paper or in an ASCII diagram the desired layout. This will often reveal something that you hadn't considered.

3. With the layout decided upon, create a `GridSpec`- and `GridSpecFromSubplotSpec`-based collection of subplots with *empty axes*. Don't add any plot data. Your grid-tweaking should happen at this point.

4. With your girds ironed out, update your axes with the desired plots.

Further explorations in customization

We have covered two areas of customization that come up frequently in various online forums. The other topics in advanced matplotlib customization include the creation of axes, scales, projections, and backends for some particular data or project requirements. Each of these have tutorials or examples that are provided by the matplotlib project, and given your newly attained comfort level with reading the matplotlib sources directly, these are now within your reach.

Several of these are worth mentioning specifically:

- The API example code for `custom_projection_example.py` provides a highly detailed look into the means by which you can create custom projections. Another example of this is the radar plot that we created earlier in this chapter. If you view the library files for this chapter, you will see that we based the work on the polar projection that comes with matplotlib.

- The API example code for `custom_scale_example.py` shows how to create a new scale for the *y* axis, which uses the same system as that of the **Mercator map projection**. This is a smaller amount of code, which is more easily digestible than the preceding projection example.

- The **matplotlib Transformations Tutorial** will teach you how to create data transforms between coordinate systems, use axes transforms to keep the text bubbles in fixed positions while zooming, and blend transformations for the highlighting portions of the plotted data.

Finally, Joe Kington, a geophysicist, created an open source project for equal-angle **Stereonets** in matplotlib. Stereonets, or **Wulff net** are used in geological studies and research, and Dr. Kington's code provides excellent examples of custom transforms and projections. All of this has been documented very well. This is an excellent project to examine in detail after working on the `matplotlib.org` tutorials and examples on creating custom projections, scales, and transformations.

Configuration

We've just covered some examples of matplotlib customization. Hand in hand with this topic is that of configuration—the tweaking of predefined values to override default behaviors. The matplotlib module offers two ways to override the default values for the configuration settings—you can either run the control files, or run the control parameters that are stored in-memory to make changes to a running instance.

The run control for matplotlib

While commonly expanded to the *run control*, the `.rc` extension and `-rc` suffix trace their origins to 1965 and the **Multics** (short for **Multiplexed Information and Computing Service**) operating system, where `rc` stood for the *run command*. Like many software systems that were developed on UNIX- or BSD-based machines, matplotlib has an `rc` file where the control of matplotlib may be configured. This control is not limited to configuration files; one may also access an `rc` object via the matplotlib API. Each of these is covered in the following few sections.

File and directory locations

The configuration of matplotlib is possible through the creation and editing of the `matplotlibrc` file. The matplotlib module will search for this file in the following locations:

- The current working directory
- The `$HOME/.matplotlib` directory
- `INSTALL/matplotlib/mpl-data/`, where `INSTALL` is the Python site-packages directory where matplotlib was installed
- A temporary directory created by Python, in case `$HOME/.matplotlib` is not writable
- The directory defined by the `MPLCONFIGDIR` environment variable (if defined, this directory will override the use of `$HOME/.matplotlib`)

You can use matplotlib to find the location of your configuration directory by using the following code:

```
In [30]: mpl.get_configdir()
Out[30]: '/Users/yourusername/.matplotlib'
```

Similarly, you can display the currently active `matplotlibrc` file with the help of the following code:

```
In [31]: mpl.matplotlib_fname()
Out[31]: '/Users/yourusername/mastering-matplotlib/.venv-mmpl/lib/
python3.4/site-packages/matplotlib/mpl-data/matplotlibrc'
```

Using the matplotlibrc file

There are hundreds of configuration options that are available to you via the `matplotlibrc` file:

```
In [32]: len(mpl.rcParams.keys())
Out[32]: 200
```

You can have a look at some of these with the following code:

```
In [33]: dict(list(mpl.rcParams.items())[:10])
Out[33]: {'axes.grid': False,
          'mathtext.fontset': 'cm',
          'mathtext.cal': 'cursive',
          'docstring.hardcopy': False,
          'animation.writer': 'ffmpeg',
          'animation.mencoder_path': 'mencoder',
          'backend.qt5': 'PyQt5',
          'keymap.fullscreen': ['f', 'ctrl+f'],
          'image.resample': False,
          'animation.ffmpeg_path': 'ffmpeg'}
```

The configuration options that you need depend entirely upon your use cases, and thanks to matplotlib's ability to search multiple locations, you can have a global configuration file as well as per-project configurations.

We've already run into a special case of matplotlib configuration—the contents of the style files that we saw at the beginning of this chapter. If you were so inclined, all of those values could be entered into a `matplotlibrc` file, thus setting the default global look and feel for matplotlib.

A complete template for the `matplotlbrc` file is available in the matplotlib repository on GitHub. This is the canonical reference for all your matplotlib configuration needs. However, we will point out a few that may be helpful if you keep them in mind, including some that may be used to decrease the render times:

- `agg.path.chunksize: 20000`: This improves the speed of operations slightly and prevents an `Agg` rendering failure
- `path.simplify: true`: This removes the invisible points to reduce the file size and increase the rendering speed
- `savefig.jpeg_quality: xx`: This lowers the default `.jpg` quality of the saved files
- `axes.formatter.limits`: This indicates when you use scientific notations for exponents
- `webagg.port`: This is the port that you should use for the web server in the `WebAgg` backend
- `webagg.port_retries`: With this, the number of other random ports will be tried until the one that is available is found

Updating the settings dynamically

In addition to setting the options in the `matplotlibrc` file, you have the ability to change the configuration values on the fly by directly accessing the `rcParams` dictionary that we saw earlier:

```
In [34]: mpl.rcParams['savefig.jpeg_quality'] = 72

Out[34]: mpl.rcParams['axes.formatter.limits'] = [-5, 5]
```

If you either find out that your changes have caused some problems, or you want to revert to the default values for any reason, you can do so with `mpl.rcdefaults()`, which is demonstrated in the following code:

```
In [35]: mpl.rcParams['axes.formatter.limits']

Out[35]: [-5, 5]

In [36]: mpl.rcdefaults()

In [37]: mpl.rcParams['axes.formatter.limits']

Out[37]: [-7, 7]
```

Options in IPython

If you are using matplotlib via IPython, as many do, there are IPython matplotlib configuration options that you should be aware of, especially if you regularly use different backends or integrate with different event loops. When you start up IPython, you have the ability to configure matplotlib for interactive use by setting a default matplotlib backend in the following way:

```
--matplotlib=XXX
```

In the preceding code, XXX is one of `auto`, `gtk`, `gtk3`, `inline`, `nbagg`, `osx`, `qt`, `qt4`, `qt5`, `tk`, or `wx`. Similarly, you can enable a GUI event loop integration with the following option:

```
--gui=XXX
```

In the preceding code, XXX is one of `glut`, `gtk`, `gtk3`, `none`, `osx`, `pyglet`, `qt`, `qt4`, `tk`, or `wx`.

While you may see the `--pylab` or `%pylab` option being referred to in older books and various online resources (including some of matplotlib's own official documentation), its use has been discouraged since IPython version 1.0. It is better to import the modules that you will be using explicitly and not use the deprecated pylab interface at all.

Summary

In this chapter, we covered two areas of detailed customization—the creation of custom styles, as well as complex subplots. In the previous chapters, you have been exposed to the means by which you can discover more of matplotlib's functionality through its sources. It was in this context that the additional topics in customization were mentioned. With this, we transitioned into the topic of matplotlib configuration via files as well as `rcParams`. This is a transitional topic that will be picked up again at the beginning of the next chapter, where we will cover matplotlib deployments.

7
Deploying matplotlib in Cloud Environments

With this chapter, we will move into the topics that focus on the computationally intensive matplotlib tasks. This is not something that is usually associated with matplotlib directly, but rather with libraries like NumPy, Pandas, or scikit-learn, which are often brought to bear on large number-crunching jobs. However, there are a number of situations in which organizations or individual researchers need to generate a large number of plots. In the remainder of the book, our exploration of matplotlib in advanced usage scenarios will rely on the free or low-cost modern techniques that are available to the public. In the early 1960s, the famous computer scientist John McCarthy predicted a day when computational resources would be available like the public utilities of electricity and water. This has indeed come to pass, and we will now turn our focus to these types of environments.

We will cover the following topics in this chapter:

- Making a use case for matplotlib in the Cloud
    - Preparing a well-defined workflow
    - Choosing technologies

- AWS and Docker
    - Local setup
    - Using Docker
    - Thinking about deployment
    - Working with AWS
    - Running matplotlib tasks

To follow along with this chapter's code, clone the notebook's repository and start up IPython by using the following code:

```
$ git clone https://github.com/masteringmatplotlib/cloud-deploy.git
$ cd cloud-deploy
$ make
```

Making a use case for matplotlib in the Cloud

At first blush, it may seem odd that we are contemplating the distributed use of a library that has historically been focused on desktop-type environments. However, if we pause to ponder over this, we will see its value. You will have probably noticed that with large data sets or complex plots, matplotlib runs more slowly than we might like. What should we do when we need to generate a handful of plots for very large data sets or thousands of plots from diverse sources? If this sounds far-fetched, keep in mind that there are companies that have massive PDF-generating *farms* of servers for such activities.

This chapter will deal with a similar use case. You are a researcher working for a small company, tracking climactic patterns and possible changes at both the poles. Your team is focused on the Arctic and your assignment is to process the satellite imagery for the east coast of Greenland, which includes not only the new images as they come (every 16 days), but also the previously captured satellite data. For the newer material (2013 onwards), you will be utilizing the Landsat 8 data, which was made available through the combined efforts of the **United States Geological Survey (USGS)** and the NASA Landsat 8 project and the USGS EROS data archival services.

The data source

For your project, you will be acquiring data from the EROS archives by using the USGS EarthExplorer site (downloads require a registered user account, which is free). You will use their map to locate *scenes* — specific geographic areas of satellite imagery that can be downloaded using the EarthExplorer **Bulk Download Application (BDA)**. Your initial focus will be data from `scoresbysund`, the largest and longest fjord system in the world. Your first set of data will come from the `LC82260102014232LGN00` scene ID, a capture that was taken in August 2014 as shown in the following screenshot:

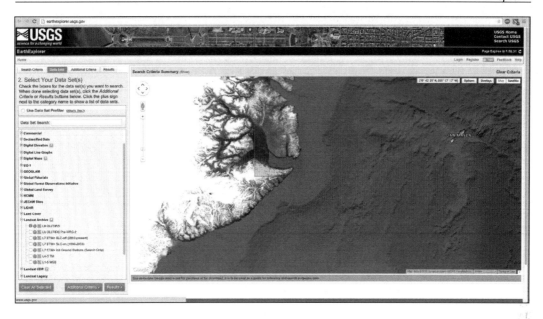

Once you have marked the area in EarthExplorer, click the **Data Sets** view, expand **Landsat Archive**, and then select **L8 OLI/TIRS**. After clicking on **Results**, you will be presented with a list of scenes, each with a preview. You can click on the thumbnail image to see the preview, to check whether you have the right scene. Once you have located the scene, click on the tiny little *package* icon (it will be light brown/tan in color). If you haven't logged in, you will be prompted to. Add it to your cart, and then go to your cart to complete the free order.

Next, you will need to open the BDA and download your order from there (when the BDA opens, it will show the pending orders and present you with the option of downloading them). BDA will download a tarball (tar archive) to the given directory. From that directory, you can create a scene directory and unpack the files.

Defining a workflow

Before creating a Cloud workflow, we need to step through the process manually to identify all the steps and indicate those that may be automated. We will be using a data set from a specific point in time, but what we will define here should be usable by any Landsat 8 data, and some of it will be usable by the older satellite remote sensing data.

We will start by organizing the data. The BDA will save its downloads to a specific location (different for each operating system). Let's move all the data that you've taken with the EarthExplorer BDA to a location that we can easily reference in our IPython Notebook — /EROSData/L8_OLI_TIRS. Ensure that your scene data is in the LC82260102014232LGN00 directory.

Next, let's perform the necessary imports and the variable definitions, as follows:

```
In [1]: import matplotlib
        matplotlib.use('nbagg')
        %matplotlib inline
In [2]: from IPython.display import Image
        import sys
        sys.path.append("../lib")
        import eros
```

With the last line of code, we bring in the custom code created for this chapter and task (based on the demonstration code by Milos Miljkovic, which he delivered as a part of a talk at the PyData 2014 conference). Here are the variables that we will be using:

```
In [3]: path = "/EROSData/L8_OLI_TIRS"
        scene_id = "LC82260102014232LGN00"
```

With this in place, we're ready to read some Landsat data and write them to the files in the following way:

```
In [4]: rgb_image = eros.extract_rgb(path, scene_id)
```

If you examine the source for the last two function calls, you will see that identifying the files that are associated with the Landsat band data, extracting them from the source data, and then creating a data structure to represent the red, blue, and green channels needed for digital color images. The Landsat 8 bands are as follows:

- **Band 1**: It's represented by deep blue and violet. It is useful for tracking coastal waters and fine particles in the air.
- **Band 2**: It's represented by visible blue light.
- **Band 3**: It's represented by visible green light.
- **Band 4**: It's represented by visible red light.
- **Band 5**: It's represented by **Near-Infrared** (**NIR**) light. It is useful for viewing healthy plants.

- **Band 6 and 7**: They are represented by **Short-Wavelength Infrared (SWIR)** light. It is useful for identifying wet and dry earth. It shows the contrast between the rocks and soil.

- **Band 8**: It's represented by a panchromatic emulsion like a black and white film; this band combines all the colors. Due to its sharp contrast and high resolution, it's useful if you want to zoom in on the details.

- **Band 9**: This is a narrow slice of wavelengths that is used by a few space-based instruments. It is useful for examining the cloud cover and very bright objects.

- **Band 10 and 11**: They are represented by a thermal infrared light. It is useful when you want to obtain the temperature of the air.

In your task, you will use bands 1 through 4 for water and RGB, 5 for vegetation, and 7 to pick out the rocks. Let's take a look at the true-color RGB image for the bands that we just extracted by using the following code:

```
In [5]: eros.show_image(
    rgb_image, "RGB image, data set " + scene_id,
    figsize=(20, 20))
```

The following image is the result of the preceding code:

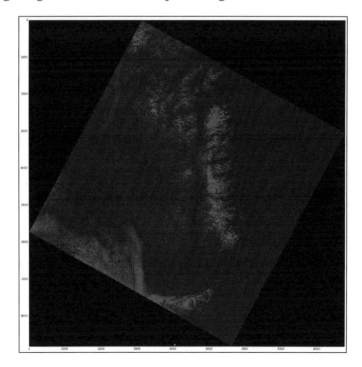

The preceding image isn't very clear. The colors are all quite muted. We can gain some insight into this by looking at a histogram of the data files for each color channel by using the following code:

```
In [6]: eros.show_color_hist(
    rgb_image, xlim=[5000,20000], ylim=[0,10000],
    figsize=(20, 7))
```

The following histogram is the result of the preceding code:

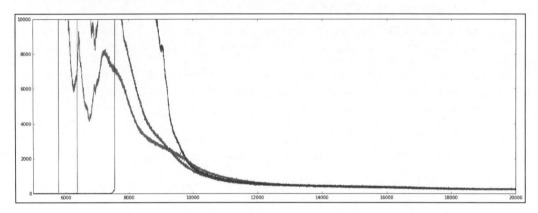

As you can see, a major part of the color information is concentrated in a narrower band, while the other data is still included. Let's create a new image by using ranges based on a visual assessment of the preceding histogram. We'll limit the red channel to the range of 5900-11000, green to 6200-11000, and blue to 7600-11000:

```
In [7]: rgb_image_he = eros.update_image(
    rgb_image,
    (5900, 11000), (6200, 11000), (7600, 11000))
        eros.show_image(
    rgb_image_he, "RGB image, histogram equalized",
    figsize=(20, 20))
```

The following image is the result of the preceding code:

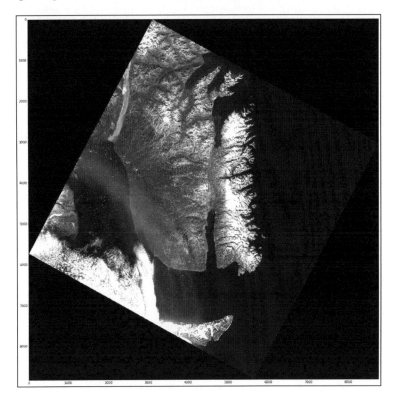

With the preceding changes, the colors really pop out of the satellite data. Next, you need to create your false-color image.

You will use the Landsat 8 band 1 (coastal aerosol) as blue, band 5 (NIR) as green, and band 7 (SWIR) as red to gain an insight into the presence of water on land, ice coverage, levels of healthy vegetation, and exposed rock or open ground. These will be used to generate a **false color** image. You will use the same method as with the previous image—generating a histogram, analyzing it for the best points of the color spectrum, and then displaying the image. This can be done with the help of the following code:

```
In [8]: swir2nirg_image = eros.extract_swir2nirg(path, scene_id)

In [9]: eros.show_color_hist(
    swir2nirg_image, xlim=[4000,30000], ylim=[0,10000],
    figsize=(20, 7))
```

The following histogram is the result of the preceding code:

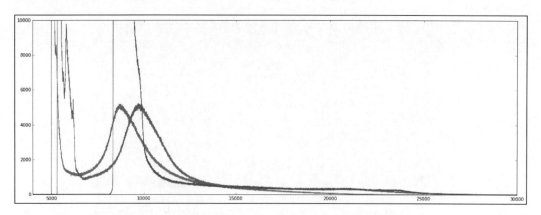

Let's create the image for the histogram using the following code:

```
In[10]: swir2nirg_image_he = eros.update_image(
    swir2nirg_image,
    (5900, 15000), (6200, 15000), (7600, 15000))
        eros.show_image(swir2nirg_image_he, "",
    figsize=(20, 20))
```

The following is the resultant image:

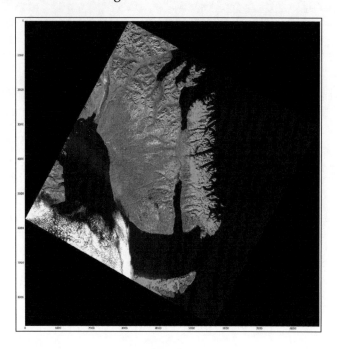

On a 2009 iMac (Intel Core i7, 8 GB RAM), the processing of the Landsat 8 data and the generation of the associated images took about 7 minutes with the RAM usage peaking at around 9 GB. For multiple runs, the IPython kernel needs to be restarted just to free up the RAM quickly enough. It's quite clear that performing these tasks on a moderately equipped workstation would be a logistically and economically unfeasible proposition for thousands (or even hundreds) of scenes.

So, you will instead accomplish these tasks with the help of utility computing. The following are the necessary steps that are used to carry out the tasks:

1. Define a Landsat 8 scene ID.

2. Ensure that the data is available.

3. Extract the coastal/aerosol, RGB, NIR, and SWIR data.

4. Identify the optimum ranges for display in each channel. We'll skip this step when we automate. However, this is an excellent exercise for the motivated readers.

5. Generate the image files for the extracted data.

These need to be migrated to the desired Cloud platform and augmented according to the needs of the associated tools. This brings us to the important question: Which technology should we use?

Choosing technologies

There is a dizzying array of choices when it comes to selecting a combination of a vendor, an operating system, vendor service options, a configuration management solution, and deployment options for Cloud environments. You can select one of the several OpenStack providers, such as Google Cloud Platform, Amazon AWS, Heroku, and Docker's dotCloud. Linux or BSD is probably the best choice for the host and guest OS, but even that leaves open many possibilities. Some vendors offer RESTful web services, SOAP, or dedicated client libraries that either wrap one of these or provide direct access.

In your case, you've done some testing on the speed needed to transfer considerably large files that are approximately 150 MB in size for each Landsat 8 band from a storage service to a running instance. Combining the speed requirements with usability, you found out that at the current time, Amazon's AWS came up as the winner in a close race against its contending Cloud service platforms. Since we will be using the recent versions of Python (3.4.2) and matplotlib (1.4.2) and we need a distribution that provides these pre-built, we have opted for Ubuntu 15.04. You will spin up the guest OS instances to run each image processing job, but now you need to decide how to configure these and determine the level of automation that is needed.

Configuration management

It was in this capacity that Docker made its way into the Linux world of configuration management. Systems administrators were looking for more straightforward solutions to problems that did not require the feature sets and complexities of larger tools. Configuration management can encompass topics such as version control, packaging, software distribution, build management, deployment, and change control, just to name a few. For our purposes, we will focus on configuration management as it concerns the following:

- High-level dependency management
- The creation and management of baseline systems as well as the task of building on the same
- Deployment of a highly specified system to a particular environment

In the world of open source software configuration management, there are two giants that stand out—**Chef** and **Puppet**. Both of these were originally written in Ruby, with the Chef server having been rewritten in Erlang. In the world of Python, Salt and Ansible have risen to great prominence. Unfortunately, neither of the Python solutions currently support Python 3. Systems like Chef and Puppet are fairly complex and suited to addressing the problems of managing large numbers of systems with a multitude of possible configurations under continually changing circumstances. Unless one already has an expertise in these systems, their use is outside the scope of our current task.

This brings us to an interesting option that is almost outside the realm of configuration management—Docker. **Docker** is a software that wraps access to the Linux container technology, allowing the fast creation of operating system images that can then be run on a host system. Thus, this software utilizes a major part of the underlying system while providing an isolated environment, which can be customized according to the specific needs.

It was in this capacity that Docker made its way into the Linux world of configuration management via the system administrators, who were looking for more straightforward solutions for problems that did not require the feature sets and complexities of larger tools. Likewise, it is a perfect match for our needs. As a part of this chapter, we have provided various baselines for your use. These baselines are as follows:

- `masteringmatplotlib/python`: This is a Python 3.4.2 image built on the official Ubuntu 15.05 Docker image
- `masteringmatplotlib/scipy`: This is a NumPy 1.8.2, SciPy 0.14.1, and matplotlib 1.4.2 image that is based on the `masteringmatplotlib/python` image

- `masteringmatplotlib/eros`: This is a custom image that contains not only the software used in this chapter based on the `masteringmatplotlib/scipy` image, but also the Python **Python Imaging Library** (PIL) and `scikit-image` libraries

We will discuss the Docker images in more detail shortly.

Types of deployment

Docker had its genesis in a Cloud platform and as one might guess, it is ideally suited for deployments on multiple Cloud platforms including the likes of Amazon AWS, Google Cloud Platform, Azure, OpenStack, dotCloud, Joyent, and OpenShift. Each of these differs from the others—only slightly when it comes to some features and enormously with regard to the others. Conceptually though, they offer utility-scale virtualization services, which is something that is particularly well suited to Docker. Which one is the best for your general needs depends on many of the same criteria that exist for any hosting scenario, regardless of the underlying technology.

Each of these will also let you spin up multiple Docker containers, allowing for entire application stacks to run an assortment of Docker images. With Docker's support of orchestration with a new set of tools, the number of possibilities for deployment options and the associated flexibility has been greatly increased.

As mentioned previously, in your tests for the Landsat 8 data scenario, you assessed AWS as the best fit. You looked at Elastic Beanstalk, but opted for a very simple solution that offers you more control—you will deploy a large **Elastic Compute Cloud** (EC2) Linux instance and use it to fire up the satellite-data-processing Docker containers as needed.

An example – AWS and Docker

The rest of this chapter is dedicated to the running of the `matplotlib` USGS/EROS image generation task in AWS using EC2, S3, and Docker. We are going to need to perform two stages of preparation—work that needs to be done locally and the setup that needs to happen in the Cloud. With these complete, we will be ready to execute our prepared task.

Getting set up locally

Your local setup will include an installation of Docker (and `boot2docker` if you are using Mac or Windows). It will create or download `Dockerfiles`, generate images from these files, extend the base images as necessary, and start up a Docker image to ensure that everything is in working order.

Requirements

Here's what you will need for the remainder of this chapter:

- Docker
- `boot2docker` (for easily using Docker from Windows or Mac)

If you're running Linux, you can skip the rest of this section. If you haven't run `boot2docker` before, you'll need to run the following command first:

```
$ boot2docker init
```

If you have previously initiated `boot2docker`, you can just do the following code:

```
$ boot2docker up
```

At this point, you will see an output that looks like the following:

```
Waiting for VM and Docker daemon to start......ooo
Started.
Writing ~/.boot2docker/certs/boot2docker-vm/ca.pem
Writing ~/.boot2docker/certs/boot2docker-vm/cert.pem
Writing ~/.boot2docker/certs/boot2docker-vm/key.pem
To connect the Docker client to the Docker daemon, please set:
export DOCKER_CERT_PATH=~/.boot2docker/certs/boot2docker-vm
export DOCKER_TLS_VERIFY=1
export DOCKER_HOST=tcp://192.168.59.103:2376
```

You can either manually export the **environment variables**, or run the following code from your shell prompt:

```
$ $(boot2docker shellinit)
```

The preceding code will set the appropriate variables in your shell environment for you automatically. At this point, Docker is ready for use.

Dockerfiles and the Docker images

The heart of configuration management is the `Dockerfile`. This will be used to generate the Docker image that you need to run the Docker containers, which is where your matplotlib tasks will actually happen. If you are unfamiliar with Docker, here's a quick summary of how to think about the components that we have just mentioned:

- **Dockerfile**: This is the specification that is used to build extendible images

- **The Docker image**: This is a read-only template, which is somewhat like a filesystem
- **The Docker container**: This is an isolated and secure application platform; this is what actually gets run

One of the features of Docker is that through its underlying use of a unification file system one is able to load images, starting with a base image and adding increasingly more specific images until the desired configuration state is achieved. This is exactly what we will do. The company that you work for, as stated earlier, is a Python 3 shop. So, they've built a Docker image that has all the basic goodies for Python 3 on Ubuntu 15.04. Furthermore, since the research and computation groups make heavy use of NumPy, SciPy, Pandas, and matplotlib, a second image has been created by using the Python 3 image as a base.

Here's what the Python 3 `Dockerfile` looks like:

```
In [11]: cat ../docker/python/Dockerfile
        FROM ubuntu:vivid
        MAINTAINER Duncan McGreggor <oubiwann@gmail.com>
        ENV DEBIAN_FRONTEND noninteractive
        RUN apt-get update
        RUN apt-get upgrade -y
        RUN apt-get install -y -q apt-utils
        RUN apt-get install -y -q \
            ca-certificates git build-essential
        RUN apt-get install -y -q \
            libssl-dev libcurl4-openssl-dev
        RUN apt-get install -y -q curl
        RUN apt-get install -y -q \
            cython3 libpython3.4-dev python3.4-dev \
            python3-setuptools python3-pip
        CMD python3
```

Note that this `Dockerfile` has not been created from scratch. Rather, it is based on another Docker image—the official `ubuntu:vivid` image. It has a maintainer that sets an environment variable, which will be available for each of the RUN and CMD directives as well as when the Docker image is running (with and without an interactive session). Each of the RUN commands is executed when building the Docker image. The CMD command is what will be run by default when executing Docker run on the command line.

This `Dockerfile` has been used to generate an image, which has been published to **Docker Hub** with the `masteringmatplotlib/python` tag. As such, you will not need to build this yourself.

The next `Dockerfile` that we will look at is the one that your group uses for the majority of its scientific computing tasks. Here is a `Dockerfile`:

```
In [12]: cat ../docker/scipy/Dockerfile
         FROM masteringmatplotlib/python
         MAINTAINER Duncan McGreggor <oubiwann@gmail.com>
         ENV DEBIAN_FRONTEND noninteractive
         RUN apt-get install -y -q \
             libatlas3-base libblas-dev libblas3 \
             libatlas-base-dev libatlas-dev \
             liblapack-dev gfortran
         ENV LAPACK /usr/lib/liblapack.so
         ENV ATLAS /usr/lib/libatlas.so
         ENV BLAS /usr/lib/libblas.so
         RUN apt-get install -y -q \
             python3-six python3-flake8 \
             python3-dateutil python3-pyparsing \
             python3-numpy python3-scipy \
             python3-matplotlib python3-pandas
         RUN pip3 install seaborn
         CMD python3
```

In this case, the `Dockerfile` is based on the Python 3 `Dockerfile`. It is extended by additional installations of the libraries that are commonly needed for scientific computing that is performed by using Python. The `Dockerfile` is used to create an image and pushed to Docker Hub using the `masteringmatplotlib/scipy` tag. This is the one that we will be extending for our task.

Extending a Docker image

The preceding `scipy` Docker image has almost everything we need. It's just missing a few dependencies, which are available in this chapter's Git repository. These dependencies include the following:

- PIL
- The `scikit-image` library

- A custom code to work with the USGS EROS/NASA Landsat 8 data

So, how can we customize the scipy image to include the preceding dependencies? There are two ways to do this:

- Make changes to the image and commit these changes
- Create a Dockerfile that is based on the image

We will use the second option so that we are able to easily track changes in the source code of the Dockerfile. We've provided the following file in the notebook repository:

```
In [13]: cat ../docker/simple/Dockerfile
         FROM masteringmatplotlib/scipy
         MAINTAINER Py3 Hacker <you@py.hacker>
         ENV HOME /root
         ENV REPO cloud-deploy
         RUN cd $HOME && \
             git clone \
             https://github.com/masteringmatplotlib/${REPO}.git
         RUN cd $HOME/$REPO && \
             make docker-setup
         CMD PYTHONPATH=$HOME/$REPO/lib:$PYTHONPATH \
             python3
```

Points to note:

- The preceding Dockerfile extends the masteringmatplotlib/scipy Docker image.
- Being able to use the standard development workflows that we are used to, like cloning the required code, is an incredibly powerful tool, which is quite easy to accomplish thanks to the simple design of Docker.
- For ease of demonstration, we're going to simply use the notebook repository and add it to PYTHONPATH. In most situations, you have to create a setup.py file for your Python library and install it with pip in the Dockerfile build steps. Thus, you don't have to mess with PYTHONPATH when running your commands in the Dockerfile.

Building a new image

Let's build a new image! First, run the following code:

```
$ docker build -t yourname/eros ./docker/simple/Dockerfile
```

The `-t` parameter instructs `docker` to *tag* the image with the provided name once it's built. The prefix before / should match the name used on Docker Hub if you're going to publish the image there. This can be a username or an organization.

Once you execute the preceding command, you will see the following output:

```
Sending build context to Docker daemon   2.56 kB
Sending build context to Docker daemon
Step 0 : FROM ipython/scipystack
 ---> 113395173d25
Step 1 : MAINTAINER Py Hacker <you@py.hacker>
 ---> Using cache
 ---> fd520c92b33b


[snip]


Removing intermediate container 90983e9fdd54
Step 6 : CMD PYTHONPATH=./cloud-deploy/lib:$PYTHONPATH python3
 ---> Running in b7a022f2ac29
 ---> abde2bb0eeaa
Removing intermediate container b7a022f2ac29
Successfully built abde2bb0eeaa
```

Let's make sure that the library is present in our new image by using the `-i` option for `docker run` to indicate that we will need an interactive session with the container (this keeps `STDIN` open):

```
$ docker run -t -i yourname/eros python3
>>> import eros
>>> ^D
$
```

Looks like our simple image that was built on the top of `masteringmatplotlib/scipy` worked like a charm. Now, let's make some changes to it.

Preparing for deployment

We need to make a couple of changes to the simple case so that it fulfills the following conditions:

- Our code will know that it's being called from Docker (used to set the backend to something that doesn't require a DISPLAY environment)

- We can execute a dispatch function, which will generate the desired type of satellite image

Both of the preceding conditions can be fulfilled simply by changing the Docker CMD directive in the following way:

```
In [14]: cat ../docker/eros/Dockerfile
FROM masteringmatplotlib/scipy
MAINTAINER Py3 Hacker <you@py.hacker>
ENV HOME /root
ENV REPO cloud-deploy
RUN cd $HOME && \
    git clone https://github.com/masteringmatplotlib/${REPO}.git
RUN cd $HOME/$REPO && \
    make docker-setup
CMD DOCKER_CONTAINER=true \
    PYTHONPATH=${HOME}/${REPO}/lib:$PYTHONPATH \
    python3 -c "import eros;eros.s3_generate_image();"
```

The s3_generate_image function is the dispatcher, and depending upon the environment variables that are set when running Docker, it will take different actions. We will discuss this more in a later section.

Getting the setup on AWS

Having prepared the local machine to create the Docker images that we will use in the Cloud, we now need to set up the other end—getting the Cloud ready for our images. In the following sections, we will copy the Landsat image data to a remote storage service, create a virtual machine in the Cloud that will be the host OS for the Docker images, and finally ensure that we can read and write data in our images to and from the storage service.

Pushing the source data to S3

The Landsat 8 data files that we are working with are sizable, with each file ranging from about 150 MB to 600 MB. As such, we want to be selective with regard to what we'll be pushing to S3. For your project, the following Landsat bands are needed:

- Coastal/aerosol (band 1)
- Red, green, and blue (bands 4, 3, and 2)
- SWIR, 2100-2300 nm (band 7)
- NIR, 845-885 nm (band 5)

All the files for a particular scene weigh over 2 GB, so we'll just want to push the files for the bands we need as per the Landsat bands that were noted in the preceding section. Given that we define the following shell variables:

```
$ SCENE_PATH="/EROSData/L8_OLI_TIRS"
$ SCENE=LC82260102014232LGN00
```

The files that we need to upload can be identified with the help of the following code:

```
$ find $SCENE_PATH/$SCENE \
    -name "*_B[1-5,7].TIF" \
    -exec basename {} \;
LC82260102014232LGN00_B1.TIF
LC82260102014232LGN00_B2.TIF
LC82260102014232LGN00_B3.TIF
LC82260102014232LGN00_B4.TIF
LC82260102014232LGN00_B5.TIF
LC82260102014232LGN00_B7.TIF
```

Before running the following commands, you need to make sure that the user associated with the access and secret keys has the appropriate S3 permissions (for example, the ability to upload the files). This is done in the AWS Management Console in the IAM screen through various means (your preference with regard to the combination of users, groups, roles, and policies).

Let's start by setting some AWS shell variables in a terminal window on your local machine by using the following code:

```
$ export AWS_ACCESS_KEY_ID=YOURACCESSKEY
$ export AWS_SECRET_ACCESS_KEY=YOURSECRETKEY
```

These will be used by the aws command-line utility, which was installed when you ran the make command in the IPython Notebook repository at the beginning of the chapter. Let's also set a bucket name variable by using the following code:

```
$ S3_BUCKET=scoresbysund
```

Note that the Amazon S3 bucket names are global like DNS. As such, this bucket may already exist. So, be ready with an alternate name.

Now we can create the S3 bucket in the following way:

```
$ aws s3 mb s3://$S3_BUCKET
```

With the new bucket in place, we can now upload the selected Landsat 8 scene files:

```
$ for FILE in "$SCENE_PATH"/$SCENE/*_B[2-5,7].TIF
    do
    aws s3 cp "$FILE" s3://$S3_BUCKET
    done
```

That's a total of about 888 MB. So, depending on the upload speed of your Internet connection, you may be in for a wait.

The files that the satellite image processing task will need have been uploaded. The next step is to set up a server on which the Docker container tasks will run.

Creating a host server on EC2

In the previous testing, you discovered that an m3/xlarge EC2 instance, along with its 15 GB RAM, will be required due to the intensive memory requirements for the task of image processing. The next step involved an instance the requires a 7.5 GB RAM; this generated out-of-memory errors, indicating that the RAM was insufficient for the instance.

To create an EC2 instance on AWS, perform the following steps:

1. Log in to the AWS console and click on the **Launch Instance** button.
2. Select your preferred **Volume Type** (for example, Red Hat, SUSE, Ubuntu, and so on). We will use an Ubuntu 64 EC2 **Amazon Machine Image** (**AMI**) with 4 virtual CPUs and 15 GB of RAM.
3. Select or create the security group that will allow an in-bound **Secure Shell** (**SSH**) access (port 22) to the EC2 instance from your workstation.
4. Launch the EC2 instance.

The following screenshot shows the **Review Instance Launch** step:

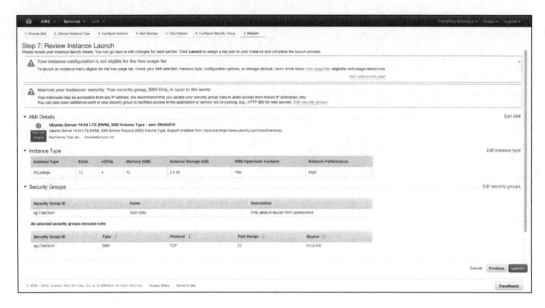

Once the instance is up and running, get the IP address from the AWS Management Console from where you launched it and use it to SSH into it:

```
$ ssh -i /path/to/your-ec2-key-pair.pem \
    ubuntu@instance-ip-address
```

Once you have activated SSH into the running EC2 instance, prep the instance by installing Docker and saving your AWS credentials on the filesystem. You will need access to these credentials when you start up the Docker containers so that the Python script on the container can read from and write to S3:

```
ubuntu@ip-address:~$ sudo apt-get install -y docker.io

ubuntu@ip-address:~$ sudo mkdir /etc/aws

ubuntu@ip-address:~$ sudo vi /etc/aws/access

ubuntu@ip-address:~$ sudo vi /etc/aws/secret

ubuntu@ip-address:~$ sudo chmod 600 /etc/aws/*

ubuntu@ip-address:~$ sudo chown ubuntu /etc/aws/*
```

Using Docker on EC2

Now, you need to pull down the Docker image that we've created for this task and then run a container by using this image in the interactive mode with the help of Python as the shell. You can use either the Docker image that you created or the one that we did (`masteringmatplotlib/eros`):

```
ubuntu@ip-address:~$ sudo docker run -i \
    -t masteringmatplotlib/eros python3
Python 3.4.3 (default, Feb 27 2015, 02:35:54)
[GCC 4.9.2] on linux
Type "help", "copyright", "credits" or "license" for more information.
>>>
```

This will attempt to run the `masteringmatplotlib/scipy` Docker image, which won't be present on your EC2 instance. So, it will then download it from Docker Hub (also downloading all the images upon which it is built). Once this finishes, do a quick test to make sure that everything is in place:

```
>>> import eros
>>>
```

You should get no errors. This will indicate that you are all set for the next step!

Reading and writing with S3

In order to read your scene data from the files that you uploaded to S3, you'll need to do the following:

1. Update your bucket permissions with a policy that allows your EC2 instance to access it.
2. Obtain the HTTP URL for your bucket on the **S3** screen in the AWS Console.
3. Keep the IP address of your newly started EC2 instance handy.

The easiest way to read data from S3 in EC2 is to open the HTTP URL for the file in question. To do this, you need to do the following:

1. Go to the **S3** section in the AWS Console.
2. Click on the bucket that you will be using.
3. In the new page that loads, click on **Properties**.

4. In the **Properties** section, click on **Edit bucket policy**.

5. In the form that appears, paste the following, substituting your EC2 IP address:

```
{
    "Version": "2012-10-17",
    "Id": "S3ScoresbySundGetPolicy",
    "Statement": [
        {
            "Sid": "IPAllow",
            "Effect": "Allow",
            "Principal": "*",
            "Action": "s3:*",
            "Resource": "arn:aws:s3:::scoresbysund/*",
            "Condition" : {
                "IpAddress" : {
                    "aws:SourceIp": "YOUREC2IPADDRESS/32"
                }
            }
        }
    ]
}
```

The following screenshot shows the code pasted in the **Bucket Policy Editor**:

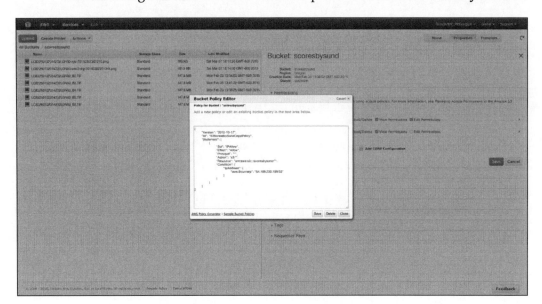

With this change, your storage dependencies are now complete and your scripts on the EC2 instance, which use the appropriate AWS access credentials, will be able to read from and write to S3.

Running the task

As it is evident from the work that we have done till now, the operation of processing in remote environments requires a great deal of preparation and attention to detail. We have now made the way clear for our matplotlib satellite image generation task. We are ready to pass the parameters to Docker, which will let us flexibly handle many tasks with one image. We are also going to first tweak the Python code to handle these parameters and then finally execute our task.

Environment variables and Docker

When the EC2 instance starts up a Docker container that has to build images from the Landsat 8 data files, the Docker container will need to know a few things, which are as follows:

- The Landsat 8 scene ID
- The AWS access key that is used to access S3
- The AWS secret key that is used to access S3

We can pass this information to the Docker container by using the -e flag, which will set the environment variables in the container once it starts. Before we try using this in a script, let's make sure that the feature behaves according to our expectations by starting up a Docker container in the EC2 instance in the following way:

```
ubuntu@ip-address:~$ sudo docker run -i \
  -e "PYTHONPATH=/root/cloud-deploy" \
  -e "EROS_SCENE_ID=LC82260102014232LGN00" \
  -e "AWS_ACCESS_KEY_ID=`cat /etc/aws/access`" \
  -e "AWS_SECRET_ACCESS_KEY=`cat /etc/aws/secret`" \
  -t masteringmatplotlib/eros \
  python3
```

This will drop us into a Python prompt in the container, where we can check out the environment variables:

```python
>>> import os
>>> os.getenv("EROS_SCENE_ID")
'dummy001'
>>> os.getenv("AWS_ACCESS_KEY_ID")
'YOURACCESSKEY'
>>> os.getenv("AWS_SECRET_ACCESS_KEY")
'YOURSECRETACCESSKEY'
```

Everything worked perfectly, just as one might have expected.

Changes to the Python module

Now that you've confirmed that you can get the data that you need into the Docker containers, you can update your code to check for some specific data that you will set when running a container to generate satellite images. For instance, towards the beginning of the `lib/ec2s3eros.py` module, we have the following:

```python
bucket_name = os.environ.get("S3_BUCKET_NAME")
scene_id = os.environ.get("EROS_SCENE_ID")
s3_path = os.environ.get("S3_PATH")
s3_title = os.environ.get("S3_IMAGE_TITLE")
s3_filename = os.environ.get("S3_IMAGE_FILENAME")
s3_image_type = os.environ.get("S3_IMAGE_TYPE", "").lower()
access_key = os.environ.get("AWS_ACCESS_KEY_ID")
secret_key = os.environ.get("AWS_SECRET_ACCESS_KEY")
```

The preceding lines of code are what the code will use to create the suitable image and save it to the appropriate place with the expected name. You can see this clearly if you scroll towards the end of the file. Here's an example of one of these variables getting used to dispatch the appropriate image-generating function:

```python
def s3_generate_image():
    if s3_image_type == "rgb":
        s3_image_rgb()
    elif s3_image_type == "swir2nirg":
        s3_image_swir2nirg()
```

There's another important change that we had to make. In order for matplotlib to run successfully on EC2, we need to set an explicit backend. The matplotlib module is only smart enough to choose a backend based on the operating system. As it has been designed for use with GUIs, it makes an assumption that you not only have a DISPLAY environment variable set, but more importantly, there is an actual display to which this variable points.

On EC2 and other Cloud environments, this will almost always not be the case. If you look at the top of the lib/ec2s3eros.py module, you will see the following:

```
import matplotlib as mpl
if  os.environ.get("DOCKER_CONTAINER") == "true":
    mpl.use("Agg")
```

The environment variable that you see in the preceding code is the one that set in the CMD directive of the Dockerfile:

```
CMD DOCKER_CONTAINER=true \
    PYTHONPATH=${HOME}/${REPO}/lib:$PYTHONPATH \
    python3 -c "import eros;eros.s3_generate_image();"
```

As you can see in the module, we used the environment variable to determine whether the module is being used in a Docker container (with no variable set). If it is being used in Docker, we explicitly set the backend to something that will not throw errors if there is no display.

In the preceding example, we have done this in the code, since the file already existed and it was just a two-line change. However, we can also provide a custom matplotlibrc file, which will set the default backend. For the long term, this is probably the better approach because of the following reasons:

- The new file will only need to be created once in the Dockerfile that installs matplotlib (for us, this was the one that generated the masteringmatplotlib/scipy Docker image)

- The images that extend that one will then benefit from the presence of the matplotlibrc file, and you will not need to make any code changes to run in virtualized environments.

Subsequently, the developer and user experience for these Docker images will be greatly improved. The administrators who are responsible for the creation of new images with these as the basis will have less work to do and the users will have one less error to face when getting started.

Back on your workstation, having made the necessary changes to your custom `Dockerfile`, you can now create an updated version of your Docker image with the help of the following code:

```
$ docker build -t yourname/eros ./docker/eros/
```

Next, you'll need to publish the image to Docker Hub so that you can pull it down on your EC2 instance:

```
$ docker push yourname/eros
```

On your EC2 instance, get the latest version of `yourname/eros` that you just published:

```
ubuntu@ip-address:~$ sudo docker pull yourname/eros
```

With the last step, everything is now in place and your jobs are ready to be executed.

Execution

At this point, you can run a Docker container from your latest Docker image to generate a file for the RGB satellite image data by using the following code:

```
ubuntu@ip-address:~$ export S3_BUCKET=scoresbysund
ubuntu@ip-address:~$ export SCENE=LC82260102014232LGN00
ubuntu@ip-address:~$ export IMGTYPE=rgb
ubuntu@ip-address:~$ sudo docker run \
  -e "S3_IMAGE_TITLE=RGB Image: Scene $SCENE" \
  -e "S3_IMAGE_TYPE=$IMGTYPE" \
  -e "S3_IMAGE_FILENAME=$SCENE-$IMGTYPE-`date "+%Y%m%d%H%M%S"`.png" \
  -e "S3_BUCKET_NAME=$BUCKET" \
  -e "S3_PATH=https://s3-us-west-2.amazonaws.com/$S3_BUCKET" \
  -e "EROS_SCENE_ID=$SCENE" \
  -e "AWS_ACCESS_KEY_ID=`cat /etc/aws/access`" \
  -e "AWS_SECRET_ACCESS_KEY=`cat /etc/aws/secret`" \
  -t yourname/eros
```

As the task runs, you will see the following output:

```
Generating scene image ...
Saving image to S3 ...
0.0/100
```

```
27.499622350156933/100
54.99924470031387/100
82.4988670504708/100
100.0/100
```

Remember that on a relatively modern iMac, this job took about 7 to 8 minutes. Executing it on EC2 just now only took about 15 seconds.

For the false-color short-wave and the IR image, you can run a similar command, as follows:

```
ubuntu@ip-address:~$ export IMGTYPE=swir2nirg
ubuntu@ip-address:~$ sudo docker run \
  -e "S3_IMAGE_TITLE=False-Color Image: Scene $SCENE" \
  -e "S3_IMAGE_TYPE=$IMGTYPE" \
  -e "S3_IMAGE_FILENAME=$SCENE-$IMGTYPE-`date "+%Y%m%d%H%M%S"`.png" \
  -e "S3_BUCKET_NAME=$BUCKET" \
  -e "S3_PATH=https://s3-us-west-2.amazonaws.com/$S3_BUCKET" \
  -e "EROS_SCENE_ID=$SCENE" \
  -e "AWS_ACCESS_KEY_ID=`cat /etc/aws/access`" \
  -e "AWS_SECRET_ACCESS_KEY=`cat /etc/aws/secret`" \
  -t yourname/eros
Generating scene image ...
Saving image to S3 ...
0.0/100
26.05542715379233/100
52.11085430758466/100
78.16628146137698/100
100.0/100
```

You can confirm that both of the images have been saved to your bucket by refreshing the S3 screen in your AWS Console.

Though it may seem awkward to parameterize the Docker container with so many environment variables, this allows you to easily change the data that you pass without having to regenerate the Docker image. Your Docker image produces containers that are generally useful for the task at hand—and potentially many other tasks—allowing you to process any scene without any code changes.

Summary

We covered some interesting ground in this chapter. We explored the fascinating world of satellite imagery, showing with just a few lines of code how to work with it. Hitting the hardware limitations of a modest workstation, we uncovered a straightforward use case to put matplotlib in the Cloud. Docker provides a fresh outlook towards the world of configuration management and does so in a way that has a very low barrier to entry. It uses the existing Linux skills that many developers may have already gained by the time they reach the early stages of an advanced level. Working with Docker in EC2 and S3 proved to be painless, as it offers an array of potential ways to extend the initial workflow. Furthermore, the use of Docker provides for a no-lock-in scenario with the Cloud vendors. As soon as you identify a provider with better data transfer rates, features on instances, or price, you'll be able to make the switch due to the ubiquity of Docker in Cloud environments. In the next chapter, we will continue with our foray into the Cloud environments and distributed workloads, where we will explore some topics in the arena of large datasets.

8
matplotlib and Big Data

In the spirit of adapting the established tools to new challenges, the last chapter saw us finding ways to work around the limitations of matplotlib on a single workstation. In this chapter, we will explore ways around some of the other limitations that matplotlib users may run up against when working on problems with very large datasets. Note that this investigation will often cause us to bump up against the topic of clustering. We will be setting these explorations aside for now though. Lest you feel that a critical aspect of the problem domain is being ignored, take heart—this will be the primary focus of the next chapter.

The material in the final two chapters of this book attempt to provide the reader with enough additional context to easily understand the origins of these technologies and their uses and thus apply them to their own computation, analysis, and ultimately their plotting needs.

There are two major areas of the problem domain that we will cover in this chapter:

- Preparing large data for use by matplotlib
- Visualizing the prepared data

These are the two distinct areas, each with their own engineering problems that need to be solved and with which matplotlib needs to be able to function. We will take a look at several aspects of each area.

We will cover the following topics in this chapter:

- Big data and its use in matplotlib
- Working with large datasets
    - Data on local filesystems
    - Distributed data

- Visualizing large datasets
  - ○ Determining the limits of matplotlib
  - ○ Working around the limits

To follow along with this chapter's code, clone the notebook's repository, start up IPython, and execute the following command lines:

```
$ git clone https://github.com/masteringmatplotlib/big-data.git
$ cd big-data
$ make
```

Big data

The term "big data" is semantically ambiguous due to the varying contexts to which it is applied and the motivations of the users applying it. The first question that may have occurred to you on seeing this chapter's title is "how is this applicable to matplotlib or even plotting in general?" Before we answer this question though, let's establish a working definition of *big data*.

The Wikipedia article on big data opens with the following informal definition:

> *"Big data is a broad term for data sets so large or complex that traditional data processing applications are inadequate."*

This description is honest, as it admits that the definition is imprecise. It also implies that the definition may change given the differing contexts. The words *large* and *complex* are relative, and the term *traditional data processing* is not going to mean the same thing in different segments of the industry. In fact, different departments in a single organization may have widely varying data processing "traditions".

The canonical example of big data is related to its origins in web search. Google is generally credited with starting the big data movement with the publication of the paper *MapReduce: Simplified Data Processing on Large Clusters*, by Jeffrey Dean and Sanjay Ghemawat. The paper describes the means by which Google was able to quickly search an enormous volume of textual data (crawled web pages and log files, for example) amounting, in 2004, to around 20 terabytes of data. In the decade that followed, more and more companies, institutions, and even individuals were faced with the need to quickly process datasets varying in sizes, from hundreds of gigabytes to multiples of exabytes.

Every scenario encompassed in this spectrum can be viewed as a big data-related problem. To a small business that used to manage hundreds of megabytes and is now facing several orders of magnitude in data sources for analysis, 250 gigabytes is considered big data. For intelligence agencies storing information from untold data sources, even a few terabytes is a small amount of data. For them, hundreds of petabytes is considered big data.

For each organization though, the general problem remains the same—what worked before on smaller datasets is no longer feasible. New methodologies, novel approaches towards the usage of hardware, communication protocols, data distribution, search, analysis, and visualization, among many others, are required.

Finally, no matter which methodologies are used to support a big data project, one of the last steps in most of them is the presentation of the analyzed data to human eyes. This can be anything from a decision maker to an end user, but the need is the same—a visual representation of the data collected, searched, and analyzed. This is where tools such as matplotlib come into play.

Working with large data sources

Most of the data that users feed into matplotlib when generating plots is from NumPy. NumPy is one of the fastest ways of processing numerical and array-based data in Python (if not *the* fastest), so this makes sense. However by default, NumPy works on in-memory database. If the dataset that you want to plot is larger than the total RAM available on your system, performance is going to plummet.

In the following section, we're going to take a look at an example that illustrates this limitation. But first, let's get our notebook set up, as follows:

```
In [1]: import matplotlib
        matplotlib.use('nbagg')
        %matplotlib inline
```

Here are the modules that we are going to use:

```
In [2]: import glob, io, math, os
        import psutil
        import numpy as np
        import pandas as pd
        import tables as tb
        from scipy import interpolate
        from scipy.stats import burr, norm
```

```
import matplotlib as mpl
import matplotlib.pyplot as plt
from IPython.display import Image
```

We'll use the custom style sheet that we created earlier, as follows:

```
In [3]: plt.style.use("../styles/superheroine-2.mplstyle")
```

An example problem

To keep things manageable for an in-memory example, we're going to limit our generated dataset to 100 million points by using one of SciPy's many statistical distributions, as follows:

```
In [4]: (c, d) = (10.8, 4.2)
        (mean, var, skew, kurt) = burr.stats(c, d, moments='mvsk')
```

The **Burr distribution**, also known as the **Singh–Maddala distribution**, is commonly used to model household income. Next, we'll use the burr object's method to generate a random population with our desired count, as follows:

```
In [5]: r = burr.rvs(c, d, size=100000000)
```

Creating 100 million data points in the last call took about 10 seconds on a moderately recent workstation, with the RAM usage peaking at about 2.25 GB (before the garbage collection kicked in).

Let's make sure that it's the size we expect, as follows:

```
In [6]: len(r)
Out[6]: 100000000
```

If we save this to a file, it weighs in at about three-fourths of a gigabyte:

```
In [7]: r.tofile("../data/points.bin")
In [8]: ls -alh ../data/points.bin
        -rw-r--r-- 1 oubiwann staff 763M Mar 20 11:35 points.bin
```

This actually does fit in the memory on a machine with a RAM of 8 GB, but generating much larger files tends to be problematic. We can reuse it multiple times though, to reach a size that is larger than what can fit in the system RAM.

Before we do this, let's take a look at what we've got by generating a smooth curve for the probability distribution, as follows:

```
In [9]:  x = np.linspace(burr.ppf(0.0001, c, d),
```

```
                    burr.ppf(0.9999, c, d), 100)
         y = burr.pdf(x, c, d)
In [10]: (figure, axes) = plt.subplots(figsize=(20, 10))
         axes.plot(x, y, linewidth=5, alpha=0.7)
         axes.hist(r, bins=100, normed=True)
         plt.show()
```

The following plot is the result of the preceding code:

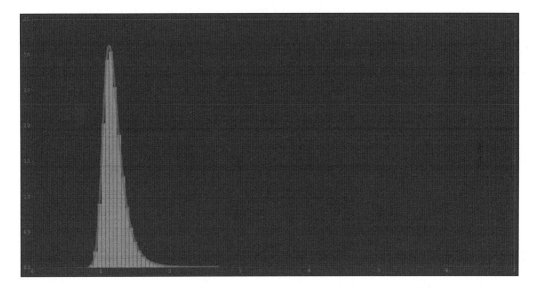

Our plot of the Burr probability distribution function, along with the 100-bin histogram with a sample size of 100 million points, took about 7 seconds to render. This is due to the fact that NumPy handles most of the work, and we only displayed a limited number of visual elements. What would happen if we *did* try to plot all the 100 million points? This can be checked by the following code:

```
In [11]: (figure, axes) = plt.subplots()
         axes.plot(r)
         plt.show()
formatters.py:239: FormatterWarning:
Exception in image/png formatter: Allocated too many blocks
```

After about 30 seconds of crunching, the preceding error was thrown—the Agg backend (a shared library) simply couldn't handle the number of artists required to render all the points. We'll examine this sort of situation towards the end of the chapter and discuss ways to work around it.

But for now, this case clarifies the point that we stated a while back—our first plot rendered relatively quickly because we were selective about the data we chose to present, given the large number of points with which we are working.

However, let's say we have data from the files that are too large to fit into the memory. What do we do about this? Possible ways to address this include the following:

- Moving the data out of the memory and into the filesystem
- Moving the data off the filesystem and into the databases

We will explore examples of these in the following section.

Big data on the filesystem

The first of the two proposed solutions for large datasets involves not burdening the system memory with data, but rather leaving it on the filesystem. There are several ways to accomplish this, but the following two methods in particular are the most common in the world of NumPy and matplotlib:

- **NumPy's memmap function**: This function creates memory-mapped files that are useful if you wish to access small segments of large files on the disk without having to read the whole file into the memory.
- **PyTables**: This is a package that is used to manage hierarchical datasets. It is built on the top of the HDF5 and NumPy libraries and is designed to efficiently and easily cope with extremely large amounts of data.

We will examine each in turn.

NumPy's memmap function

Let's restart the IPython kernel by going to the IPython menu at the top of notebook page, selecting **Kernel**, and then clicking on **Restart**. When the dialog box pops up, click on **Restart**. Then, re-execute the first few lines of the notebook by importing the required libraries and getting our style sheet set up.

Once the kernel is restarted, take a look at the RAM utilization on your system for a fresh Python process for the notebook:

```
In [4]: Image("memory-before.png")
Out[4]:
```

The following screenshot shows the RAM utilization for a fresh Python process:

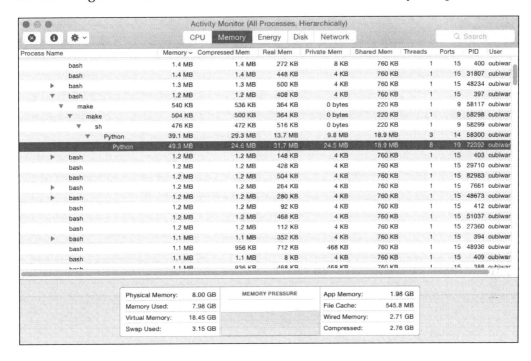

Now, let's load the array data that we previously saved to disk and recheck the memory utilization, as follows:

```
In [5]: data = np.fromfile("../data/points.bin")
        data_shape = data.shape
        data_len = len(data)
        data_len
Out[5]: 100000000
In [6]: Image("memory-after.png")
Out[6]:
```

The following screenshot shows the memory utilization after loading the array data:

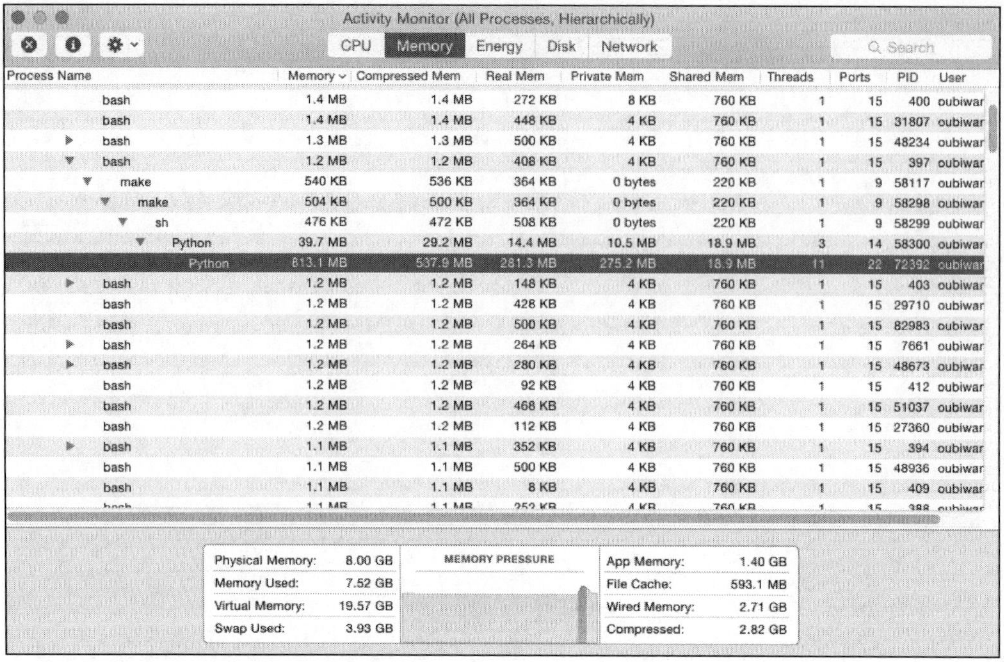

This took about five seconds to load, with the memory consumption equivalent to the file size of the data. This means that if we wanted to build some sample data that was too large to fit in the memory, we'd need about 11 of those files concatenated, as follows:

```
In [7]: 8 * 1024
Out[7]: 8192
In [8]: filesize = 763
        8192 / filesize
Out[8]: 10.73656618610747
```

However, this is only if the entire memory was available. Let's see how much memory is available right now, as follows:

```
In  [9]: del data
In [10]: psutil.virtual_memory().available / 1024**2
Out[10]: 2449.1796875
```

That's 2.5 GB. So, to overrun our RAM, we'll just need a fraction of the total. This is done in the following way:

```
In [11]: 2449 / filesize
Out[11]: 3.2096985583224114
```

The preceding output means that we only need four of our original files to create a file that won't fit in memory. However, in the following section, we will still use 11 files to ensure that data, if loaded into the memory, will be much larger than the memory.

How do we create this large file for demonstration purposes (knowing that in a real-life situation, the data would already be created and potentially quite large)? We can try to use `numpy.tile` to create a file of the desired size (larger than memory), but this can make our system unusable for a significant period of time. Instead, let's use `numpy.memmap`, which will treat a file on the disk as an array, thus letting us work with data that is too large to fit into the memory.

Let's load the data file again, but this time as a memory-mapped array, as follows:

```
In [12]: data = np.memmap(
             "../data/points.bin", mode="r", shape=data_shape)
```

The loading of the array to a `memmap` object was very quick (compared to the process of bringing the contents of the file into the memory), taking less than a second to complete. Now, let's create a new file to write the data to. This file must be larger in size as compared to our total system memory (if held on in-memory database, it will be smaller on the disk):

```
In [13]: big_data_shape = (data_len * 11,)
         big_data = np.memmap(
             "../data/many-points.bin", dtype="uint8",
             mode="w+", shape=big_data_shape)
```

The preceding code creates a 1 GB file, which is mapped to an array that has the shape we requested and just contains zeros:

```
In [14]: ls -alh ../data/many-points.bin
         -rw-r--r-- 1 oubiwann staff 1.0G Apr 2 11:35 many-points.bin
In [15]: big_data.shape
Out[15]: (1100000000,)
In [16]: big_data
Out[16]: memmap([0, 0, 0, ..., 0, 0, 0], dtype=uint8)
```

Now, let's fill the empty data structure with copies of the data we saved to the 763 MB file, as follows:

```
In [17]: for x in range(11):
             start = x * data_len
             end = (x * data_len) + data_len
             big_data[start:end] = data
         big_data
Out[17]: memmap([ 90, 71, 15, ..., 33, 244, 63], dtype=uint8)
```

If you check your system memory before and after, you will only see minimal changes, which confirms that we are not creating an 8 GB data structure on in-memory. Furthermore, checking your system only takes a few seconds.

Now, we can do some sanity checks on the resulting data and ensure that we have what we were trying to get, as follows:

```
In [18]: big_data_len = len(big_data)
         big_data_len
Out[18]: 1100000000
In [19]: data[100000000 - 1]
Out[19]: 63
In [20]: big_data[100000000 - 1]
Out[20]: 63
```

Attempting to get the next index from our original dataset will throw an error (as shown in the following code), since it didn't have that index:

```
In [21]: data[100000000]
-----------------------------------------------------------
IndexError                      Traceback (most recent call last)
...
IndexError: index 100000000 is out of bounds ...
```

But our new data does have an index, as shown in the following code:

```
In [22]: big_data[100000000
Out[22]: 90
```

And then some:

```
In [23]: big_data[1100000000 - 1]
Out[23]: 63
```

We can also plot data from a memmaped array without having a significant lag time. However, note that in the following code, we will create a histogram from 1.1 million points of data, so the plotting won't be instantaneous:

```
In [24]: (figure, axes) = plt.subplots(figsize=(20, 10))
         axes.hist(big_data, bins=100)
         plt.show()
```

The following plot is the result of the preceding code:

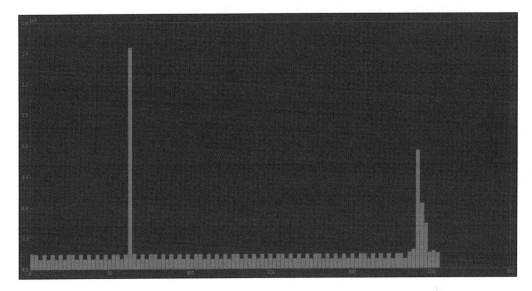

The plotting took about 40 seconds to generate.

The odd shape of the histogram is due to the fact that, with our data file-hacking, we have radically changed the nature of our data since we've increased the sample size linearly without regard for the distribution. The purpose of this demonstration wasn't to preserve a sample distribution, but rather to show how one can work with large datasets. What we have seen is not too shabby. Thanks to NumPy, matplotlib can work with data that is too large for memory, even if it is a bit slow iterating over hundreds of millions of data points from the disk.

Can matplotlib do better?

HDF5 and PyTables

A commonly used file format in the scientific computing community is **Hierarchical Data Format (HDF)**. HDF is a set of file formats (namely HDF4 and HDF5) that were originally developed at the **National Center for Supercomputing Applications (NCSA)**, a unit of the University of Illinois at Urbana-Champaign, to store and organize large amounts of numerical data.

> The NCSA is a great source of technical innovation in the computing industry—a Telnet client, the first graphical web browser, a web server that evolved into the Apache HTTP server, and HDF, which is of particular interest to us, were all developed here. It is a little known fact that NCSA's web browser code was the ancestor to both the Netscape web browser as well as a prototype of Internet Explorer that was provided to Microsoft by a third party.

HDF is supported by Python, R, Julia, Java, Octave, IDL, and MATLAB, to name a few. HDF5 offers significant improvements and useful simplifications over HDF4. It uses **B-trees** to index table objects and, as such, works well for write-once/read-many time series data. Common use cases span fields such as meteorological studies, biosciences, finance, and aviation. The HDF5 files of multiterabyte sizes are common in these applications. Its typically constructed from the analyses of multiple HDF5 source files, thus providing a single (and often extensive) source of grouped data for a particular application.

The **PyTables** library is built on the top of the Python HDF5 library and NumPy. As such, it not only provides access to one of the most widely used large data file formats in the scientific computing community, but also links data extracted from these files with the data types and objects provided by the fast Python numerical processing library.

PyTables is also used in other projects. Pandas wraps PyTables, thus extending its convenient in-memory data structures, functions, and objects to large on-disk files. To use HDF data with Pandas, you'll want to create `pandas.HDFStore`, read from the HDF data sources with `pandas.read_hdf`, or write to one with `pandas.to_hdf`. Files that are too large to fit in the memory may be read and written by utilizing chunking techniques. Pandas does support the disk-based `DataFrame` operations, but these are not very efficient due to the required assembly on columns of data upon reading back into the memory.

One project to keep an eye on under the **PyData** umbrella of projects is *Blaze*. It's an open wrapper and a utility framework that can be used when you wish to work with large datasets and generalize actions such as the creation, access, updates, and migration. Blaze supports not only HDF, but also SQL, CSV, and JSON. The API usage between Pandas and Blaze is very similar, and it offers a nice tool for developers who need to support multiple backends.

In the following example, we will use PyTables directly to create an HDF5 file that is too large to fit in the memory (for an 8 GB RAM machine). We will follow the following steps:

- Create a series of CSV source data files that take up approximately 14 GB of disk space
- Create an empty HDF5 file
- Create a table in the HDF5 file and provide the schema metadata and compression options
- Load the CSV source data into the HDF5 table
- Query the new data source once the data has been migrated

Remember the temperature precipitation data for St. Francis, in Kansas, USA, from a previous notebook? We are going to generate random data with similar columns for the purposes of the HDF5 example. This data will be generated from a normal distribution, which will be used in the guise of the temperature and precipitation data for hundreds of thousands of fictitious towns across the globe for the last century, as follows:

```
In [25]: head = "country,town,year,month,precip,temp\n"
         row = "{},{},{},{},{},{}\n"
         filename = "../data/{}.csv"
         town_count = 1000
         (start_year, end_year) = (1894, 2014)
         (start_month, end_month) = (1, 13)
         sample_size = (1 + 2
                         * town_count * (end_year - start_year)
                         * (end_month - start_month))
         countries = range(200)
         towns = range(town_count)
         years = range(start_year, end_year)
         months = range(start_month, end_month)
         for country in countries:
             with open(filename.format(country), "w") as csvfile:
                 csvfile.write(head)
                 csvdata = ""
```

```
weather_data = norm.rvs(size=sample_size)
weather_index = 0
for town in towns:
    for year in years:
        for month in months:
            csvdata += row.format(
                country, town, year, month,
                weather_data[weather_index],
                weather_data[weather_index + 1])
            weather_index += 2
csvfile.write(csvdata)
```

Note that we generated a sample data population that was twice as large as the expected size in order to pull both the simulated temperature and precipitation data at the same time (from the same set). This will take about 30 minutes to run. When complete, you will see the following files:

```
In [26]: ls -rtm ../data/*.csv
         ../data/0.csv, ../data/1.csv, ../data/2.csv,
         ../data/3.csv, ../data/4.csv, ../data/5.csv,
         ...
         ../data/194.csv, ../data/195.csv, ../data/196.csv,
         ../data/197.csv, ../data/198.csv, ../data/199.csv
```

A quick look at just one of the files reveals the size of each, as follows:

```
In [27]: ls -lh ../data/0.csv
         -rw-r--r-- 1 oubiwann staff 72M Mar 21 19:02 ../data/0.csv
```

With each file that is 72 MB in size, we have data that takes up 14 GB of disk space, which exceeds the size of the RAM of the system in question.

Furthermore, running queries against so much data in the .csv files isn't going to be very efficient. It's going to take a long time. So what are our options? Well, to read this data, HDF5 is a very good fit. In fact, it is designed for jobs like this. We will use PyTables to convert the .csv files to a single HDF5. We'll start by creating an empty table file, as follows:

```
In [28]: tb_name = "../data/weather.h5t"
         h5 = tb.open_file(tb_name, "w")
         h5
```

```
Out[28]: File(filename=../data/weather.h5t, title='', mode='w',
            root_uep='/', filters=Filters(
                complevel=0, shuffle=False, fletcher32=False,
                least_significant_digit=None))
        / (RootGroup) ''
```

Next, we'll provide some assistance to PyTables by indicating the data types of each column in our table, as follows:

```
In [29]: data_types = np.dtype(
            [("country", "<i8"),
            ("town", "<i8"),
            ("year", "<i8"),
            ("month", "<i8"),
            ("precip", "<f8"),
            ("temp", "<f8")])
```

Also, let's define a compression filter that can be used by PyTables when saving our data, as follows:

```
In [30]: filters = tb.Filters(complevel=5, complib='blosc')
```

Now, we can create a table inside our new HDF5 file, as follows:

```
In [31]: tab = h5.create_table(
            "/", "weather",
            description=data_types,
            filters=filters)
```

With that done, let's load each CSV file, read it in chunks so that we don't overload the memory, and then append it to our new HDF5 table, as follows:

```
In [32]: for filename in glob.glob("../data/*.csv"):
            it = pd.read_csv(filename, iterator=True, chunksize=10000)
            for chunk in it:
                tab.append(chunk.to_records(index=False))
            tab.flush()
```

Depending on your machine, the entire process of loading the CSV file, reading it in chunks, and appending to a new HDF5 table can take anywhere from 5 to 10 minutes.

However, what started out as a collection of the `.csv` files that weigh in at 14 GB is now a single compressed 4.8 GB HDF5 file, as shown in the following code:

```
In [33]: h5.get_filesize()
Out[33]: 4758762819
```

Here's the metadata for the PyTables-wrapped HDF5 table after the data insertion:

```
In [34]: tab
Out[34]: /weather (Table(288000000,), shuffle, blosc(5)) ''
  description := {
  "country": Int64Col(shape=(), dflt=0, pos=0),
  "town": Int64Col(shape=(), dflt=0, pos=1),
  "year": Int64Col(shape=(), dflt=0, pos=2),
  "month": Int64Col(shape=(), dflt=0, pos=3),
  "precip": Float64Col(shape=(), dflt=0.0, pos=4),
  "temp": Float64Col(shape=(), dflt=0.0, pos=5)}
  byteorder := 'little'
  chunkshape := (1365,)
```

Now that we've created our file, let's use it. Let's excerpt a few lines with an array slice, as follows:

```
In [35]: tab[100000:100010]
Out[35]: array([(0, 69, 1947, 5, -0.2328834718674, 0.06810312195695),
          (0, 69, 1947, 6, 0.4724989007889, 1.9529216219569),
          (0, 69, 1947, 7, -1.0757216683235, 1.0415374480545),
          (0, 69, 1947, 8, -1.3700249968748, 3.0971874991576),
          (0, 69, 1947, 9, 0.27279758311253, 0.8263207523831),
          (0, 69, 1947, 10, -0.0475253104621, 1.4530808932953),
          (0, 69, 1947, 11, -0.7555493935762, -1.2665440609117),
          (0, 69, 1947, 12, 1.540049376928, 1.2338186532516),
          (0, 69, 1948, 1, 0.829743501445, -0.1562732708511),
          (0, 69, 1948, 2, 0.06924900463163, 1.187193711598)],
        dtype=[('country', '<i8'), ('town', '<i8'),
            ('year', '<i8'), ('month', '<i8'),
            ('precip', '<f8'), ('temp', '<f8')])
In [36]: tab[100000:100010]["precip"]
Out[36]: array([-0.23288347,  0.4724989 , -1.07572167,
```

```
       -1.370025   ,   0.27279758,  -0.04752531,
       -0.75554939,   1.54004938,   0.8297435 ,
       0.069249   ])
```

When we're done with the file, we do the same thing that we would do with any other file-like object:

```
In [37]: h5.close()
```

If we want to work with it again, simply load it, as follows:

```
In [38]: h5 = tb.open_file(tb_name, "r")
         tab = h5.root.weather
```

Let's try plotting the data from our HDF5 file:

```
In [39]: (figure, axes) = plt.subplots(figsize=(20, 10))
         axes.hist(tab[:1000000]["temp"], bins=100)
         plt.show()
```

Here's a plot for the first million data points:

This histogram was rendered quickly, with a much better response time than what we've seen before. Hence, the process of accessing the HDF5 data is very fast. The next question might be "What about executing calculations against this data?" Unfortunately, running the following will consume an enormous amount of RAM:

```
tab[:]["temp"].mean()
```

We've just asked for *all* of the data—all of its 288 million rows. We are going to end up loading everything into the RAM, grinding the average workstation to a halt. Ideally though, when you iterate through the source data and create the HDF5 file, you also crunch the numbers that you will need, adding supplemental columns or groups to the HDF5 file that can be used later by you and your peers.

If we have data that we will mostly be selecting (extracting portions) and which has already been crunched and grouped as needed, HDF5 is a very good fit. This is why one of the most common use cases that you see for HDF5 is the sharing and distribution of the processed data.

However, if we have data that we need to process repeatedly, then we will either need to use another method besides the one that will cause all the data to be loaded into the memory, or find a better match for our data processing needs.

In the following section, we will look at the last point in more detail. However before that, let's give HDF5 another chance.

We saw in the previous section that the selection of data is very fast in HDF5. What about calculating the mean for a small section of data? If we've got a total of 288 million rows, let's select a divisor of the number that gives us several hundred thousand rows at a time—2,81,250 rows, to be more precise. Let's get the mean for the first slice, as follows:

```
In [40]: tab[0:281250]["temp"].mean()

Out[40]: 0.0030696632864265312
```

This took about 1 second to calculate. What about iterating through the records in a similar fashion? Let's break up the 288 million records into chunks of the same size; this will result in 1024 chunks. We'll start by getting the ranges needed for an increment of 281,250 and then, we'll examine the first and the last row as a sanity check, as follows:

```
In [41]: limit = 281250
         ranges = [(x * limit, x * limit + limit)
             for x in range(2 ** 10)]
         (ranges[0], ranges[-1])
Out[41]: ((0, 281250), (287718750, 288000000))
```

Now, we can use these ranges to generate the mean for each chunk of 281,250 rows of temperature data and print the total number of means that we generated to make sure that we're getting our counts right, as follows:

```
In [42]: means = [tab[x * limit:x * limit + limit]["temp"].mean()
           for x in range(2 ** 10)]
         len(means)
Out[42]: 1024
```

Depending on your machine, that should take between 30 and 60 seconds. With this work done, it's now easy to calculate the mean for all of the 288 million points of temperature data:

```
In [43]: sum(means) / len(means)
Out[43]: -5.3051780413782918e-05
```

Through HDF5's efficient file format and implementation, combined with the splitting of our operations into tasks that would not copy the HDF5 data into memory, we were able to perform calculations across a significant fraction of a billion records in less than a minute. HDF5 even supports parallelization. So, this can be improved upon with a little more time and effort.

However, there are many cases where HDF5 is not a practical choice. You may have some free-form data, and preprocessing it will be too expensive. Alternatively, the datasets may be actually too large to fit on a single machine. This is when you may consider using matplotlib with distributed data.

Distributed data

We've looked at the following two ways to handle data that is too large for the memory:

- NumPy's memmap function
- The general HDF5 format wrapped by PyTables

However, there is another situation that may come into play for projects that need to use matplotlib to visualize all or parts of large data sets — data that is too large to fit on a *hard drive*. This can be anything from large datasets, such as the ones created by super-colliders and radio telescopes, to the high-volume streaming data used in systems analysis (and social media) and financial markets data. All of these are either too large to fit on a machine, or too ephemeral to store and need to be processed in real time.

The latter of these is the realm of projects such as **Apache Spark** (developed at the UC Berkeley AMPLab), **Apache Storm** (originally developed at BackType and then acquired by Twitter), **Apache Kafka** (created at LinkedIn), and Amazon's **Kinesis**. We will not discuss these in this notebook. Instead, we will focus on the former — processing large datasets in a distributed environment; in particular, we will concentrate on MapReduce. Understanding how to use matplotlib and NumPy with a MapReduce framework will provide the foundation necessary for the reader to extend this to the scenarios that involve streaming data.

Even though we have chosen to demonstrate a solution with MapReduce, there are many other options to address problems like these—distributed RDMSes and NoSQL solutions such as Riak, Redis, and Cassandra, to name a few.

MapReduce

So what is MapReduce, and why are we looking at it in the context of running computations against large sets of data? Wikipedia gives the following definition:

> *MapReduce is a programming model for processing and generating large data sets with a parallel, distributed algorithm on a cluster. A MapReduce program is composed of a Map procedure that performs filtering and sorting, and a Reduce procedure that performs a summary operation. The "MapReduce System" orchestrates the processing by marshalling the distributed servers, running the various tasks in parallel, managing all communications and data transfers between the various parts of the system, and providing for redundancy and fault tolerance.*

A little context as to why it is potentially very useful to visualize large datasets with matplotlib will make the definition more clear.

Between 1999 and 2004, Google engineering had created hundreds of proprietary, special-purpose functions, scripts, and programs to process the huge amounts of data that were generated by web crawling, HTTP access logs, and so on. The many kinds of processing tasks that were developed were in large part used to create the page-ranked search results of Google search. At the time, this was a vast improvement over the other search engine results. Though each individual computation was pretty straightforward and nothing about it was new, the manner in which these were combined was unique and provided a vastly improved experience for users.

However, in a span of five years, the computation tasks needed to be split across hundreds, and later thousands, of machines in order to finish in a timely manner. The difficulties of parallelizing code were introduced—not only the decomposition of tasks into parallelizable parts, but also the parallelization of data and handling failures. As a result of these difficulties as well as some related issues, engineers were no longer able to easily add new features to the system

After five years, inspiration struck and Google adopted a new paradigm for distributed, parallelized workloads.

Interestingly enough, the muse behind this new approach to Google's problem came from the second oldest programming language that is still in use—Lisp (Fortan being the oldest). The authors of the Google MapReduce paper were reminded of the fact that many of their processing jobs consisted of a simple action against a dataset. Here's a simple illustration of this pattern using **Lisp Flavored Erlang** (LFE), a modern Lisp:

```
> (set data "some words to examine")
"some words to examine"
> (lists:map #'length/1 (string:tokens data " "))
(4 5 2 7)
```

The preceding code represents a common pattern in functional programming languages where, in this example, the tokenized data is mapped over a length function.

What's more is that Google didn't just stop here. Their engineers were then performing additional operations on the processed data. Here's an example that takes the preceding processed list and creates a new result by "folding" the results into a secondary analytical result:

```
> (lists:foldl #'+/2 0 (4 5 2 7))
18
```

The preceding function is called folding due to the fact that there is a recursive operation in place, with each item in the list being folded into an accumulator after being applied to a function. In this case, the folding function is the function that performs the operation of *addition* (with a parity of 2, thus the +/2). The initial value for the first fold that was provided is 0. Note that if the folding function created items in a list rather than adding two integers for a sum, the initial value would have been a list (empty or otherwise).

The map and fold operations can be combined in the fashion that is typical of higher-order functions, as follows:

```
> (lists:foldl
    #'+/2
    0
    (lists:map
      #'length/1
      (string:tokens data " ")))
18
```

As you may have guessed by now (or known already), there is another term by which folding is known. It is named not for the process employed, but by the nature of the results it creates — *reduce*. In this case, a list of integers is reduced to a single value by the means of the addition function that we provided.

To summarize, given an initial dataset, we executed a `length` function (with a parity of one) against every element of the data that has been split on the "space" character. The results were integers representing the length of each word in the dataset. Then, we folded the list of length values with the + function, one element at a time, into an accumulator with an initial value of 0. The end result represented the sum of all the word lengths. If we wanted a running average instead of a running sum, we would have supplied a different function. It still would take two arguments and add them. It would just divide that result by two, as follows:

```
> (defun ave (number accum)
     (/ (+ number accum) 2))
ave
> (lists:foldl
     #'ave/2
     0
     (lists:map
       #'length/1
       (string:tokens data " ")))
4.875
```

The average word length in our data is `4.875` ASCII characters.

The last example makes the latent power clear in solutions like these — for completely new results, we only need to change one function.

Various Lisps and functional programming languages have the `fold` or `reduce` functionality, but this is not just the domain of functional programming. Python 3 has a library dedicated to the functional programming idioms — `functools`. Here's how the preceding examples will be implemented in Python:

```
>>> data = "some words to examine"
>>> [x for x in map(len, data.split(" ")]
[4, 5, 2, 7]
>>> functools.reduce(operator.add, [4, 5, 2, 7], 0)
18
```

Similarly, these may be composed in Python, as follows:

```
>>> functools.reduce(operator.add,
...                     map(len, data.split(" ")),
...                     0)
18
```

To calculate the running average, we will use the following code:

```
>>> def ave(number, accum):
...         return (number + accum) / 2
...
>>> functools.reduce(ave,
...                     map(len, data.split(" ")),
...                     0)
4.875
```

The really important part to realize here—given the context of Google's needs in 2004 and the later fluorescence of MapReduce via the Hadoop project—is that each map call of `len` is independent of all the others. Therefore, these can be called on the same machine in the same process or in different processes, on different cores, or on another machine altogether (given the appropriate framework, of course). In a similar fashion, the data provided to the `reduce` function can be from any number of local or remote sources. In fact, the `reduce` step can be split across multiple computational resources. It will just need a final reduce step to aggregate the reduce results.

This insight led to an innovation in the development process at Google in support of the tasks that had steadily grown in complexity and had been encumbered by reduced maintainability. They created such infrastructure so that engineers only needed to create their own mapper and reducer functions; these could then be run against the desired data sources on the appropriate MapReduce clusters. This approach to the problem space allowed for the automated parallelization of tasks as well as the distribution of workload across a number of servers running in Google's large computation clusters in their data centers.

What started by applying old techniques from an old language resulted in a whole new industry dominated by the Java MapReduce implementation, Hadoop, but utilized extensively by Python programmers who use the Hadoop streaming. In the next section, we will take a look at Hadoop and others in the open source community of big data frameworks. Let's first close this section with a return to the practical world—what is MapReduce good for, other than for the counting of letters and words?

The main benefit that MapReduce offers is the ability to split a specific class of data processing problems across a potentially large number of machines without the need for specialized hardware. Once a MapReduce framework is in place, developers only need to focus on creating new tasks and need not worry, for the most part, about how all the pieces of infrastructure fit together or whether those pieces need to be adjusted for a different job. A caveat here is that authors of mappers and reducers do need to be aware of the tradeoffs between the computation and communication costs in their distributed environment when running the particular tasks that they have designed. We will examine this topic in more detail in the next chapter when we tackle parallelization and clustering.

MapReduce is useful in a wide range of applications, which includes the following:

- Distributed pattern-based searching
- Distributed sorting
- Web link-graph reversal
- **Singular Value Decomposition (SVD)**
- Web access log statistics
- Inverted index construction
- Document clustering
- Machine learning
- Statistical machine translation

Moreover, the MapReduce model has been adapted to several computing environments, which include the following:

- Multi-core systems
- Desktop grids
- Volunteer computing environments
- Dynamic cloud environments
- Mobile environments

As great an impact as MapReduce has had on the industry, nothing is permanent and evolution continues to push products and services to new uses and improved user experiences. In 2014, Google announced that it had stopped relying on MapReduce for its petabyte-scale operations. Since then, it moved on to technologies such as Percolator, Flume, and MillWheel, which offer streaming operations and updates instead of batch processing. This allowed them to integrate live search results without rebuilding the complete search index.

Furthermore, these technologies are not limited to the concept of map and reduce workflows. Rather, they are open to the more general concept of data pipeline workflows.

Despite this news, MapReduce certainly isn't dead; the frameworks that support it aren't going away. We have been seeing an evolution in the industry since Google popularized the concept of distributed workloads across commodity hardware with MapReduce, and both proprietary and open source solutions are offering their users the fruits of these innovations, such as the previously mentioned Apache Spark project. We will likely see MapReduce platforms such as Hadoop offer more generalized workflows, with MapReduce being just one of many workflows available to the users.

Open source options

We've mentioned Hadoop several times now, and most readers who may have just a passing familiarity with big data must have heard of Hadoop. A member project of the Apache Software Foundation, Hadoop is an open source distributed storage and processing framework designed to work with very large datasets on commodity hardware computing clusters. The distributed storage part of the project is called HDFS and the processing part is named MapReduce. When a user uploads data to the Hadoop filesystem, the files are split into pieces and then distributed across the cluster nodes. When a user creates some code to run on Hadoop MapReduce, the custom mappers and reducers—similar in concept to what we saw in the previous section—are copied to the MapReduce nodes in the cluster, which are then executed against the data stored at each node.

Hadoop's predecessor was created at the Internet Archive in 2002 in an attempt to build a better web page crawler and indexer. When the papers on the Google File System and Google's MapReduce were published in 2003 and 2004 respectively, the creators of Hadoop re-envisioned their project and created a framework upon which it could run more efficiently. This led to the creation of Hadoop. Yahoo! invested heavily in the project a few years later and open sourced it and at the same time provided its researchers an access to a testing cluster. The last project sowed the seed for Hadoop's very strong role in the field of machine learning.

Though Hadoop is the primary driver for the big data market—projected to generate 23 billion USD by 2016—it is not the only big data framework available in the open source community. A notable, if quiet, contender is the **Disco** project.

In 2008, the Nokia Research Center needed a tool that would allow them to process enormous amounts of data in real time. They wanted their researchers—many of them proficient in Python—to be able to easily and quickly create MapReduce jobs against their large datasets.

They also needed their system to be fault-tolerant and scalable. They built the server on top of the Erlang distributed programming language and created a protocol and a Python client that could talk to it, thus allowing their users to continue using the language they knew so well.

Since then, Disco has continued to evolve. It provides a generalized workflow on top of its distributed file system—the Disco pipelines. The pipeline workflow enables data scientists to create distributed processing tasks, which go beyond the original vision of MapReduce.

The functionality of MapReduce is no longer available only in the domain of the MapReduce frameworks. The rise of NoSQL databases, which subsequently extended their functionality to distributed data, have started offering MapReduce features in their products. For instance, the Redis clusters make it easy for you to implement the MapReduce functionality. Riak is a distributed NoSQL key-value data store that is based on the Amazon Dynamo paper (not to be confused with the DynamoDB product from Amazon). This data store offers built-in MapReduce capabilities and an API to execute the MapReduce jobs against the nodes in a cluster and is supported by the Python Riak client library. MongoDB is another NoSQL database that offers built-in support for MapReduce.

In our case though, we will focus on the Hadoop implementation of MapReduce, utilizing its support for Python via its streaming protocol. In particular, we will take advantage of a service provider that allows us to quickly and easily set up the Hadoop clusters. We will use Amazon's **Elastic MapReduce (EMR)** service.

An example – working with data on EMR

We are now going to return to the data that we generated to build the large `.csv` files for the HDF5 example. In this case though, we're not going to take advantage of the speed offered by HDF5. Instead, we're going to use the data to simulate the experience of working with extremely large datasets. This will be a simulation for practical reasons. The generation of a large dataset for demonstration purposes is prohibitively expensive with regard to both time as well as the computing resources. That being said, this simulation will offer all the insight that is necessary to adapt a small dataset to much larger ones.

In this section, we will use Hadoop on Amazon EMR service and perform the following tasks:

- Create a cluster
- Push a dataset to the cluster
- Write the mapper and reducer functions in Python

- Test the mapper and reducer functions against small local data
- Add nodes to the EMR cluster to prepare it for our job
- Execute the MapReduce job against the EMR cluster that we created
- Examine the results

In the previous chapter, the `aws` command-line tool was installed. We will use `aws` extensively for the rest of this section. To ensure that you have access to it, you will need to activate the Python virtual environment in your terminal. From the directory for this chapter's notebook `git` repository (see the beginning of this chapter), execute the following code:

```
$ . ../.venv-mmpl/bin/activate
```

The preceding code will provide the visual result of adding (`.venv-mmpl`) to your system prompt. You should now have an access to the `aws` tool. You can confirm your access using the usual technique, as follows:

```
$ which aws
/Users/oubiwann/lab/mastering-matplotlib/.venv-mmpl/bin/aws
```

This section assumes that you have created a key pair on AWS for use in ssh'ing to the EC2 instances and, as we will soon implement, ssh'ing to the EMR master nodes.

We will now ready to create a Hadoop cluster on EMR:

```
$ aws emr create-cluster --name "Weather" --ami-version 3.6.0 \
    --applications Name=Hue Name=Hive Name=Pig Name=HBase \
    --use-default-roles --ec2-attributes KeyName=YourKeyName \
    --instance-type c1.xlarge --instance-count 3
j-63JNVV2BYHC
```

We have enabled the standard Hadoop tools—Hue, Hive, Pig, and HBase. However, we will not use them in the following section. These tools are provided in case you would like to use them in further explorations. We've given our cluster a name, configured it to use the EMR system image version (3.6.0), which supports the 2.4.0 version of Hadoop, and supplied the SSH key name that we will use to log into the master server.

 The key name that you provide should only be a name and should not contain the `.pem` file extension.

The `create-cluster` command returned a single value—the ID for the cluster that we just created. We're going to need this cluster ID. So, let's export it as a shell variable. We're also going to use the full path to the .pem file. Hence, we'll set one for that too, as follows:

```
$ export CLUSTER_ID=j-63JNVV2BYHC
$ export AWS_PEM=/path/to/YourKeyName.pem
```

You can check the state of the cluster with the help of the following code:

```
$ aws emr describe-cluster --cluster-id $CLUSTER_ID |grep STATUS
STATUS   RUNNING
STATUS   RUNNING
STATUS   WAITING
```

The first STATUS output is for the master node. Once it returns the state of the node as RUNNING, we can start copying files to it. The following command will copy just a few files to the cluster:

```
$ for FILE in data/{0,1,2}.csv
  do
    aws emr put \
      --src $FILE \
      --cluster-id $CLUSTER_ID \
      --key-pair-file $AWS_PEM
  done
```

We'll start with just a few files (remember, they're about 73 MB each) to make sure that everything's working, but we'd like to demonstrate a fuller experience of MapReduce. Therefore, we'll copy all the files. If you'd prefer to avoid the incurrence of data costs for the same, you can still run the demo with just a few files. To make sure that we don't run out of space, we'll switch to a remote file system that has plenty of room, as follows:

```
$ for FILE in data/*.csv
  do
    aws emr put \
      --src $FILE \
      --dest /mnt1 \
      --cluster-id $CLUSTER_ID \
      --key-pair-file $AWS_PEM
  done
```

Now that the .csv files have been copied to the Hadoop master node, we can login to the server and copy the data to HDFS, as follows:

```
$ aws emr ssh --cluster-id $CLUSTER_ID --key-pair-file $AWS_PEM
```

Now, you are on the master node where you uploaded your data. Let's copy this data into the Hadoop cluster's filesystem, as follows:

```
[hadoop@ip-10-255-7-47 ~]$ hdfs dfs -mkdir /weather

[hadoop@ip-10-255-7-47 ~]$ hdfs dfs -put /mnt1/*.csv /weather
```

With the two preceding commands, we created an HDFS directory for our data and then started the process by which the 14 gigabytes of .csv files will be pushed out to the worker nodes. This process may take some time, possibly as much as 30 minutes, depending on Amazon.

Once the last command has been executed, we can check whether the files exist on HDFS with the following command:

```
[hadoop@ip-10-255-7-47 ~]$ $ hdfs dfs -ls /weather|head -10

Found 200 items

-rw-r--r--   1 hadoop g    75460820 2015-03-29 18:46 /weather/0.csv
-rw-r--r--   1 hadoop g    75456830 2015-03-29 18:47 /weather/1.csv
-rw-r--r--   1 hadoop g    76896036 2015-03-30 00:16 /weather/10.csv
-rw-r--r--   1 hadoop g    78337868 2015-03-30 00:16 /weather/100.csv
-rw-r--r--   1 hadoop g    78341694 2015-03-30 00:16 /weather/101.csv
-rw-r--r--   1 hadoop g    78341015 2015-03-30 00:16 /weather/102.csv
-rw-r--r--   1 hadoop g    78337662 2015-03-30 00:16 /weather/103.csv
-rw-r--r--   1 hadoop g    78336193 2015-03-30 00:16 /weather/104.csv
-rw-r--r--   1 hadoop g    78336537 2015-03-30 00:16 /weather/105.csv
```

With our data in place, we're now ready to write some Python code for the MapReduce task. Before we do so, let's remind ourselves what the data looks like by using the following code:

```
[hadoop@ip-10-255-7-47 ~]$ head /mnt1/0.csv

country,town,year,month,precip,temp

0,0,1894,1,0.8449506929198441,0.7897647433139449

0,0,1894,2,0.4746140099538822,0.42335801512344756

0,0,1894,3,-0.7088399152900952,0.776535509023379

0,0,1894,4,-1.1731692311337918,0.8168558530942849

0,0,1894,5,1.9332497442673315,-0.6066233105016293
```

```
0,0,1894,6,0.003582147937914687,0.2720125869889254
0,0,1894,7,-0.5612131527063922,2.9628153460517272
0,0,1894,8,0.3733525007455101,-1.3297078910961062
0,0,1894,9,1.9148724762388318,0.6364284082486487
```

The Python code that we will write will consist of two files, one for each part of the MapReduce job. Just like what we saw when reviewing the history of MapReduce, we will need a mapper function and a reducer function.

In our case, we want to perform the same task that we performed dealing with the HDF5 file when we used PyTables — the calculation of the mean value for all the simulated temperatures across all the simulated countries and towns over a period of 120 years. The mapper function will extract the temperature value from each line of every .csv files in HDFS. The reducer function will add these and then calculate the mean.

Keeping in mind that you are still ssh'ed into the Hadoop master node on EMR, save the following code in a file named mapper.py:

```python
#!/usr/bin/env python
import sys

def parse_line(line):
    return line.strip().split(",")

def is_header(line):
    return line.startswith("country")

def main():
    for line in sys.stdin:
        if not is_header(line):
            print(parse_line(line)[-1])

if __name__ == "__main__":
    main()
```

The MapReduce code interacts with the Hadoop nodes via stdin and stdout. The code will receive input via stdin and send results to Hadoop via stdout, one line at a time. We will check to make sure that the line that we receive is not the CSV header, and then, we will use a simple line parser to extract the last value, which is the temperature field.

Save the following code in the file `reducer.py`:

```python
#!/usr/bin/env python
import sys

def to_float(data):
    try:
        return float(data.strip())
    except:
        return None

def main():
    accum = 0
    count = 0
    for line in sys.stdin:
        temp = to_float(line)
        if temp == None:
            continue
        accum += temp
        count += 1
    print(accum / count)

if __name__ == "__main__":
    main()
```

Now, we will make them executable:

```
[hadoop@ip-10-255-7-47 ~]$ chmod 755 *.py
```

Before we execute the preceding code against the cluster, let's perform a quick check on one of the .csv files that we uploaded, as follows:

```
[hadoop@ip-10-255-7-47 ~]$ head /mnt1/0.csv | ./mapper.py
0.7897647433139449
0.42335801512344756
0.776535509023379
0.8168558530942849
-0.6066233105016293
0.2720125869889254
2.9628153460517272
-1.3297078910961062
0.6364284082486487
```

Looks good! Now, let's add the reducer to the mix, as follows:

```
[hadoop@ip-10-255-7-47 ~]$ head 0.csv | ./mapper.py | ./reducer.py
0.526826584472
```

A quick manual check confirms that the generated average is correct for the values parsed by the mapper. This combination of tasks via the command-line pipes highlights the flexible and inherently composable nature of the MapReduce flows.

With our Python code tested and working, we're almost ready to run it on Hadoop. First, we're going to switch to a local terminal session and create some more nodes in our cluster. This is more of an exercise to gain familiarity with the process than anything else since, in our case, the extra nodes won't have too much of an impact:

```
$ aws emr add-instance-groups \
    --cluster-id $CLUSTER_ID \
    --instance-groups \
      InstanceCount=6,InstanceGroupType=task,InstanceType=m1.large \
      InstanceCount=10,InstanceGroupType=task,InstanceType=m3.xlarge
j-63JNVV2BYHC

INSTANCEGROUPIDS    ig-ZCJCUQU6RU21

INSTANCEGROUPIDS    ig-3RXZ98RUGS7OI
```

We obtained not only the cluster ID like we did before, but also the IDs for the two new instance groups that we asked for. We can check the creation and setup progress of the nodes by querying the cluster, as follows:

```
$ aws emr describe-cluster --cluster-id $CLUSTER_ID
CLUSTER        False  j-63JNVV2BYHC ec2-54-70-11-85.us-west-2.compute.
amazonaws.com Weather      189    3.6.0  3.6.0  EMR_DefaultRole      False
True

APPLICATIONS hadoop 2.4.0

APPLICATIONS Hue

BOOTSTRAPACTIONS      Install Hue   s3://us-west-2.elasticmapreduce/libs/
hue/install-hue

BOOTSTRAPACTIONS      Install HBase s3://us-west-2.elasticmapreduce/
bootstrap-actions/setup-hbase

EC2INSTANCEATTRIBUTES       us-west-2b    OubiwannAWSKeyPair   sg-fea0e9cd
sg-fca0e9cf   EMR_EC2_DefaultRole

INSTANCEGROUPS      ig-3M0BXLF58BAO1      MASTER c1.xlarge      ON_DEMAND
MASTER 1      1

STATUS RUNNING
```

```
STATECHANGEREASON

TIMELINE       1427653325.578       1427653634.541

INSTANCEGROUPS       ig-1YYKNHQQ27GRM     CORE    c1.xlarge     ON_DEMAND
CORE    2      2

STATUS RUNNING

STATECHANGEREASON

TIMELINE       1427653325.579       1427653692.548

INSTANCEGROUPS       ig-3RXZ98RUGS7OI     TASK    m3.xlarge     ON_DEMAND
task    10     0

STATUS RESIZING

STATECHANGEREASON     Expanding instance group

TIMELINE       1427676271.495

INSTANCEGROUPS       ig-ZCJCUQU6RU21     TASK    m1.large     ON_DEMAND
task    6      0

STATUS RESIZING

STATECHANGEREASON     Expanding instance group

TIMELINE       1427676243.42

STATUS WAITING

STATECHANGEREASON     Waiting after step completed

TIMELINE       1427653325.578       1427653692.516
```

That's a lot of information to parse, but if you scan the bottom of the code, you will see the two groups that we just added have a status of RESIZING. Keep an eye on these until they've finished. Once it's done, we can move back to the terminal window where we've SSH'ed into the Hadoop master.

Getting back to the Hadoop cluster, let's execute the map-reduce task against the data that we've updated to the cluster and saved to HDFS, as follows:

```
[hadoop@ip-10-255-7-47 ~]$ hadoop \
  jar contrib/streaming/hadoop-*streaming*.jar \
  -D mapred.reduce.tasks=1 \
  -files mapper.py,reducer.py \
  -mapper mapper.py \
  -reducer reducer.py \
  -combiner reducer.py \
  -input /weather/*.csv \
  -output /weather/total-mean-temp
```

That will only take about a minute and a half to run. To see the results, we just need to take a look at the file that was dumped to the output directory that we indicated previously. This can be accomplished with the help of the following code:

```
[hadoop@ip-10-255-7-47 ~]$ hdfs dfs -ls /weather/total-mean-temp

Found 2 items

-rw-r--r-- 1 hadoop g  0 2015-03-29 20:20 /weather/total-mean-temp/_
SUCCESS

-rw-r--r-- 1 hadoop g 18 2015-03-29 20:20 /weather/total-mean-temp/part-
00000

[hadoop@ip-10-255-7-47 ~]$ hdfs dfs \

    -cat /weather/total-mean-temp/part-00000

-5.30517804131e-05
```

The output is within an order of magnitude of the result that was obtained by manually slicing the HDF5 file:

```
In [44]: sum(means)/len(means)

Out[44]: -5.3051780413782918e-05
```

Without an in-depth analysis, one might venture to guess that the difference between these two values may be due to the floating point calculations on different platforms that use different versions of Python (the Python version on the Hadoop cluster was 2.6; we're using 3.4.2). At any rate, the calculated mean meets our expectations, that is, close to zero for a normal distribution that is centered around zero.

So, we've come out on the other side of Hadoop with our result, but what does this mean to us as matplotlib users? The standard use case for matplotlib is on a workstation, often at an interactive Python or IPython prompt. In such scenarios, we are used to crunching our data by calculating the means, standard deviations, and so on – and then plotting them. All of this is achieved with the help of a few commands (and seconds), and then execution is completed in a span of few seconds.

In the world of big data, that experience changes drastically. What was an implicit understanding that one's data is in-process and it is easy to copy and perform analytical operations on the same is now an involved process comprising of cluster deployments, configuration management, distributed data, communication latencies, and the like. The only thing that remains the same is that it's our data and we need to *plot* it.

When the data was too large for the memory but we were still able to fit the same in a single hard drive, HDF5 and PyTables gave us the means by which we could use our old approaches with very little change in our analytical workflows.

Once our data becomes too large for a hard drive or a file server, the workflows have to change. We can't even pretend it's the same data world that we lived in previously. We have to think in terms of the partitioned data and our tasks running against the partitions.

We still get to use NumPy, but the work is not being done on our machine in the IPython shell. It's being done remotely on a cluster comprising of distributed nodes. Our work in the interactive shells is transformed to a testbed, where we operate on a small sample set to prepare for the task of pushing out a job to the cluster. Additionally, every new big data project has the potential to be legitimately different from any other big data project. For every organization that needs to work with big data, for each set of data, the particulars of the day-to-day analytics workflows are likely to change.

In the end though, our jobs will run and we will have distilled a few tens of millions of data points that are needed in the final analysis from the octillions of data points, and it is this data that will be provided to matplotlib for the task of plotting. Though big data requires that the preparation of data for the operation of plotting move outside the familiarity of an interactive Python prompt, the essence remains the same. We need to know what we have and ways to distill what we have. Furthermore, we should be able to visualize it.

Visualizing large data

The majority of this notebook has been dedicated to processing large datasets and plotting histograms. This was done intentionally because by using such an approach, the number of artists on the matplotlib canvas is limited to something in the order of hundreds, which is better than attempting to plot millions of artists. In this section, we will address the problem of displaying the actual elements of large datasets. We will then return to the last HDF5 table in the remainder of the chapter.

As a refresher on the volume that we're looking at, the number of data points in our dataset can be calculated in the following way:

```
In [45]: data_len = len(tab)
         data_len
Out[45]: 288000000
```

Again, our dataset has nearly one third of a billion points. That is almost certainly more than matplotlib can handle. In fact, one often sees comments online that warn users not to attempt plotting more than ten thousand or one hundred thousand points.

However, is this a good advice? It might be better to advise users to switch to PyTables or `numpy.memmap` and then, based on that, make a recommendation about the upper limits for the plotting of the data points. Let's use our data to establish a baseline for matplotlib's comfort zone.

Finding the limits of matplotlib

We're going to attempt plotting an increasing number of points from our dataset. We'll use the HDF5 table and start modestly with 1000 points, as follows:

```
In [46]: limit = 1000
         (figure, axes) = plt.subplots()
         axes.plot(tab[:limit]["temp"], ".")
         plt.show()
```

The following plot is the result of the preceding code:

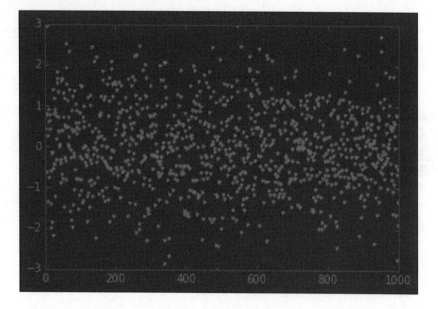

The output was rendered very quickly—most likely under a second. Let's bump up our dataset size by an order of magnitude, as follows:

```
In [47]: limit = 10000
         (figure, axes) = plt.subplots()
         axes.plot(tab[:limit]["temp"], ".")
         plt.show()
```

The following plot is the result of the preceding code:

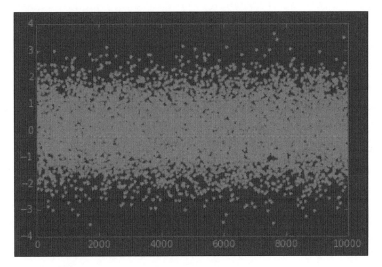

Again, that was very fast. There was no noticeable difference between this render and the previous one. Let's keep going by again increasing the order of magnitude, as follows:

```
In [48]: limit = 100000
         (figure, axes) = plt.subplots()
         axes.plot(tab[:limit]["temp"], ".")
         plt.show()
```

The following plot is the result of the preceding code:

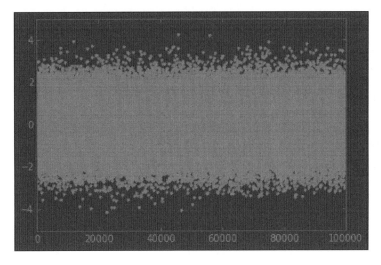

At 100,000 points, you will start seeing a tiny delay. The previous code took about a second to render. This looks better than what we had been led to believe. Let's try a million and then ten million points, as follows:

```
In [49]: limit = 1000000
         (figure, axes) = plt.subplots()
         axes.plot(tab[:limit]["temp"], ".")
         plt.show()
```

The following plot is the result of the preceding code:

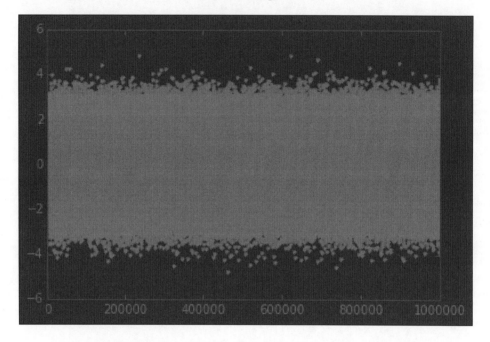

```
In [50]: limit = 10000000
         (figure, axes) = plt.subplots()
         axes.plot(tab[:limit]["temp"], ".")
         plt.show()
```

The following plot is the result of the preceding code:

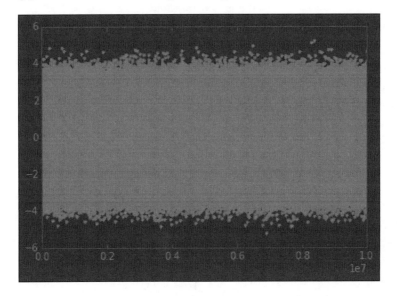

One million points were rendered in about 2 to 3 seconds, which is pretty good considering the fact that we were expecting a limit of around 10,000! However, if we had to plot hundreds or thousands of datasets like these for a project, the delay for the same would be prohibitive. 10 million points took about 15 seconds. Therefore, that wouldn't be an option for even a moderate number of plots that needed to be rendered in a timely manner.

Agg rendering with matplotlibrc

If we use lines instead of points in our plot, we will hit another limit—the inability of the Agg backend to handle a large number of artists. We can see this when we switch from the preceding point plots to the matplotlib default of line plots, as follows:

```
In [51]: (figure, axes) = plt.subplots()
         axes.plot(tab[:10000000]["temp"])
         plt.show()
...
FormatterWarning: Exception in image/png formatter:
Allocated too many blocks
...
<matplotlib.figure.Figure at 0x160587240>
```

If you run into an error like this, it may be worth tweaking an advanced configuration value in the `matplotlibrc` file—chunksize. Normally, the `Agg` path `chunksize` is configured and has a value of 0, but a recommended value to start off with is 20,000. Let's give this a try and then attempt to render again, as follows:

```
In [52]: mpl.rcParams["agg.path.chunksize"] = 20000
In [53]: (figure, axes) = plt.subplots()
         axes.plot(tab[:10000000]["temp"])
         plt.show()
```

The following plot is the result of the preceding code:

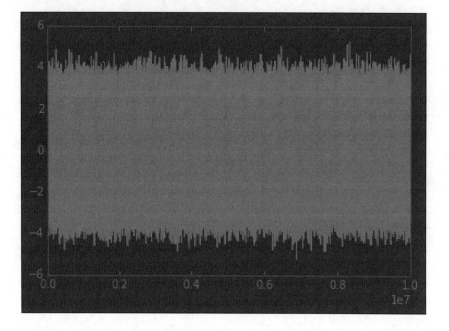

This feature was marked as an experimental in 2008, and it has remained so even in 2015. A warning to the user—enabling the `Agg` backend to plot in chunks instead of doing so all at once may introduce visual artifacts into the plots. In the case of quickly checking one's data in IPython, this might not be a concern for you. However, sharing experimental results in publications will make the plots worthless.

More practically though, we lucked out. It just so happened that the presence of 10 million lines in our data was something that our backend could handle when using the chunked approach. Another order of magnitude or so, and we'd likely be back in the same situation. As the dataset sizes grow beyond the capabilities of matplotlib, we must turn to some other approaches.

Decimation

One way of preparing large datasets to render carries the unfortunate name of the brutal practice employed by the Roman army against large groups that were guilty of capital offenses—"the removal of a tenth", which is more commonly known by its Latin name, *decimation*. We will use this term in the book more generally. It indicates the removal of a fraction, which is sufficient to give us our desired performance that, as it turns out, will be much more than a tenth.

As you may have noticed in our preceding exploration, we couldn't spot any appreciable visual difference in the nature of the plots after 100,000 points. There are certainly some additional outliers that we can point to, but the structure is hidden by the sheer numbers after the threshold is passed.

If we want to limit our plot to 100,000 points but cover the entire spectrum of our dataset, we just need to divide the size of the dataset by the desired point number to calculate the decimation value, as follows:

```
In [54]: frac = math.floor(data_len / 100000)
         frac
Out[54]: 2880
```

Because PyTables uses the NumPy arrays, we can take advantage of an array-slicing feature that lets us extract every nth value—data[::n]. Let's use this to plot a representation of the dataset across its entire spectrum, as follows:

```
In [55]: xvals = range(0, data_len, frac)
         (figure, axes) = plt.subplots()
         axes.plot(xvals, tab[::frac]["temp"], ".", alpha=0.2)
         plt.show()
```

The following plot is the result of the preceding code:

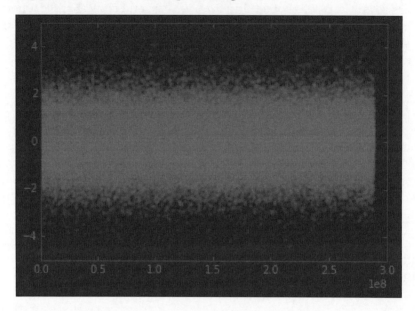

We also provided *x* values that matched the *skipping* that we did when selecting every *y* value. Had we not done this, the *x* axis would have ranged from 0 to 100,000. As you can see, it ranges instead to 300 million, showing our data's end at 288 million.

When taking an approach like this, we need to keep in mind that we're essentially dumping data from our plot. Potentially important data points (such as significant outliers) might be removed in this process. Furthermore, depending on the distribution, statistical values may be altered. However, the most significant issue with this approach is that it has the potential to exaggerate the outliers that *remain* in the dataset. This form of distortion is known as *aliasing*, and there are filtering techniques that one can employ to minimize it.

If you are working with digital signals or periodic data, you may find the `scipy.signal.decimate` and `scipy.signal.resmple` functions useful.

Additional techniques

Even with an approach as simple as decimation, we need to consider applying filters. Depending on one's data, there are a number of additional techniques that one may utilize to make large datasets more digestible. Data can be quantized or binned. In particular, we took advantage of binning data by using the histogram plots early in this chapter and thus sidestepping the need to worry about rendering plots with massive dataset sizes. Similarly, matplotlib, Seaborn, and several other libraries offer heat maps and hexbin plots. When applied intelligently, these features can provide invaluable insights without the need to display every single point from a dataset.

Other visualization tools

The matplotlib module was originally designed for use on workstations and desktops, not servers. Its design did not arise from use cases for high-volume or large datasets. However, as you saw in this chapter, by using the right tools and taking the appropriate measures, matplotlib can perform admirably with hundreds of millions of data points.

Should you ever hit insurmountable barriers for matplotlib (such as real-time visualization and user interaction with billions of data points), you can make use of the following open source projects that were originally designed by keeping large datasets in mind:

- **ParaView** (`http://www.paraview.org/`): This is an open source, multiplatform data analysis and visualization application. ParaView was developed to analyze extremely large datasets by using distributed memory computing resources. It can be run on supercomputers to analyze datasets of petascale size as well as on laptops for smaller data. Paraview also offers the Python Scripting Interface.

- **VisIt** (`https://wci.llnl.gov/simulation/computer-codes/visit`): This is an open source, interactive, scalable tool for visualization, animation, and analysis. VisIt has a parallel and distributed architecture that allows users to interactively visualize and analyze data, which ranges in scale from small (fewer than 102 cores) desktop-sized projects to large (more than 105 cores) computing facility simulation campaigns. VisIt is capable of visualizing data from over 120 different scientific data formats. It offers a Python interface.

- **Bokeh** (`http://bokeh.pydata.org/en/latest/`): As mentioned previously, Bokeh is a Python interactive visualization library that targets modern web browsers for presentation. Its goal is to not only provide elegant, concise construction of novel graphics in the style of D3.js, but also deliver this capability with high-performance interactivity over very large or streaming datasets.

- **Vispy** (`http://vispy.org/`): This is a new 2D and 3D high-performance visualization library that can handle very large datasets. Vispy uses the OpenGL library and GPUs for increased performance. With Vispy, users can interactively explore plots that have hundreds of millions of points. A basic knowledge of OpenGL is very helpful when using Vispy.

That being said, matplotlib is a powerful, well-known tool in the scientific computing community. Organizations and teams have uncountable years of cumulative experience building, installing, augmenting, and using matplotlib and the libraries of related projects, such as NumPy and SciPy. If there is a new way to put old tools to use without having to suffer the losses in productivity and the re-engineering of infrastructure associated with platform changes, it is often in everyone's best interest to do so.

Summary

The most important thing to keep in mind when working with large datasets and matplotlib is to use data wisely and take advantage of NumPy and tools such as PyTables. When moving to distributed data, a large burden with regard to infrastructure is taken on compared to working with data on a single machine. As datasets approach terabytes and petabytes, the greatest work involved really has less to do with plotting and visualization and has more to do with deciding *what* to visualize and how to actually get there. An increasingly common aspect of big data is real-time analysis, where matplotlib might be used to generate hundreds or thousands of plots of a fairly small set of data points. Not all problems in big data visualization are about visualizing big data!

Finally, it cannot be overstated that knowing your data is the most crucial component when tackling large datasets. It is very rare that an entire raw dataset is what you want to present to your colleagues or end users. Gaining an intuition with the help of your data through an initial process of exploration will enable you to select the appropriate presentation approaches, which may involve the process of binning your data in a simple histogram, decimating data, or simply providing statistical summaries. The biggest problem of big data that users face is how not to get lost in either the sheer size of it or the complex ecosystem of tools and fads that have grown up around the buzz of big data. Careful thinking and an eye towards simplicity will make all the difference in having a successful experience with large datasets in matplotlib.

9
Clustering for matplotlib

In the final chapter of this book, we will address a topic that has been alluded to several times—clustering and parallel programming for matplotlib. Our motivation to discuss this is nearly identical to that which drove our investigation into working with large datasets. Although matplotlib lib *itself* isn't a library that makes direct use of large datasets or provides an API that can be used with clusters, advanced users of the library will very likely encounter situations where they may want to utilize matplotlib.

Not to put too fine a point on this, we live in a new world of computing. This was presented exceptionally well in the oft-quoted article, *The Free Lunch Is Over*, by Herb Sutter. With the drastic limitations faced by the semiconductor industry, yearly gains in computing power are no longer a result of faster chips. Instead, we get this benefit through the addition of cores in a single machine. Unfortunately, common practices in programming that have persisted over the past half century leave us ill-prepared to take advantage of this increasingly common form of additional computing power. Programmers need to learn new skills.

One of the most effective means of utilizing multiple cores is parallelization, which is achieved by either converting some old code to execute in parallel, or adopting infrastructure and code paradigms that allow us to easily start with parallelization from the start. The programmer who wants to make full use of multiple cores will benefit greatly from learning parallel programming. Fortunately, matplotlib coders can also take advantage of this.

To provide an entry point to learn more about this topic in the context of matplotlib and scientific computing, we will cover the following topics in this chapter:

- Clustering and parallel programming
- Creating a custom worker cluster by using ZeroMQ
- Using IPython to create clusters
- Further clustering options

To follow along with this chapter's code, clone the notebook's repository and start up IPython, as follows:

```
$ git clone https://github.com/masteringmatplotlib/clustering.git
$ cd clustering
```

 To compile all the dependencies in this chapter's notebook, you may need to set the CC environment variable, for example export CC=gcc. If you are using Mac OS X, you can use export CC=clang.

Now, you can finish the chapter start-up, as follows:

```
$ make
```

Clustering and parallel programming

The term **clustering** may have a number of operational definitions depending on the situation that one is facing or the organization that one is working with. In this chapter, we will use the term in a very general sense to indicate a system of computing nodes across which a task may be split and whose parts may be executed in *parallel* with all the system nodes. We won't specify what nodes are, as they may be anything from a collection of processes on the same machine or a computer network to virtual machines or physical computers on a network.

The word "cluster" alludes to a logical collection, but in our definition there is a more important word—*parallel*. For our purposes, clusters exist to make running code in parallel more efficient or convenient. The topic of parallel computing is a vast one and has an interesting history. However, it rose to greater prominence in 2003 due to the physical limitations that were encountered by the chip-making industry— increased CPU heat, power consumption, and current leakage problems in circuits. As such, CPU performance gains started coming from the addition of more cores to a system. This was discussed in detail by Herb Sutter in his article, *The Free Lunch Is Over*, which was published in 2005. Ever since, a greater number of mainstream programmers have become interested in taking advantage of the increased number of system cores through the application of parallel programming techniques.

In essence, parallel programming describes scenarios where computationally intensive code may be broken down into smaller code, which can then be run concurrently by taking advantage of a larger number of processing resources and solving problems in a shorter span of time. There are several ways in which one may write parallel code, but our focus will be on the following:

- **Data parallelization**: In this, the same calculation is performed on different datasets (and sometimes on the same datasets)

- **Task parallelization**: In this, a task is broken down into subtasks, and the subtasks are executed in parallel

The sort of problems that are amenable to parallelization include the following:

- **N-body problems** (for example, simulating physics to understand the structure of physical reality such as the work done on *Millennium Run*)
- **Structured grid problems** (for example, computational fluid dynamics)
- **The Monte Carlo simulation** (for example, computational biology, artificial intelligence, and investment evaluations in finance)
- **Combinational logic** (for example, the brute-force cryptographic techniques)
- **Graph traversal** (for example, calculating the least expense and least time for shipping companies)
- **Dynamic programming** (for example, mathematical and computational optimizations, RNS structure prediction, and optimal consumption and saving in economic modeling)
- **Bayesian networks** (for example, risk analysis, decision systems, document classification, and biological belief modeling)

However, the reader will be relieved to know that we will focus on a simple example in order to more clearly apply the basic principles of parallel programming. In particular, the examples in this chapter will utilize a parallelizable means to estimate the value of π.

The custom ZeroMQ cluster

In this section, we will create a task *pipeline*, which is a messaging pattern that we mentioned briefly when discussing the Disco project's answer to MapReduce. Task pipelines can be viewed as a generalization of MapReduce in that they support data flows through a sequence of steps, where each step provides the results from its processing to the next step in the flow. We will accomplish this by using ZeroMQ to create a messaging topology that is suitable for the execution of *embarrassingly parallel* code in a number of worker processes.

> The descriptive term *embarrassingly parallel* was adopted in online parallelization discussions after its use in an article named *Matrix Computation on Distributed Memory Multiprocessors* that was written by Cleve Moler. The parallelizing of serially biased code is notoriously difficult, and problems that were obviously or easily parallelizable were described by using this phrase.

ZeroMQ is an asynchronous messaging framework, which evolved from the experience and lessons learned from the work on the **Advanced Message Queuing Protocol (AMQP)**. Its primary purpose is to allow programmers to quickly and easily interconnect various software components from a system written in any networking-capable programming language.

We will adapt some Python examples from the ZeroMQ Guide (from the *Divide and Conquer* and *Handling Errors and ETERM* sections) to create a task pipeline cluster. We will then use it to estimate the value of π.

Estimating the value of π

Blaise Barney from Lawrence Livermore National Laboratory created a series of pages and tutorials on the topic of parallel computing that offers as an example a means to estimate the value of π by using a parallel approach. The method used is as follows:

1. Inscribe a circle in a square.
2. Randomly generate points in the square.
3. Determine the number of points in the square that fall within the inscribed circle.
4. Let π be represented by the ratio of the areas.

This can be clearly and unambiguously expressed by using the equations for the area of the square and the circle. We will start with the following equations:

$$A_{square} = (2r)^2$$
$$A_{circle} = \pi r^2$$

We can find the value for r2 in both the preceding cases, as follows:

$$r^2 = \frac{A_{square}}{4}$$
$$r^2 = \frac{A_{circle}}{\pi}$$

Knowing that each value of r2 is equal to the other, we may now solve for π, as follows:

$$\frac{A_{square}}{4} = \frac{A_{circle}}{\pi}$$

$$\pi = 4\frac{A_{circle}}{A_{square}}$$

Letting the random placement of points in the respective areas uniformly represent the areas themselves, we can use this to estimate the value of π.

A graphic representation of this may be helpful. The following code assumes that you have opened and run the notebook for this chapter and executed the first few cells, which import all the necessary libraries:

```
In [4]: xs = np.random.uniform(-1, 1, 10000)
        ys = np.random.uniform(-1, 1, 10000)
        points_inside = []
        points_outside = []
        for point in zip(xs, ys):
            (x, y) = point
            if (x ** 2 + y ** 2) <= 1:
                points_inside.append(point)
            else:
                points_outside.append(point)
```

The preceding code generates random numbers for the x and y values between -1 and 1. Using the equation of a unit circle, it then calculates whether the points constructed from these x and y values fall within the area of the circle or not.

Let's plot these two sets of points by using the following code:

```
In [5]: (figure, axes) = plt.subplots(figsize=(10,10))
        axes.scatter(*zip(*points_inside), color=colors[1],
                    alpha=0.5)
        axes.scatter(*zip(*points_outside), color=colors[0],
                    alpha=0.5)
        circle = plt.Circle((0, 0), 1, fill=False)
        axes.set_xlim((-1.1, 1.1))
```

```
axes.set_ylim((-1.1, 1.1))
axes.add_artist(circle)
axes.set_title("Visualization of estimating $\pi$",
               fontsize=28)
nbutil.hide_axes(axes)
plt.show()
```

The following plot (**Visualization of estimating π**) is the result of the preceding code:

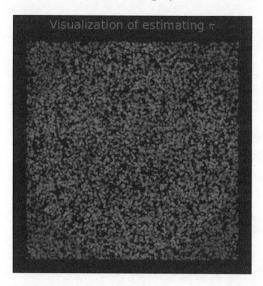

The C and Fortran π estimation code provided in the example given in the **Lawrence Livermore National Laboratory (LLNL)** parallel programming tutorial can be easily converted to Python, as follows:

```
In [6]: def estimate_pi(points):
            in_circle = 0
            for _ in range(int(points)):
                (x, y) = (random.random(), random.random())
                if (x ** 2 + y ** 2) <= 1:
                    in_circle += 1
            return 4 * in_circle / points
```

When we run the preceding code with 100 million points and track the execution time on a moderate workstation, it takes over a minute, which is depicted in the following code:

```
In [7]: %%time
        print(estimate_pi(1e8))
3.14157116
CPU times: user 1min 10s, sys: 151 ms, total: 1min 10s
Wall time: 1min 11s
```

The preceding code offers a baseline against which we will soon be able to compare our parallel results.

Creating the ZeroMQ components

In order to use the ZeroMQ pipeline pattern (dispatching tasks to workers and having the workers forward the results to a collector), we'll need to create each of the following components:

- A distributor
- Multiple instances of a worker
- A collector (for the results)

As stated before, the code for the components were adapted from the code from the ZeroMQ guide, which was originally contributed by Lev Givon and Jeremy Avnet. We've made several changes, one of which is to utilize the Python `multiprocessing` module, which lets us run the example in a single terminal window rather than three. Naturally, this also lets us easily run the example in an IPython Notebook.

We've decided to implement the cluster in several small modules in order to keep things as clear and organized as possible. This should make it fairly obvious which code is responsible for which functionality. All the modules are available in the `lib` directory of the repository for this chapter's notebook. We'll start where everything begins—the `demo` module:

```
import multiprocessing, random, time
import zmq
import collector, democfg, distributor, worker


def main(tasks):
    # Initialize random number generator
    random.seed()
```

```
    print("Starting task workers ...")
    for worker_id in range(democfg.worker_pool_size):
        worker_proc = multiprocessing.Process(
            target=worker.work, args=[worker_id])
        worker_proc.start()
    print("Starting task collector ...")
    collector_proc = multiprocessing.Process(
            target=collector.collect)
    collector_proc.start()
    time.sleep(democfg.pause_time)
    print("Starting task distributor ...")
    distributor.distribute(tasks)


if __name__ == "__main__":
    tasks = [1e8 / democfg.task_count] * democfg.task_count
    main(tasks)
```

The `main` function performs the following tasks:

- It creates a worker pool with a worker count, as configured in the `democfg` module
- It starts the collector process, which will be responsible for the processing of results from the workers
- It starts the distributor process, passing it the tasks that are defined at the end of the module before the `main` function is called

Though you can't tell right now, the `distributor.distribute` function is the one that starts the process of passing messages across the cluster. Now, let's take a look at this code in the `distributor` module:

```
import time
import zmq
import democfg


def distribute(tasks):
    context = zmq.Context()
    # Socket to send messages on
    sender = context.socket(zmq.PUSH)
    sender.bind(democfg.routing_table["receiver"])
```

```
# Socket with direct access to the sink used to
synchronize
# start of batch
syncher = context.socket(zmq.PUSH)
syncher.connect(democfg.routing_table["sender"])
# Give 0MQ time to start up
time.sleep(democfg.pause_time)
syncher.send(democfg.start_flag)
for task in tasks:
    sender.send_pyobj(task)
# Give 0MQ time to deliver message
time.sleep(democfg.pause_time)
```

The `distribute` function takes as an argument a list of tasks that it will be passing to the workers. Before it gives out any jobs though, it sets up the ZeroMQ sockets to communicate with the other components:

- The `sender` ZeroMQ socket to pass jobs
- The `syncher` ZeroMQ socket to kick off the batch

If you're not familiar with ZeroMQ, don't be alarmed that the `worker.work` function isn't called. Instead, what happens is this—a message gets passed to the ZeroMQ queue that the worker is listening. As we'll shortly see, the work function will pull task data off the queue to which the `distribute` function sent it.

Next up, the worker:

```
import random
import zmq
import democfg, tasker


def is_done(socks, controller):
    if (socks.get(controller) == zmq.POLLIN and
        controller.recv() == democfg.done_msg):
        return True
    return False


def work(worker_id):
    context = zmq.Context()
    # Socket to receive messages on
```

```
receiver = context.socket(zmq.PULL)
receiver.connect(democfg.routing_table["receiver"])
# Socket to send messages to
sender = context.socket(zmq.PUSH)
sender.connect(democfg.routing_table["sender"])
# Socket for control input
controller = context.socket(zmq.SUB)
controller.connect(democfg.routing_table ["controller"])
controller.setsockopt(zmq.SUBSCRIBE, b"")
# Process messages from receiver and controller
poller = zmq.Poller()
poller.register(receiver, zmq.POLLIN)
poller.register(controller, zmq.POLLIN)
# Process messages from both sockets
run_loop = True
while run_loop:
    socks = dict(poller.poll())
    if socks.get(receiver) == zmq.POLLIN:
        task_data = receiver.recv_pyobj()
        # Process task data
        result = tasker.task(task_data)
        sender.send_pyobj(result)
    if is_done(socks, controller):
        run_loop = False
```

The worker.work function creates a worker that listens on a ZeroMQ PULL connection, where it will take the task data that the *distributor* PUSH-ed. The worker then calls another function that will do the actual computation for the task. Once this is done, the worker will send the result to the *collector*.

The code for the worker is a little more complex than the distributor, primarily because the worker polls the following two separate queues:

- A queue from which it will pull the task data
- A queue on which it is listening for the control messages — in particular, a stop message

The result that gets sent to the collector is created in a separate `tasker` module, as follows:

```
import random
import zmq
import democfg


def task(task_data):
    in_circle = 0
    for _ in range(int(task_data)):
        (x, y) = (random.random(), random.random())
        if (x ** 2 + y ** 2) <= 1:
            in_circle += 1
    return 4 * in_circle / task_data
```

This code might look familiar. It's very close to the code that we used to create a area plot to demonstrate the method for estimating the value of π. In the `tasker` module, we will see what the task data, which was originally passed to the `main` function, is actually used for—it is the number of points that will be created to estimate the value of π.

The `worker` function executes the `task` function, and when the function gets the results, it sends a message to the queue upon which the collector is listening. Here's the `collector` module:

```
import time
import zmq
import democfg, processor


def collect():
    context = zmq.Context()
    # Socket to receive messages on (collect results from worker)
    receiver = context.socket(zmq.PULL)
    receiver.bind(democfg.routing_table["sender"])
    # Socket for worker control
    controller = context.socket(zmq.PUB)
    controller.bind(democfg.routing_table["controller"])
    # Wait for start signal
```

```
assert receiver.recv() == democfg.start_flag
processor.process(receiver)
# Let workers know that all results have been processed
controller.send(democfg.done_msg)
# Finished, but give 0MQ time to deliver
time.sleep(5 * democfg.pause_time)
```

This code is almost as simple as that for the distributor. The `collector.collect` function does a few things, which includes the following tasks:

- It PULL-s the data that was PUSH-ed by the workers
- It calls `processor.process` on the data that it PULL-ed
- It sends a control message to stop the function as soon as it finishes processing the results

 Using `time.sleep` repeatedly to ensure that the different parts of the system have completed their tasks is a fragile and slow process. As with the official ZeroMQ examples upon which this code is based, it is used here only for pedagogical clarity. A more robust solution will be to use **Pub-Sub** synchronization. For more information, see the ZeroMQ Guide sections, *Node-Coordination* and *Getting the Message Out*.

In the same way that we separated the ZeroMQ code and task code in the worker, we will separate the collector code and the code that processes the results. Here is the `processor` module:

```
import time
import zmq
import democfg


def process(receiver):
    return get_results(receiver)


def get_results(receiver):
    data = []
    # Process results from the workers
    for _ in range(democfg.task_count):
        result = receiver.recv_pyobj()
```

```
    print("Processing result: {}".format(result))
    data.append(result)
# Calculate final result
print("Final result: {}".format(sum(data)/len(data)))
return data
```

The `get_results` function's primary purpose is to print out the mean value for π based on the values obtained from all the workers. The fact that we split this into distinct functions may seem useless right now, but this will provide some convenience when we update the code to plot our data.

We will take a moment here to review what we've seen:

- The source code that initializes the cluster components (the `demo` module)
- The source code for each of the components of the ZeroMQ pipeline cluster — the distributor, worker, and collector
- The source code that does the actual calculation (in the `tasker` module)
- The source code that renders the final result (in the `processor` module)

We could have easily left the `tasker` code in the `worker` module and the `processor` code in the `collector` module. So why did we split these out? This separation highlights the very different concepts of each. The `worker.work` function doesn't care what it does. The work that it represents is abstract in nature — *tell me what to do, and I'll do it*. The same goes for `collector.collect` — *tell me what to collect, and I will do that*. The distributor, worker, and collector are not concerned with the execution of the Python code and the returning of the results. Instead, they are concerned with the sending and receiving of messages in various special-purpose queues that we set up. These three components are the message-passing architecture, which is the core of the pipeline cluster.

On the other hand, the `tasker.task` and `processor.process` functions are the ones that care about executing the Python code and gathering results. What they do is completely unrelated to what the pipeline architecture code does, so much so that we can rip them out and insert the new `task` and `process` functions that solve completely different problems. All of this can be accomplished without touching the pipeline modules. In fact, we will do a bit of this at the end of the next section.

We discussed the message-passing pipeline architecture and the conceptually orthogonal computational work done by the other modules, but we need to make sure that we don't lose sight of another key element — the parallelization. Where does it live?

When we start the program by calling main, we don't give any indication of what gets parallelized. Also, we don't explicitly state where the parallelization occurs in any of the modules. In fact, it is spread across a couple of features, some of which are as follows:

- Before we call main, we divide the original value—the total number of points that we want to process—by the number of workers that we will be creating

- These split point counts are then sent to the distributor component, which iterates over these and sends them (via a queue) to the workers

- Finally, the results are then assembled at the end in the collector component

It is important to note that it is these three conceptual elements that work together that carry out the hard work of finding the solution to a parallelizable problem. However, the last bit of hidden implicitness is the most difficult of all—identifying the problems that may be parallelized and then figuring out how to do so. We brushed over this in the introduction to this section, but it is without doubt where all the hard work lies.

Before we try implementing the cluster, there's one more module that we should look at so that there's no mystery and the source is shared—the democfg module that is referenced by the others:

```
worker_pool_size = 8
task_count = 8
delay_range = (1, 100) # milliseconds
pause_time = 1 # seconds
start_flag = b"0"
done_msg = b"DONE"
routing_table = {
    "receiver": "tcp://127.0.0.1:7557",
    "sender": "tcp://127.0.0.1:7558",
    "controller": "tcp://127.0.0.1:7559"}
```

With this bit of code, we have reviewed all the components of our system and are ready to run it!

Working with the results

If you review the code in the demo module, you may recall that when the module is called from the command line, it performs the following tasks:

- It gets a total task count
- It partitions this total task count into equal segments that represent the task
- It calls the main function and passes this partitioned data

Let's try calling the demo module now:

```
In [15]: %%time
         %%bash
         python ../lib/demo.py
Starting task workers ...
Starting task collector ...
Starting task distributor ...
Processing result: 3.14210336
Processing result: 3.1415472
Processing result: 3.14151648
Processing result: 3.14219872
Processing result: 3.14187168
Processing result: 3.14149984
Processing result: 3.14178592
Processing result: 3.14194304
Final result: 3.14180828
CPU times: user 3.05 ms, sys: 8.41 ms, total: 11.5 ms
Wall time: 25.4 s
```

As you might have expected, the parallel version runs faster than—more than twice as fast as—the single-process version. However, we don't even get close to eight times as fast. From this, you can infer that there is overhead above and beyond the simple computation that we parallelized. It is likely that this is due to our extensive use of time.sleep. Generally though, to understand exactly what impacts the performance of any given code, we need to profile the code and analyze the results. This is left as an exercise for curious readers, as a great deal of literature was produced in the past half century of computing research on parallel computing and its performance characteristics.

We will set this aside though and connect our example to matplotlib. The next thing that we'd like to be able to do is plot our results. However, our data is handled in separate processes. We can use any number of approaches to solve this problem (for examples, anything from databases to creating an on-notebook ZeroMQ socket to receive data), but let's do something simple instead. Make the following changes to `./lib/processor.py`:

```
import numpy as np

def process(receiver):
    results = get_results(receiver)
    np.save("../data/results.npy", np.array(results))
    return results
```

We haven't muddied the logic coded in the `get_results` function, and because we're still using the `process` function, no code in the other modules needs to be updated. We do need to reload some modules though, as follows:

```
In [16]: import imp
         imp.reload(collector)
         imp.reload(processor)
         imp.reload(demo)
Out[16]: <module 'demo' from '../lib/demo.py'>
```

Let's run the `demo.main` function in the following way, passing it some tasks, the results of which will be saved to our NumPy file:

```
In [17]: tasks = [1e8 / democfg.task_count] * democfg.task_count
         demo.main(tasks)
Starting task workers ...
Starting task collector ...
Starting task distributor ...
```

If you didn't see the expected output and you've checked the system process table to find out that eight Python processes are not running at high CPU specs, then the job is finished and you might need to flush `stdout`, as follows:

```
In [18]: sys.stdout.flush()
Processing result: 3.14124992
Processing result: 3.14037024
Processing result: 3.1411328
Processing result: 3.14301344
Processing result: 3.1412272
```

```
Processing result: 3.14260256
Processing result: 3.14093152
Processing result: 3.1416672
Final result: 3.14152436
```

With the data saved, we can load it and plot it, as follows:

```
In [19]: results = np.load("../data/results.npy")
         (figure, axes) = plt.subplots(figsize=(16, 8))
         axes.scatter([x + 1 for x in range(len(results))],
                     results,
                     color=colors[0])
         axes.set_title("Estimated values of $\pi$", fontsize=28)
         axes.set_ylabel("~$\pi$", fontsize=24)
         axes.set_xlabel("Worker Number", fontsize=20)
         plt.show()
```

The following plot is the result of the preceding code:

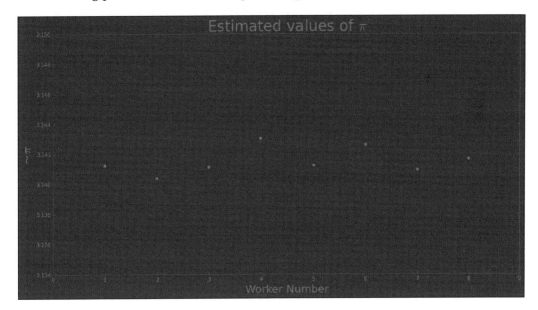

This brings us to the end of our ZeroMQ cluster exploration, but it serves as an excellent introduction because IPython also uses ZeroMQ for its clustering features, and this is what we shall discuss next.

Clustering with IPython

As explained in the IPython documentation for parallel computing, IPython has built-in support for parallelism. This came as a result of the architectural overhaul that IPython received when the project finished migrating to ZeroMQ in 2011. The architecture that resulted can be summarized with the following components, all of which are present in the IPython.parallel package:

- **The IPython engine**: This is a Python interpreter that accepts Python commands over a network connection. Multiple engines form the basis of IPython's parallel computing capabilities.

- **The IPython hub**: This is the process that keeps track of engine connections, schedulers, clients, task requests, and results. Its primary purpose is to facilitate queries that are made from the cluster state.

- **The IPython schedulers**: The actions that can be performed on an engine go through a scheduler. They also provide a fully asynchronous interface to a set of engines.

- **The controller client**: This is the user interface for developers who wish to access a set of engines. It is what we will be using subsequently in the code examples (in particular, the different *views*).

The following figure shows us the IPython architecture:

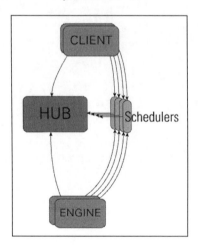

Thanks to the aforementioned architecture, IPython supports the following different styles of parallelism:

- Single program, multiple data
- Multiple programs, multiple data

- Passing messages by using **Message Passing Interface (MPI)**
- Task farming
- Parallel data
- Combinations of the aforementioned approaches
- Custom user-defined approaches

Practically speaking, this allows the IPython users to tackle the following use cases:

- Quickly parallelize algorithms that are embarrassingly parallel by using a number of simple approaches. Many simple things can be parallelized interactively in one or two lines of code.
- Steer the traditional MPI applications on a supercomputer from an IPython session on your laptop.
- Analyze and visualize large datasets (that may be remote and/or distributed) interactively by using IPython and tools such as matplotlib or TVTK.
- Develop, test, and debug new parallel algorithms (that may use MPI) interactively.
- Tie together the multiple MPI jobs that run on different systems into a giant distributed and parallel system.
- Start a parallel job on your cluster and then have a remote collaborator connect to it and pull back data into their local IPython session for plotting and analysis.
- Run a set of tasks on a set of CPUs by using dynamic load balancing.

Getting started

To use IPython for parallel computing, you need to initialize an instance of the controller and one or more instances of the engine. Initially, it is best to simply start a controller and engines on a single host by using the `ipcluster` command. To initialize a controller and 4 engines on your localhost, switch to a terminal window with this notebook's virtual environment activated and execute the following command:

```
$ ipcluster start -n 4
```

This will run the `ipcluster` app in the foreground and show the following output:

```
2015-04-28 09:50:29.584 [IPClusterStart] Using existing profile dir: '/
Users/oubiwann/.ipython/profile_default'
2015-04-28 09:50:29.587 [IPClusterStart] Starting ipcluster with
[daemon=False]
```

```
2015-04-28 09:50:29.589 [IPClusterStart] Creating pid file: /Users/
oubiwann/.ipython/profile_default/pid/ipcluster.pid
```

```
2015-04-28 09:50:29.589 [IPClusterStart] Starting Controller with
LocalControllerLauncher
```

```
2015-04-28 09:50:30.593 [IPClusterStart] Starting 4 Engines with
LocalEngineSetLauncher
```

With an IPython cluster running, we're ready to start using it. There are several ways via which one can interact with an IPython cluster. The connection is made with a client object. However, the client object offers *views* for an actual interaction with the cluster. The following views are available:

- The direct view
- The load-balanced view
- The IPython parallel magic functions

Though not a view per se, the IPython cluster provides *magic functions* to interact with clusters, thus acting very much like a view. In an IPython Notebook, the parallel magic functions will often be what you want to use. For both the direct and load-balanced views, you will need to create a cluster client, as follows:

```
In [20]: from IPython.parallel import Client
         client = Client()
         client.ids
```

The `client.ids` attribute holds the IDs for each IPython cluster engine that was started by the call to the preceding `ipcluster`.

The direct view

The direct view is called so because the `DirectView` object offers an interface to the cluster that doesn't go through the schedulers. Instead, it offers direct, manual execution control.

Here's how you create a direct view from the `client` object:

```
In [21]: view = client.direct_view()
         view
Out[21]: <DirectView all>
```

Direct views are also available on the client via indices. The `all` part in the `view` object representation is an oblique reference to the fact that you have not selected some of the direct view instances on the object (such as the view index number or slicing), but have rather asked for all of them.

By default, when executing functions in parallel, an asynchronous `result` object is returned, which is demonstrated in the following code:

```
In [22]: async_result = view.apply(np.random.rand, 2, 2)
         async_result
Out[22]: <AsyncResult: finished>
```

When the results are ready to be obtained, the `result` object representation will provide a clue to this fact by displaying `finished`. To get the result values, simply call the `get` method, as follows:

```
In [23]: values = async_result.get()
         values
Out[23]: [array([[ 0.07792881,  0.21319405],
                 [ 0.20925777,  0.74999169]]),
          array([[ 0.07792881, 0.21319405],
                 [ 0.20925777,  0.74999169]]),
          array([[ 0.07792881,  0.21319405],
                 [ 0.20925777,  0.74999169]]),
          array([[ 0.07792881,  0.21319405],
                 [ 0.20925777,  0.74999169]])]
```

As you might expect, we can also use the results in further parallel calls, as follows:

```
In [24]: async_result = view.apply(np.linalg.eigvals, values)
         async_result
Out[24]: <AsyncResult: eigvals>
In [25]: async_result.get()
Out[25]: [array([[ 0.01706021,  0.81086029],
                 [ 0.01706021,  0.81086029],
                 [ 0.01706021,  0.81086029],
                 [ 0.01706021,  0.81086029]]),
          array([[ 0.01706021,  0.81086029],
                 [ 0.01706021,  0.81086029],
                 [ 0.01706021,  0.81086029],
                 [ 0.01706021,  0.81086029]]),
          array([[ 0.01706021,  0.81086029],
                 [ 0.01706021,  0.81086029],
                 [ 0.01706021,  0.81086029],
```

```
              [ 0.01706021,   0.81086029]]),
       array([[ 0.01706021,   0.81086029],
              [ 0.01706021,   0.81086029],
              [ 0.01706021,   0.81086029],
              [ 0.01706021,   0.81086029]])]
```

The load-balanced view

In contrast to the direct view, IPython offers a view that does not bypass the schedulers. Instead, this view executes based on the configured load-balancing scheme.

There are a variety of valid ways to determine where the jobs should be assigned in a load-balancing situation. IPython supports several standard schemes and even provides the means by which developers can easily add their own. The scheme can be selected either via the scheme argument to `ipcontroller`, or in the `TaskScheduler.schemename` attribute of a controller `config` object.

The following built-in routing schemes are provided by IPython:

- `lru`: Least recently used
- `plainrandom`: Plain random
- `twobin`: Two-bin random
- `leastload`: Least load (default)
- `weighted`: Weighted two-bin random

To select one of the aforementioned schemes, simply use the `ipcontroller` command-line tool, as follows:

```
$ ipcontroller –scheme=twobin
```

Call the client with the appropriate method to get the load-balanced view, as follows:

```
In [26]: lb_view = client.load_balanced_view()
         lb_view
Out[26]: <LoadBalancedView None>
```

The basic usage is the same as the direct view:

```
In [27]: serial_result = map(lambda x:x**10, range(32))
         parallel_result = lb_view.map(lambda x:x**10, range(32))
In [28]: list(serial_result) == parallel_result.get()
Out[28]: True
```

The load-balanced view provides a convenient decorator to create parallel functions. In form, the parallel functions look just like their serially executed cousins. However, with `@parallel`, the function obtains a `map` method, which will distribute the execution of the function across the cluster, as follows:

```
In [29]: @lb_view.parallel()
         def f(x):
             return 10.0*x**4


         f.map(range(32)).get()
Out[29]: [0.0,
          10.0,
          160.0,
          810.0,
          2560.0,
          6250.0,
          12960.0,
          24010.0,
          40960.0,
          65610.0,
          100000.0,
          146410.0,
          207360.0,
          285610.0,
          384160.0,
          506250.0,
          655360.0,
          835210.0,
          1049760.0,
          1303210.0,
          1600000.0,
          1944810.0,
          2342560.0,
          2798410.0,
          3317760.0,
          3906250.0,
          4569760.0,
```

```
        5314410.0,
        6146560.0,
        7072810.0,
        8100000.0,
        9235210.0]
```

The parallel magic functions

If you are unfamiliar with IPython, then you may not know that IPython has a set of predefined functions that are referred to as the *magic functions* or simply *magics*. Some apply these functions only to a single line (the ones with the % prefix). However, some apply them to the entire cell (these have the %% prefix).

IPython comes with magics, which ease the user experience of executing code in parallel. If your parallel code requires libraries, you can use the following code to import them to all the engines:

```
In [30]: with view.sync_imports():
             import numpy

importing numpy on engine(s)
```

Now, let's execute the code that we used in the section on the direct view, as follows:

```
In [31]: %px async_result = numpy.random.rand(2, 2)
In [32]: %px numpy.linalg.eigvals(async_result)
         Out[0:2]: array([ 1.69123631,  0.0052597 ])
         Out[1:2]: array([ 1.4345667 ,  0.15208336])
         Out[2:2]: array([ 1.24709664, -0.06577105])
         Out[3:2]: array([ 0.39707627,  1.01065811])
```

An example – estimating the value of π

Let's use the clustering features of IPython to execute the same job that we did during the implementation of the ZeroMQ pipeline pattern. Go ahead and stop the cluster with four nodes and restart it with eight nodes, as follows:

```
$ ipcluster start -n 8
```

Let's get a fresh connection that is aware of the new nodes, as follows:

```
In [33]: client = Client()
         client.ids
Out[33]: [0, 1, 2, 3, 4, 5, 6, 7]
```

Next, we're going to do something different — we'll demonstrate working with blocking, synchronous results by explicitly setting a flag. Also, since the `estimate_pi` function uses an imported module, we're going to have each engine import it, as follows:

```
In [34]: view = client.direct_view()
         view.block = True
         with view.sync_imports():
             import random
         importing random on engine(s)
```

Now, let's execute the π-estimating function in the new IPython cluster, timing it with the `%%time` magic function, as follows:

```
In [35]: %%time
         node_count = 8
         results = view.apply(estimate_pi, 1e8 / node_count)
         pi_est = sum(results)/len(client.ids)
         print("Result: {}".format(pi_est))
         Result: 3.1414122399999997
         CPU times: user 6.76 s, sys: 624 ms, total: 7.38 s
         Wall time: 19.1 s
```

The preceding code runs faster than our custom multiprocessing ZeroMQ example. It is almost four times faster than the original serial example that we gave, but all things being equal, its biggest advantage is that it's *much* easier to set up. However, thanks to the work we did in the previous section, we have an idea of what's going on behind the scenes due to the fact that IPython uses ZeroMQ to create and manage its clusters.

In addition to it being easy to set up, it's easier to plot the results. This is demonstrated in the following code:

```
In [36]: (figure, axes) = plt.subplots(figsize=(16, 8))
         axes.scatter([x + 1 for x in range(len(results))],
                      results, color=colors[0])
         axes.set_title("Estimated values of $\pi$", fontsize=28)
         axes.set_ylabel("~$\pi$", fontsize=24)
         axes.set_xlabel("Worker Number", fontsize=20)
         plt.show()
```

The following plot is the result of the preceding code:

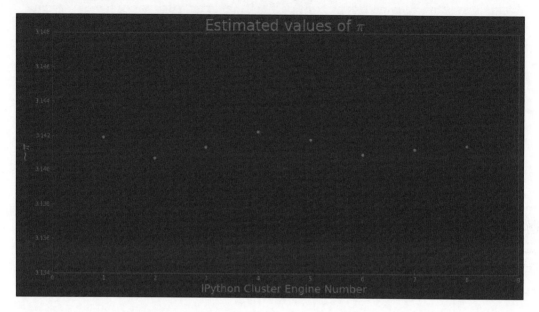

More clustering

There are other interesting options if you wish to parallelize the Python code and run it on clusters on problems that require you to visualize computationally intensive problems. Of particular interest is MIT's **StarCluster** project, which runs on Amazon AWS (EC2) and supports the Open Grid Engine (formerly known as the Sun Grid Engine). Furthermore, StarCluster has an IPython cluster plugin, which lets you easily run the IPython.parallel code on EC2. For more information on this, be sure to refer to this chapter's IPython Notebook, the StarCluster documentation, and the IPython documentation for parallel computations.

Summary

With this chapter, we reached the culmination of our adventure through the advanced topics in the world of matplotlib. Many of the topics covered in the latter half of this book crossed into other domains, as is often the case with the advanced usage of any software. These topics explored systems that did not have a direct and obvious connection with the narrow scope of matplotlib as a library. Rather, they reflected the usage patterns that are requested of software engineers working on real-world problems.

This bears further reflection. Often, computing problems in both research settings and start-ups are initially tackled quickly to get the results and examine the data as soon as possible. The next round of usage might require the addition of a bit more functionality or some other code tweaks. After a few months, you may be in any of the following situations:

- You may end up with one or two functions of enormous size with no obvious or clear path towards something that would be more maintainable

- You may discover that you are doing far more computation than what was initially expected and/or working with or generating far more data than what was anticipated

- You may come to the realization that your problem has aspects that lend themselves quite nicely to parallelization and distributed processing

In particular, you may find out that in order to plot data, you have to execute vast, monolithic functions, whose final operations produce results that get plotted by matplotlib. In many cases, you may find out that properly refactoring your code and parallelizing it will allow you to perform the expensive computations concurrently, ultimately allowing your plot rendering to happen much more quickly.

In other words, even though matplotlib doesn't directly enter the realm of parallelization, at one time or another, our matplotlib workflows may require tight coordination with computations running in clustered environments, utilizing parallel execution patterns.. Ultimately, the developer or user experience that is *perceived* to be matplotlib can be improved with the techniques outlined in this chapter and in fact, the techniques that were covered in the entire book.

Index

switch_backend() function 25
title() function 25
pyplot scripting API 52-57
PyTables 202-209
Python 3
 about 4
 Python 2, syntactical differences 4, 5
Python Imaging Library (PIL) 173

Q

Qt5 backend 2

R

read-eval-print loop (REPL) 75
RendererBase 18
run control, for matplotlib
 file and directory locations 158
 matplotlibrc file, using 158, 159
 settings, updating dynamically 160
 values, matplotlibrc file 159

S

scikit-learn 67, 95
SciPy 95
scripting layer
 about 14, 24
 pylab interface 25
 pyplot interface 24
Seaborn 3, 8, 66, 109, 111
Secure Shell (SSH) 181
setup, on AWS
 about 179
 Docker, using on EC2 183
 host server, creating on EC2 181, 182
 reading, with S3 183-185
 source data, pushing to S3 180, 181
 writing, with S3 183-185
Short-Wavelength Infrared (SWIR)
   light 167
Singh-Maddala distribution 194
spline interpolation 129
StarCluster project 260
Stereonets 157

subplots
 about 145
 implementing 151-156
 individual plots 148-150
 Pandas, revisiting 147, 148
Superhero Bootstrap theme 143
supporting components, matplotlib
   stack 26, 27
SymPy 95

T

task, Docker
 environment variables, setting 185
 execution 188, 189
 Python module, updating 186, 187
 running 185
task parallelization 237
Tornado 19

U

UCI Machine Learning Repository 146
United States Geological Survey
   (USGS) 164
United States Historical Climatology
   Network (USHCN) 112
user interface backends 16

V

VisIt
 about 233
 URL 233
Vispy
 about 233
 URL 233
visualization tools
 about 233
 Bokeh 233
 ParaView 233
 VisIt 233
 Vispy 233

W

Wulff net 157

Y

ŷhat ggplot 106

Z

Thank you for buying
Mastering matplotlib

About Packt Publishing

Packt, pronounced 'packed', published its first book, *Mastering phpMyAdmin for Effective MySQL Management*, in April 2004, and subsequently continued to specialize in publishing highly focused books on specific technologies and solutions.

Our books and publications share the experiences of your fellow IT professionals in adapting and customizing today's systems, applications, and frameworks. Our solution-based books give you the knowledge and power to customize the software and technologies you're using to get the job done. Packt books are more specific and less general than the IT books you have seen in the past. Our unique business model allows us to bring you more focused information, giving you more of what you need to know, and less of what you don't.

Packt is a modern yet unique publishing company that focuses on producing quality, cutting-edge books for communities of developers, administrators, and newbies alike. For more information, please visit our website at www.packtpub.com.

About Packt Open Source

In 2010, Packt launched two new brands, Packt Open Source and Packt Enterprise, in order to continue its focus on specialization. This book is part of the Packt Open Source brand, home to books published on software built around open source licenses, and offering information to anybody from advanced developers to budding web designers. The Open Source brand also runs Packt's Open Source Royalty Scheme, by which Packt gives a royalty to each open source project about whose software a book is sold.

Writing for Packt

We welcome all inquiries from people who are interested in authoring. Book proposals should be sent to author@packtpub.com. If your book idea is still at an early stage and you would like to discuss it first before writing a formal book proposal, then please contact us; one of our commissioning editors will get in touch with you.

We're not just looking for published authors; if you have strong technical skills but no writing experience, our experienced editors can help you develop a writing career, or simply get some additional reward for your expertise.

matplotlib Plotting Cookbook

ISBN: 978-1-84951-326-5   Paperback: 222 pages

Learn how to create professional scientific plots using matplotlib, with more than 60 recipes that cover common use cases

1. Learn plotting with self-contained, practical examples that cover common use cases.

2. Build your own solutions with the orthogonal recipes.

3. Learn to customize and combine basic plots to make sophisticated figures.

Interactive Applications Using Matplotlib

ISBN: 978-1-78398-884-6   Paperback: 174 pages

Don't just see your data, experience it!

1. Bring your users and your data closer with interactive visualizations using Matplotlib and Python.

2. Create user interfaces from scratch without needing a GUI toolkit, or insert new visualizations into your existing applications.

3. Pick up interactive aspects of Matplotlib and learn how widgets can be used to interact visually with data.

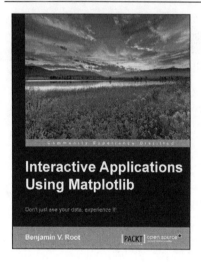

Please check **www.PacktPub.com** for information on our titles

IPython Notebook Essentials

ISBN: 978-1-78398-834-1   Paperback: 190 pages

Compute scientific data and execute code interactively
with NumPy and SciPy

1. Perform Computational Analysis interactively.

2. Create quality displays using matplotlib and
   Python Data Analysis.

3. Step-by-step guide with a rich set of
   examples and a thorough presentation
   of The IPython Notebook.

NumPy Cookbook

ISBN: 978-1-84951-892-5   Paperback: 226 pages

Over 70 interesting recipes for learning the Python
open source mathematical library, NumPy

1. Do high performance calculations with
   clean and efficient NumPy code.

2. Analyze large sets of data with
   statistical functions.

3. Execute complex linear algebra
   and mathematical computations.

Please check **www.PacktPub.com** for information on our titles

Printed in Great Britain
by Amazon